Durham

DURHAM

A thousand years of history and legend

MARTIN DUFFERWIEL

MAINSTREAM
PUBLISHING

EDINBURGH AND LONDON

All the photographs reproduced in this book are the work of the author

Copyright © Martin Dufferwiel, 1996 (text and photographs)
All rights reserved
The moral right of the author has been asserted

First published in Great Britain in 1996 by
MAINSTREAM PUBLISHING COMPANY (EDINBURGH) LTD
7 Albany Street
Edinburgh EH1 3UG

ISBN 1 85158 885 X

A catalogue record for this book is available from the British Library

Typeset in Garamond
Printed and bound in Great Britain by Butler and Tanner Ltd, Frome

For Faye and Charlotte

The ancient Citie Duram, by the Saxons called Dun-Holm, which as Beda sayth is compounded of their two words Dun, an Hill and Holm, an island, is like forme and situation as here described. The first erectors of this Citie are sayde to be the Monks of Lindisfarne which by the raging of the Danes were driven thence, and wandring farre and wyde, as last by oracle (as in those days there were maney, yf we will beleve their monkish legends) they were comanded to seat here, about the yere of grace 995, where Cuthbert their Bishop obtayned a great opinion of santitye and no lesse revenews, and authoritye.

John Speed, 1610

Contents

Acknowledgements

Firstly, I thank my wife Lynn, without whose support and encouragement I would never have started writing this book.

My special thanks go to Mary Sampson, archivist of the Royal Society, and to Mr Alan Pearce, manager of the Timothy Hackworth Victorian Railway Museum at Shildon, for their invaluable assistance in providing me with material for this book.

The diary extracts of Charles Mason and Jeremiah Dixon and quotations taken from the *Philosophical Transactions* are reproduced by kind permission of the President and Council of the Royal Society.

Thanks also go to Father Gordon Ryan and Tony Swainston, and to the staff of Durham City Reference Library, in particular to Jean Gartland, assistant reference librarian for her help, and her misfortune at always seeming to be on duty when I requested old and invariably large and heavy volumes from the archives. Last, but certainly not least, I must also thank Wendy for her time, skill and enthusiasm, without which writing this book would have proved a much more difficult, if not impossible, task.

Author's Note

It is to state the glaringly obvious to say that history is about recorded fact. About names and dates, about what happened, where and when. In order to sketch for us an accurate picture of people and events from the past, historians spend their professional lives attempting to identify the truth concealed in the tradition, to separate the fact from the fable.

But surely history is much more than facts alone. Surely the complete picture of a people's, a culture's, or indeed a region's history is one in which the bare framework of recorded fact has been fleshed out and made to come alive by the truths, half-truths and legends added to it by successive generations.

This book tells of people and events from a thousand years of history in Durham, both City and County. It is a book about history, but it is not, nor is it meant to be, a definitive historical work. That I leave to those who are qualified. Some of the subjects in the book are based firmly in fact, some are purely legendary, and others contain elements of both the truth and the tale, where the dividing line between recorded history and popular tradition has, through the passage of time, inevitably been dimmed and obscured.

So, as film director John Ford once said, 'When the legend becomes fact, print the legend.'

Martin Dufferwiel

Introduction

For the purposes of this book, our history starts in the so-called Dark Ages of Anglo-Saxon England, and the arrival in Durham, in the year 995, of the community of St Cuthbert.

That is not of course to say that the history of Durham began on that date. Remains of cultures considerably pre-dating the Anglo-Saxons can still be seen in the region today. The Romans left their mark in the area. After conquering the native Brigantes, they quickly began to build. The settlement of Concangium at Chester-le-Street; the forts of Piercebridge, of Vinovia at Binchester near Bishop Auckland, of Longovicium at Lanchester and of Vindomora at Ebchester were all at one time linked by the Roman highway of Dere Street, the supply route from York in the south to Hadrian's Wall and the border forts in the north. Much older still are the Iron and Bronze Age remains which are scattered around the county and are even to be seen in and around Durham City, with Maiden Castle a notable example.

But our story starts with the Anglo-Saxons, and the establishment of the ancient kingdom of Northumbria. The northern marches of seventh-century England were hosts to never-ending battles between pagan warlords and Christian kings, supported by missionaries from Ireland and Iona. Oswald was a Christian Prince of Northumbria, a vast kingdom which at the time extended from the Vale of York to the Scottish Borders. He had spent some time in exile with the Celtic monks of Iona, but in the year 634, after an invasion of his homeland by the pagan Welsh, Oswald returned and at the head of an army defeated and killed the Welsh King, Cadwallon of Gwynedd, at the Battle of Heavenfield near Hexham in Northumberland. With his

11

victory Oswald claimed his rightful kingship of Northumbria and, moreover, as King of Northumbria he became 'Bretwalda', the High King or Overlord of the many other kings in the England of his day.

Oswald moved quickly to spread the Christian faith throughout his realm as, although he was Christian, much of his kingdom remained pagan. He sent to Iona for monks to come and convert his subjects. The first mission to arrive in Northumbria soon returned to Iona, describing the native Northumbrians as 'wild and ungovernable men of harsh and barbarous disposition'. The man that followed was called Aidan, a monk who would be described by Bede in his *Ecclesiastical History of the English People* as being of 'singular meekness, piety and moderation, zealous in the cause of God'. In the Celtic tradition of St Columba and Iona, Aidan founded a monastic site 'in a separate place, near a chief City'; it was he who began the Celtic Christian mission on the Holy Island of Lindisfarne, within sight of the King's Royal Hall at Bamburgh.

A spiritual leader and teacher, Aidan began to expand his mission, out from the 'Thousand Acre Isle' and across the wild lands of Northumbria. Preaching in Gaelic and having others, including King Oswald, interpret for him he showed, as Bede tells us, 'the authority befitting a Bishop in rebuking the proud and mighty, and was merciful in bringing comfort to the weak and relief and protection to the poor'. It was Aidan who was to become the spiritual inspiration for a young boy from the Border hills by the name of Cuthbert, the boy who would one day himself become Bishop of Lindisfarne, be acclaimed a living saint, eventually come to be regarded as the Patron Saint of Northumbria, and whose body rests today in Durham Cathedral. It is with the tale of St Cuthbert that our book begins.

Part One

Chapter One

Beginnings

'Deliver us O Lord from the fury of the Norsemen'

A familiar prayer no doubt to early Christian monks after the first Viking raids had been visited upon their monasteries, along the north-east coast of eighth-century England. The initial bloody and destructive raids made by the Vikings, 'the hateful plague of Europe' as a contemporary scribe called the Norwegian and Danish raiders, were essentially piratical, made solely for plunder. Along the north-east coast of England, undefended coastal monastic settlements situated on sites chosen specifically for their isolation provided rich and easy pickings for the seaborne Norsemen. Once the Vikings had tasted the wealth that was to be gained from such raids, things in England were destined never to be the same again. From the late eighth century to the early eleventh, sporadic attacks continued. However, as the years passed, the small bands of armed raiders would become large, well-trained armies and rogue Norse longships would become full-scale invasion fleets bent on conquest, settlement and tribute.

On 7 June in the year 793, the monastery of the Holy Island of Lindisfarne, just off the Northumberland coast, was sacked by the Vikings. Monks were killed or taken for the slave trade, treasures were stolen, the monastery torched. The raid was to have a devastating effect on the English: *The Anglo-Saxon Chronicles* recorded that 'the ravages of heathen men miserably destroyed God's Church on Lindisfarne, with plunder and slaughter'. The contemporary English scholar Alcuin, chief adviser to Emperor Charlemagne and himself a Northumbrian, wrote:

Lo, it is almost three hundred and fifty years that we and our forefathers have dwelt in this fair land, and never has such a horror before appeared in Britain, such as we have just suffered from, the heathen, it was not thought possible that they could have made such a voyage. Behold the Church of St Cuthbert sprinkled with the blood of the priests of Christ, robbed of all its ornaments . . . in that place where, after the departure of Paulinus from York, the Christian faith had its beginnings among us, there is the beginning of woe and calamity.

Their most precious possession, however, was not revealed. For in the monastery of Lindisfarne were kept the remains of St Cuthbert, and they were to lie there in safety for almost a hundred more years. Cuthbert had been born about the year 634 and had spent his boyhood in the Lammermuir Hills on the border between England and Scotland. At the end of August in the year 651, after receiving a vision of the soul of St Aidan, the Bishop and founder of the monastery of Lindisfarne, being 'borne to heaven in the splendour of a great light and escorted by so many bands of angels', Cuthbert himself decided that he had been 'called', and that his destiny lay in holy orders. In 651 he joined the Abbey at Melrose in Scotland, where he became the protégé of the Abbot Eata. Bede records that the Prior, Boisil, 'was standing before the doors of the monastery and saw him first. Foreseeing in spirit what an illustrious man the stranger would become, he made this single remark to the bystanders: "Behold the servant of the Lord."' Before long Cuthbert decided that his mission lay not only behind the closed doors of a monastery, but also in taking the teachings of the Gospels out to the people of Northumbria. So he began the life, in turns, of a missionary, ascetic and eventually hermit, and in due time he would become the best-known and best-loved saint in the north, a divided and turbulent land.

In his youth Cuthbert travelled extensively throughout the wild lands of Northumbria. Bede in his biography of St Cuthbert tells us that 'he used to visit and preach mainly in the villages that lay far distant, among high and inaccessible mountains which others feared to visit, and whose barbarity and squalor daunted other teachers.' Northumbria would not be fully Christian until the ninth century. The land in which Cuthbert travelled and preached was a land where ancient pagan rituals were still performed. The spirits of wood and water were worshipped and people paid homage at sacred wells and trees. Christianity had made inroads and the one God was gradually driving out the many, but His progress was slow. These were times of mystery, of heroes and legends, a shadowy time of shamanism and the power of the supernatural. A dark world into which the light of Christianity was only just beginning to shine.

The reputation of Cuthbert as a preacher and healer soon began to grow.

Various miraculous events reportedly took place in his presence or following his teachings, and news of them spread throughout the countryside. It was said that people recognised in Cuthbert a special holiness and humility. When his old mentor from Melrose, Eata, became Abbot of Lindisfarne, Cuthbert joined him there and in the year 665 became Prior. By this time divisions had become apparent between the withdrawn, ascetic tradition of the Celtic Church of Aidan – and indeed of Cuthbert – and the more structured, worldly and sophisticated code of Rome. These divisions had been addressed at the Synod of Whitby in 664, where it was decided that the Roman code be adopted throughout the Church. As a result, in the Celtic north monks and Celtic churchmen began to leave the monasteries and return to Iona and Ireland. Cuthbert was a Celtic traditionalist, but by adopting the Roman code himself he was instrumental in re-stabilising a disintegrating northern Church.

As time passed Cuthbert began to seek more and more solitude for prayer and meditation. He moved out of the monastery and built a cell of stones on a tiny islet just off the shore of Lindisfarne. The islet, the remains of a building and a wooden cross can still be seen today. Eventually, however, even this sanctuary became unsatisfactory as it was accessible at low tide, and in the year 676 permission was obtained from Abbot Eata for Cuthbert to retreat, as St Aidan had done, to the isolated and inhospitable inner Farne Island, seven miles south across the sea; Bede wrote that 'The island had no water, corn or trees and being the haunt of evil spirits was very ill-suited to human habitation, but when the man of God came, he ordered the evil spirits to withdraw, and the island became quite habitable.'

For nine years on Inner Farne, Cuthbert lived the life of a recluse. With his devotion to God, his humility and his miracle working, he became recognised by the people as an exceptionally holy man. They regarded him as their very own saint. Then, in 685, he was elected Bishop of Hexham. However, such was the eminence, even then, of Cuthbert the holy man, Cuthbert the recluse, Cuthbert of Lindisfarne, that the sees of Northumbria were changed around deliberately to allow him to remain, as Bishop of Lindisfarne, a force of circumstance which pleased both Cuthbert and his followers. The incumbent Bishop, Eata, became Bishop of Hexham. Even then Cuthbert was reluctant to be ordained Bishop, but after bowing to popular pressure he was eventually persuaded by King Egfrith of Northumbria and Bishop Trumin of the Picts and was consecrated on Easter Day 685. His time as Bishop, however, was to last less than two years, but throughout that time he 'maintained the dignity of the Bishop, without abandoning the ideal of the Monk, or the virtue of the hermit'. Being aware of his forthcoming death, Cuthbert resigned his office and on 20 March in the year 687 he died. On his deathbed Cuthbert told his followers: 'I know that during my life some have despised me, yet after my death you will see what sort of man I was and that my doctrine was by no means worthy of contempt.'

Cuthbert's body was returned to Lindisfarne and was buried with great reverence. A shrine was erected and soon miracles were reported as having happened around Cuthbert's resting place. The reverence and high reputation in which he had been held during his life was now to be enhanced after his death. It was the custom of the time to open the coffin of a man of great sanctity between ten and twenty years after burial. The purpose of the exercise was ostensibly to wash the bones and wrap them in precious silks for ceremonial re-burial. But it must be remembered that in these times there was also a healthy trade in the relics of saints and holy men. In 698 Cuthbert's coffin was dutifully opened. The sight that greeted the monks offered proof, if proof were needed, of the saintliness of the man and firmly established the 'cult' of Cuthbert. It appeared to the monks of Lindisfarne that Cuthbert was lying sleeping peacefully in his coffin. After 11 years there was not a sign of corruption on the body. It is thought that it was around this time that Eadfrith, who had been a contemporary of Cuthbert, wrote the precious Lindisfarne Gospels, as a response to this singular event.

In the late ninth century great Danish fleets were invading England and further Viking attacks threatened the monastery of Lindisfarne. In the year 875 Bishop Eardulph consulted with the monks. They considered their safety and they decided to leave Lindisfarne. In reaching their decision they remembered the prophetic dying words of St Cuthbert:

> You are to remember that if you are forced to choose between two evils, I would much rather that you should lift my bones from the tomb when you leave this place, and carry them with you to rest wherever God may decree, than that in any way you should consent to evil, and put your necks under the yoke of the heathen.

So it was that the monks gathered together the coffin of St Cuthbert, relics of King Oswald and St Aidan and their precious Lindisfarne Gospels. The Holy Island of Lindisfarne was abandoned, and they set out, at the height of King Alfred the Great's wars against the Danes, seeking refuge away from the terror of the marauding Norsemen. The journey had begun which would lead them eventually to Durham.

When the community first set out they pulled the bier on which St Cuthbert's coffin was carried by hand. Eventually they obtained horses and oxen. The monk Symeon of Durham tells us that not all of the monks were allowed to touch the coffin in which the body of the saint was deposited, nor even the vehicle on which it was carried. Only seven of the company were given that privilege. The community and the 'camp followers' they attracted wandered apparently aimlessly over trackless moors and through dark forests. It was a dangerous and difficult journey across a wild and lawless land. In those times people did not travel far and to wander around the wastes of Northumbria without an attendant army was asking for trouble. Symeon tells us that 'they wandered throughout the whole District of Northumbria, having no settled dwelling place, and they were like sheep before the faces of wolves'. They travelled north to the Scottish Borders, south into what is today Yorkshire. They went west as far as the Irish Sea. There they decided to take a boat across to Ireland, but having set sail they were forced back to shore by a great storm which suddenly blew up. This they took to be a sign that St Cuthbert did not wish to leave his native land. They turned eastwards and eventually, seven years after leaving Lindisfarne, reached the old Roman centre of Chester-le-Street.

There may well still have been the substantial remains of Roman defences, perhaps giving some peace of mind to the travellers, in those troubled times. It was here therefore that they chose to settle, and here St Cuthbert's remains would rest for 113 years. Further miracles were reported at the tomb of the saint and stories of these together with the well-known accounts of the incorrupt state of his body fed the now growing 'cult' of Cuthbert. He was becoming the most powerful saint in northern England, loved by the Northumbrians and feared by their would-be enemies. His fame spread far and wide and kings, nobles and peasants alike made pilgrimage to his shrine.

In the year 934 the great Saxon King, Athelstan – 'Rex Anglorum', King of all the English, 'The very celebrated King who by the grace of God ruled all England, which prior to him many Kings shared between them' – called at Chester-le-Street on his way north to war with the Scots. At the tomb of St Cuthbert the King prostrated himself and prayed for aid in the forthcoming conflict. Opening the coffin and uncovering the saint's body, he placed copies of the Gospels at the head, put a gold arm ring, ornaments of silver and gold, two cups of 'the best money' into the coffin, and wrapped the body in a stole, maniple and girdle of eastern silk, which can still be seen today in the Durham Cathedral Treasury. The King promised rich gifts if the outcome of the war was successful; if not he told his brother to bury his body with the saint. Athelstan's attendant army, 'an army drawn from the whole of Britain' as a chronicler noted, gave to 'Cuthbert's folk' 96 pounds of silver.

In 953 Eric Bloodaxe, hero of the Norse sagas and last Viking King of York, also brought gifts and did tribute at Cuthbert's tomb. Only a year later, he would be betrayed, and would die in battle at 'a certain lonely place called Stainmore'. It is said that the 'Rey Cross' on Bowes Moor marks the spot where he fell. Such kings wished partly to have conferred upon them the blessings of the great northern saint, and partly to curry favour with the northern population. By this time the Northumbrian people were a mixture of different races, a deep-rooted society with their own social organisation and tradition. Fiercely independent, their kingdom was so far away from the southern-based Saxon kings that those kings failed to rule effectively in the lands north of the Humber. To the southern English the Northumbrians were stubborn, warlike and rebellious, but their domain was strategically important, situated as it was between the comparatively wealthy southern Saxon kingdoms and the Scots to the north.

A piece of old doggerel, written no doubt by a native of Chester-le-Street, laments the eventual removal of St Cuthbert's remains from his century-old resting place, and the great wealth that the saint's shrine would eventually attract at Durham: 'Durham lads 'ave silver an' gowld, Chester lads 'ave nowt but brass.' But the removal of the saint from Chester-le-Street was inevitable.

The late tenth century saw new and more formidable Viking raids. England was under the reign of the weak and ill-advised King Ethelred, and in 995 fears grew about new Danish incursions in the north, and so 'Cuthbert's folk' left Chester-le-Street and again took to the road. They travelled south as far as Ripon in Yorkshire, before returning north, and at last to Durham. As to exactly how they came to settle at Durham, fact is lost in legend.

> Being distressed because they were ignorant where Dunholme was, see their good fortune! As they were going, a woman that lacked hir cowe did call aloude to hir companion to know if shee did not see hir, who answered with a loude voice that hir cowe was in Dunholme – a happye and heavenly eccho to the distressed monks, who by that means were at the end of theire journie, where they should find a resting place for the body of theire honoured Saint. (*The Rites of Durham*)

The travellers reached an escarpment called Wrdelau. The noted local historian Robert Surtees suggests that this may be identified as the hill to the east of Durham, near Hetton, now known as Warden Law. The main route north through the county at the time in which the story is set did lie east to Durham. As the monks were attempting to return to Chester-le-Street, the identification of Warden Law seems a reasonable one. The story tells that at this spot 'the vehicle on which the shrine containing the holy body' was deposited inexplicably became so heavy it was impossible to move further. All efforts to move it failed: 'The shrine were fixed as if it were a mountain.' This was taken by 'Cuthbert's folk' and by Aldhune their Bishop to be a sign that the saint refused to return to Chester-le-Street. A fast of three days and three nights was ordered, for prayer and meditation. Legend has it that a revelation was granted to 'a certain religious person named Eadmer', a vision of a great and lofty church and a voice telling that they were required to take St Cuthbert's body to Dunholme and prepare a resting place there.

This revelation was received with a mixture of joy and puzzlement, joy that their journey was almost at an end and their beloved saint had chosen his final resting place, and puzzlement because none knew of a place called Dunholme. Undaunted they moved on, easily now as it required 'only very few' to move St Cuthbert's coffin. When they reached a high point called Mount Joy the monks came across two milkmaids, one of whom had lost her cow. On asking the other if she had seen the animal, she replied, yes, I've seen it on Dunholme. Overhearing this conversation the monks, now overjoyed, asked where Dunholme was to be found. The name Dunholme is Anglo-Saxon; it means 'Hill-Island', and it was to a high wooded rock surrounded on three sides by a river that the milkmaid led the monks. After years of wandering St Cuthbert's followers had at last found a permanent home, and today, one thousand years later, St Cuthbert lies there still.

On their arrival the monks began work on a shelter for their holy relics. Made of branches and the boughs of trees, it is thought that it may have been on the present site of the Church of St Mary Le Bow, now the Durham Heritage Centre. By 998 the rock had been cleared and the first stone church had been erected. From the high wooded rock a small settlement began to take shape, a settlement which would be swelled by pilgrims and made wealthy by their offerings, which would eventually become one of the most important sites of religious pilgrimage and military power in England, remaining so until the Reformation. From the high wooded rock the Prince Bishops of Durham would expand their influence outwards and rule as kings over their domain. The domain in which the land we now know as Durham County has its origins; and a domain which over the course of ten centuries would develop a culture rich in history and in legend.

The legend of the Dun Cow has been an enduring one and visitors to the cathedral can see the story depicted in a carving of the Dun Cow and the milkmaids on the north transept wall, appropriately almost overlooking Dun Cow Lane. Legend apart, however, it is obvious that the siting of their chosen resting place gave to the community of St Cuthbert an excellent defensive position, no small concern in those violent days. Over the years various 'real' reasons have been given for the community of St Cuthbert's choice of Durham, political reasons, 'deals' between the Bishops and the Northumbrian nobility, and so on. But whatever the real reason for the body of St Cuthbert coming to rest at this lofty site, surely no more splendid or fitting a resting place could have been found for the great patron saint of the Northumbrians.

Chapter Two

Cnut the Great

'My Lord, soon even the waves of the sea will obey your command.'

Towards the end of the tenth century Danish armies embarked from purpose-built training camps on the coast of Denmark, and set sail for England. At their head were two Viking leaders, two 'Sons of Odin' with names reminiscent of the legendary heroes of Norse sagas. Thorkell the Tall and King Swein Forkbeard. They came to England, they did battle, they eventually conquered and in the year 1013 Swein was accepted by the English as their king. His reign, however, was to be short as he died within a year, and it was to be his younger son who, mainly by virtue of a misinterpreted legend, was to become one of the most well-known of all the kings of England. He would became at once King of England, Denmark and Norway, the most powerful monarch in northern Europe and head of a vast Viking empire. His name was Cnut the Great, the King Canute of legend, and the same mighty king who, at the height of his power and majesty, walked barefoot, with head shaven, dressed in the garb of a penitent, to Durham, there to prostrate himself and pay homage at the shrine of St Cuthbert, and to bestow gifts of great value on 'Cuthbert's folk'.

England as a nation state had, over the course of the previous hundred years, become well organised, had attained a comparatively high level of learning and culture and was, above all, very rich. The old Saxon kingdom at the time of the great Danish invasion was 'a fruit ripe for the picking'. However, the 'Golden Age' of the great Saxon kings, of Alfred, Athelstan and Edgar, and the flowering of the kingdom of all England, would come to an ignominious end during the reign of Ethelred (the Unready). Under Ethelred, 'magnificence and power had turned to complacency and corruption'. Where his predecessors had been men strong in arms, decisive in action, just in judgement and visionary in outlook, Ethelred was none of these. Indecisive, prone to fits of cruelty, a king who did little to support his subjects and little to earn their support of himself, instead of fighting to repel successive Danish invasions he paid enormous sums of money, the 'Danegeld', to ensure the Danes would not take arms against him. Ethelred, it seems, was by nature like an over-privileged and petulant child. He presided over a Royal House riddled with moral decay where strength of purpose and concern for the people had been replaced by self-indulgence and treachery, where sycophantic courtiers encouraged a weak king's belief in his own justness and where the trust and respect of the English people had been lost. The name given Ethelred, 'Unready', is in fact a later corruption of the Saxon 'un-raed'. Raed, or rede, means advice or counsel, and one can infer from this that Ethelred was either given bad advice or he wilfully refused to take good advice.

The Danes of his time were themselves split into two factions. The warring armies, trained in Denmark, were basically professional soldiers who fought only for pay and plunder. However, by this time many Danes had been settled in England, mainly down the east of the country in an area known as the 'Danelaw', for about a hundred years. They had become farmers and traders. At the end of the tenth and beginning of the eleventh centuries there were constant hostilities between Ethelred's forces and the Danish armies, who were also now resident in England. Time after time Ethelred 'paid off' the Danes with huge consignments of Danegeld, and every time the Danes demanded more to keep the peace. On St Brice's Day, 13 November, in the year 1002, Ethelred, fearing a general Danish uprising, gave the order that all Danes living in England were to be put to the sword. Terrible atrocities were apparently committed in the name of the King against Danish settlers. Some historians have suggested that the order was meant to include only Danish soldiers, but as was usual for Ethelred things got out of hand and went badly wrong. Other historians claim there is little, if any, evidence to show the event ever happened. However, a tradition maintains that one of the victims of the St Brice's Day massacre was the sister of King Swein of Denmark, an act which was to have far-reaching consequences for Ethelred. The cycle of fighting and 'pay-offs' continued and as time went by the Danish armies became more entrenched and more threatening. By the Christmas of 1006 'the terror inspired by the host grew so great that everybody was incapable of devising or drawing up a plan to get them out of the country, or of holding this land against them'.

This then was the situation in England at the time, an old, rich kingdom led by a weak, unpopular and badly advised king. By the year 1013 the time had come for the Danes to strike the fatal blow. It was probably already in Swein's mind to take the English crown and create a unified Viking state of England, Denmark and Norway. This time there was to be no peace for

Ethelred on payment of the Danegeld. Swein's armies marched across the country, inflicting defeat after defeat on Ethelred's forces. The Danelaw willingly submitted to Swein and Ethelred's 'kingdom' was eventually reduced to an area around London. The sweeping success of Swein's campaign was to guarantee his acceptance by the English as their new king. Ethelred, now a king without a kingdom, left for exile in Normandy. On 2 February 1014, Swein Forkbeard died and his young son, Cnut, about 20 years of age at the time, was chosen as the new king. Seeing this as an opportunity to rally support in an attempt to regain his kingdom, Ethelred returned to England to lead a campaign against Cnut. It ended, as all the previous ones had done, with Ethelred paying over yet another Danegeld. On St George's Day, 23 April 1016, Ethelred, in the cutting words of one historian, 'did his country the only service that was in his power; by dying'.

Cnut was accepted and established as king but it would now be his task to consolidate his hold on his new kingdom. The senior churchmen and chief English leaders unanimously supported Cnut. He may have been young but he was very politically aware, and he quickly embraced and allied himself to the Christian Church. He took an oath that he would be loyal in affairs of state, and thus ensured the support of the English establishment. One problem remained, that of Ethelred's son, Edmund, who raised his own forces and would attack and harass Cnut's armies in an attempt to regain the throne for the Saxon Royal House. At the time, however, succession was not just a hereditary right: the King had to be 'accepted' by the English people, nobles and senior churchmen, and they were in no mood to revive the line of Ethelred. Edmund fought bravely and well, earning himself the honourable epithet 'Ironside', but his cause was doomed to failure and he was finally defeated by Cnut at the Battle of Ashingdon near Southend. Anxious to show himself as a just, wise and merciful king, Cnut announced that he would divide his kingdom and allow Edmund to rule in the west Saxon lands. They would jointly rule over England. Shortly afterwards, however, Edmund died in 'mysterious circumstances', and Cnut was finally crowned King of all the English in 1017.

Cnut was quick to reinforce his political awareness with his military strength. He was a man who recognised potential trouble and troublemakers and moved swiftly to 'remove' any possible source of rebellion. Dissenters were removed from office, potential rivals he had executed. He delegated his power to English nobles, and ruled through them, an action which would ensure him the respect of the people and would consolidate the English acceptance of his authority. Throughout his reign he moulded and reinforced his relationship with the Church, forging a firm relationship with Wulfstan, the English Archbishop of York. Cnut would make great demonstrations of his piety, making pilgrimage to Rome; and it was in 1027 after returning from

Rome that he allegedly declared to his people he would never again wear his crown of gold: 'It is not proper for me to adorn my brow with gold, when our blessed saviour wore a crown of thorns.' Legend has it that from that time his crown of state hung on the head of his wooden figure of Christ on the cross. Within ten years of his being crowned as King of the English, he was the most powerful monarch in northern Europe, head of a vast Norse empire and feared by many. He had become respected and admired as a wise and just king and, as one chronicler recorded: 'The combination of both his armies and ships was the most efficient fighting force seen in Europe since the time of Rome.'

His kingdom of England he divided into four large areas, each ruled by a trusted noble, with ultimate regal powers being retained by Cnut. These areas were Wessex, Mercia, East Anglia and the northernmost, Northumbria. In Northumbria, Cnut appointed Siward, a trusted warrior leader, to rule on his behalf. Siward was known to Cnut as being strong and effective, a warrior and a statesman, just the type of man he considered necessary to keep some sort of order in Northumbria. Indeed Siward was to be involved in some of the major events of the period, in both the fact and the fiction. For a warrior leader of the day 'The Doughty Siward', as described in Shakespeare's *Macbeth*, had a lineage that was suitably colourful. The story was told that his grandmother, a Danish princess, had been ravaged by a bear. His father had apparently borne visible traces as a result of this event, sporting 'long hairy ears; whence he was called Berne'.

In 1054, when Edward the Confessor reigned in England, Siward led an expedition into Scotland to assist his nephew, Malcolm Canmore, in his efforts to take back the Scottish crown from Macbeth. Malcolm's father, King Duncan, had since 1034 been the first general ruler of Scotland. Macbeth had been his battle commander. After Duncan had been killed in battle in 1047, Macbeth was elected as his successor, ruling Scotland for 17 years while Malcolm and his younger brother Donald Bane lived in exile with Siward. In 1057, with the help of Siward, Malcolm claimed back the Scottish throne, slew Macbeth, and began a reign which would last for 40 years. And so it came about that in 1093, as King of Scotland, Malcolm Canmore would lay one of the three foundation stones of the new Norman cathedral in Durham.

When Siward died, soon after his return from Scotland, it was a grievous blow to the people of Northumbria, for he was much loved. 'Sigward-Digr', they called him, Siward the Strong. It is said that when he realised death was approaching, he ordered his servants to dress him in his coat of mail, put on his helmet, and give him his shield: 'Lift me up, that I may die on my legs, like a soldier, and not crouching like a cow: put my battle axe in my right hand, that I may die under arms.' So passed Siward, in the tradition of his Danish forebears.

Danish immigrants had in fact been resident in Northumbria for some time. There were sizeable settlements in what is now the south of County Durham, on lands taken by the Norse King Ragnald, a hundred years earlier; in Teesdale, around Darlington; and around the ancient village of Staindrop. In fact the quiet, sleepy situation of Staindrop today belies its importance in Cnut's day. The Danish settlement there was the centre of a large manor and estate known as Staindropshire. Historians have claimed that there was even a Royal Hall situated either in Staindrop itself or on the nearby site where Raby Castle stands today. There is no archaeological evidence to confirm the Royal Hall's existence or location, although Symeon of Durham places it in Staindrop. Popular tradition, however, has it that 'Bulmers Tower', the oldest part of present-day Raby Castle, was built on the site of Cnut the Great's Royal Hall. There remains, nevertheless, a more definite connection between Cnut and the first 'Lord of Raby', for Sigen, the niece of Cnut, married Uchtred, grandson of Waltheoff the Elder, who had been Earl of Northumbria in the time of Ethelred, and it was Uchtred and Sigen who would become the first 'Lord and Lady of Raby'.

It was in Cnut's time that 'Staindropshire' became closely connected with the See of Durham, a connection which was to last until the sixteenth century. There is no record of Cnut ever having visited Staindrop, though if the story of the Royal Hall is to be believed, he may well have done so, for about the year 1027 following his pilgrimage to Rome, Cnut came north to pay homage at the shrine of St Cuthbert at Durham. It is interesting to imagine the great King breaking his journey and spending time at Staindrop, perhaps authorising an extension to the church there which dates probably from the eighth or ninth century, a pious act of devotion which fits well with his character and which would precede his pilgrimage to Durham and the shrine of the saint.

T. Cox, writing in 1730, described the shrine of St Cuthbert at the time of Cnut's pilgrimage as drawing 'multitudes of people of all qualities and degrees to it to pay their devotion, and bring choice offerings, by which means enriched it became stately and magnificent'. By this time the monastery of Durham, because of the immense drawing power of the shrine of St Cuthbert, was becoming very rich, not only in gold and jewels but also in land. Only eight years after arriving on the 'Dun-holme', Cuthbert's community had been given by 'Styr, son of Ulf' lands around Darlington, as well as lands in Coniscliffe, Cockerton and Haughton. Now it was Cnut's turn to prove his piety.

The story is told that Cnut rode towards Durham and eventually reached Trimdon, about five miles from the city. There he, his bodyguard and all his retinue unhorsed. It is said that the King then had his head shaved; indeed some have claimed the name Trimdon means 'the place of Tonsor'. Once

Cnut had had his hair 'trimmed' he divested himself of all jewellery and trappings of royalty, was dressed in the robes of a penitent and proceeded to Durham, barefoot, passing along the old Garmonds' Way, bypassing present-day Kelloe and eventually reaching a rise in the ground later known as Signing or Crossing Bank. This bank, which afforded pilgrims their first sight of the cathedral, was traditionally where they first made the sign of the cross. It must indeed have been a strange sight that day to the people of Durham; yes they were used to a stream of pilgrims to the shrine of their saint, but rarely such a distinguished visitor as this. And here he was, the great Cnut, Viking emperor, king of three kingdoms, walking with bleeding feet through the narrow streets of their emerging little city to prostrate himself before St Cuthbert.

True to form, Cnut bestowed great gifts on the community of Durham, in reverence to the saint. According to Symeon, the King gave his 'mansion house and vill which is called Staindropa together with its appurtences' – Cnapton (believed to be Snotterton), Scotton (Shotton), Rabi (Raby), Waearfeld (Walkerfield), Efenwude (Evenwood), Alclit (Aycliffe or Auckland), Elledun (Eldon), Ingleton, Thiccelea (Thickley) and Middleton (Midleston). A contemporary chronicler wrote of such extravagant gifts, which were always gratefully accepted by the Durham monastery:

> After that Aldwinus and his wandering monks had reposed the reliques of their great patron, Cuthbert, and buylded somewhat of Durham, then begged they hard, not for cantels of cheese, as other poore men doe, but for large corners of good countries, so all their professions used, and obteyned of King Cnut (whom they persuaded to goe five myles of his way barefooted to see Saint Cuthbert) the Manor of Staindrop all appendancies thereto, which were greate.

There appears to be cynicism in these words. The writer seems to be implying that the monks merely used the reputation and 'cult' of Cuthbert to further their own power and wealth. He seems to suggest that in this case they manipulated Cnut into bestowing his great gifts of wealth and land: they begged 'not for cantels of cheese, as other poore men doe, but for large corners of good countries'. It would perhaps be wrong to suggest that Cnut was easily manipulated. He may have willingly complied with the requirements of the Durham monks, but it suited him also: he was always keen on proving his piety and humility by making the 'grand gesture'; but Cnut was nobody's fool.

The legend of Cnut attempting to turn back the waves has long been a popular one in the annals of English mythology. It has served as a demonstration that whatever domain a great king may have, in the end it remains a domain only over men. The story is usually told as a lesson given to Cnut who foolishly believed he had become such a great conqueror and lord that he could even control the waves of the ocean. The origins of the legend, however, give a somewhat different version and the original story is much more in tune with what is known of Cnut's own personality.

It is said that during an endless debate at Cnut's court, the King, growing impatient and angry, cut short the proceedings by making the necessary decision. He then asked if there was general agreement among his counsellors. A sycophantic courtier ventured to suggest that of course the King had made the correct decision, and it was because of such strength of character and wise decision-making that the King had become so great and powerful and so loved by his people: 'Soon even the waves of the sea will obey your command.' There were murmurs of approval throughout the Court. Cnut smiled a wry smile to himself; his flatterers thinking it was a smile of agreement began laughing and bowing. Cnut thought about the remark and realised they needed a demonstration. He was not Ethelred, he was not 'Un-raed', and he knew exactly the extent, and the limits, of his powers, how he had achieved his position and how he maintained it.

He gave orders that he should be taken to the sea and seated in a chair on the shore, before the incoming tide. His courtiers and advisers he ordered to stand around his chair. As the waves rolled in he raised his hands in a gesture of defiance and cried, 'I Cnut the Great, King of England, Denmark and Norway, command you to go back.' The waves lapped around his chair, and about the ankles of those around him. Keeping his own feet raised above the water, he again commanded the tide to turn. By this time his attendants were getting wet, cold and disgruntled. One more command to the waves and the water around them was getting deeper. Cnut turned to his soaked and shivering subjects and ordered them to carry him, still dry, back to his Royal Hall. Cnut cast an angry sidways glance at them, and they dared not venture any comment. He had proved his point. The story is not one of the King's foolishness, as has popularly been interpreted, but shows a ruler who is fully aware, despite the flattering of sycophants, that his authority has its earthly limits.

What then do we make of Cnut the Great? In his youth he had been a true Viking warrior prince who thought nothing of killing and destroying. His prisoners, if they were lucky enough to be spared, had their noses and hands cut off. During his rise to ultimate power, he simply executed all those he thought of as potential challengers to his throne. In the end he reigned as a popular, just and pious king. He modelled his 'style' very much on the great Saxon kings of old, creating through foresight, controlling through strength and ruling the people of England by earning their respect and loyalty. Some no doubt would argue he was nothing but a brutal Norse warrior turned hypocritical opportunist, others that he was a brilliant military strategist and incomparable diplomat. Whatever the real truth about Cnut, he became respected in England and admired throughout Europe as a king who was able and strong, and whose reign brought a period of stability and relative prosperity. When Cnut died in 1036, the great Norse empire began to disintegrate and England was once again plunged into a period of instability.

Across the sea, the star of a different race was beginning to rise. Early in the tenth century a band of Vikings had landed in northern France, their leader a warrior chief named Rollo. They settled and established themselves on the lower Seine, around what is now Rouen. A direct descendant of Rollo was Duke William of Normandy, and it was he, just thirty years after Cnut's death at another time of intense internal struggle in England, who sailed at the head of an invasion fleet, the success of which was to have a devastating effect on the people of England, not least those in the north of that country.

Chapter Three

Fire and Sword

'This was a fatal day for England, a melancholy havoc of our country
. . . The Normans are a race inured to war and can hardly live
without it, fierce in attacking their enemies, and when force fails,
always ready to use guile or to corrupt by bribery.'
— William of Malmesbury

The coming of the Normans in 1066 changed the old order in England for ever. The defeat of King Harold's army and the death of many of the Anglo-Saxon aristocracy at the Battle of Hastings condemned the English to merciless subjugation at the hands of William the Conqueror and his Norman nobility. The conquest was swift and sure. The flower of the English had fallen at Hastings, and the revolts that followed were doomed to failure. As most of the great Saxon leaders were dead, there were few left able to channel the spirit of resistance into organised military strategy. What resistance was put up was pitilessly extinguished, by sword and starvation. As *The Anglo-Saxon Chronicles* tells us, 'certainly in this time people had much oppression and very many injuries'. The far north of his realm was, however, hostile to the new King's authority and remained a region remote and antagonistic, a 'grievous thorn in the side of William'. Revolt in the north was to be inevitable, and it was possibly to be the most dramatic in the course of the conquest.

As the great nephew of Edward the Confessor, William Duke of Normandy did have a genuine, if tenuous claim to the English throne. His prime objective, however, was to seize it by force at the head of a well-trained army of Norman nobles, mercenaries and freebooters, to inherit 'not by hereditary right, but in desperate battle with much spilling of people's blood'. After his victory his army had to be paid. Initially Normans were simply given land and properties left by Saxon nobles killed in battle. Other Saxon families were thrown from their lands by force of arms. But the King still needed wealth, 'the best money', to pay his soldiers. It had been the promise of massive booty, spoils from an ancient, wealthy and vanquished kingdom, that had secured William the services of much of his forces. William therefore levied on the English population huge gelds or land taxes, and it was an action that had the effect of turning the grumblings of discontent into the onset of revolt. The King's demand for money was the excuse needed for the defiant northern population to reject his authority and move against the 'yoke of Norman tyranny'. Alliances were hoped for by the northerners, perhaps with Swein of Denmark, or even Malcolm of Scotland. No alliances were made. The first uprising of 1068 ended in fiasco, the rebels simply dispersing and returning to their northern fastness. It did, however, have a marked effect on the King.

'Then the King was informed that the people in the north were gathered together and meant to make a stand against him if he came' so William decided it was time, once and for all, to impose his authority and put an end to dissent. In 1069 he personally charged a Norman noble, Robert De Comines, with the subjugation of the north. Comines rode forth with 700 fully armed knights together with foot soldiers and servants at arms. On reaching Durham on 30 January 1069, Comines disregarded Bishop Egelwin's advice not to enter the city. The Saxon Bishop was all too aware of the murderous mood of the local people. Most of the population, knowing of the coming of the Normans, had left the city seemingly in a pre-planned manoeuvre and taken to the surrounding hills and forests; others were taken prisoner and summarily executed, as an example to recalcitrants under Norman rule. Hutchinson takes up the story:

> Cumin entered the City with marks of cruelty and tyranny, and through the insolence of his own self-sufficiency permitted his troops to give themselves up to rioting and wantonness: they forcibly took possession of the houses, were dispersed through every quarter of the City, and committed various enormities against the inhabitants. The Normans, overcome with drunkenness and revelling, were totally off their guard.

And so it was that at dawn the inhabitants of Durham and the surrounding area returned, stormed the city and engaged the Norman forces. The Normans in their arrogance had not expected this. They were drunk, unordered, confused; they were forced back further into the city by the furious onset of the local people. They took refuge and were cut down in streets unfamiliar to them, but all too familiar to their assailants. Totally disorganised, the Normans were routed. Desperately they made their way back to the episcopal house, the Bishop's dwelling which Comines had made his headquarters. Barricading themselves in they shot volley after volley of arrows, down into the ranks of their attackers. Soon smoke billowed up the walls, tongues of flame licked at the timbers: the locals had set alight to the house and all inside it. Those who escaped the flames were cut down by swords or hewn with axes. Comines was dead and of his force 'all save one were killed', and it is said that the streets were 'filled with blood and carcasses'.

The success in Durham spurred on the population of the north. A rebel force was assembled and moved as far south as York, achieving some success in minor skirmishes. At York the rebels besieged the castle and the Norman garrison there. King William moved quickly. He came upon York, lifted the siege and once again the rebels were scattered. The King then sent forth an army to harry the retreating rebels. As they came north Yorkshire was laid waste; they marched as far as Elfertan, now Northallerton. There the Normans were surrounded by a dense and unyielding fog. Fearing to continue their march through the fog in unfamiliar country, they retreated to York. The monk Symeon of Durham recounted that 'St Cuthbert had sent forth this fog to protect the men of Durham and that the Normans realised its supernatural origin'.

The Conqueror himself came north with the second force. This time there was to be no mistake. This force was an army of retribution, for the revolt in Durham and for the continuing recalcitrance and open rebellion of the northern people. The people of the north, the ancient Northumbrians, had traditionally been hard for the southern Saxon kings of old to control. Their remoteness and dismissiveness towards a distant king's authority had encouraged this. It had proved no easier for the Conqueror, but his methods were more brutal; this was a man 'too relentless to care though the world might hate him'. The campaign which William led was to become known as the 'Harrying of the North'. What it would mean for the people of Durham was a savage period of ruthless killing and burning. As Surtees tells us, 'The march of the Norman army was traced in blood, the inhabitants were subject to indiscriminate slaughter, the villages were left smoking in ashes, and even the convents and monasteries were involved, undistinguished in the common destruction.'

William had a plan which if successful would end northern defiance for a generation. As he marched north, detachments were left to repair, strengthen and garrison castles and strongholds. His main force he split into two, marching through eastern and central Durham, possibly as far north as Hexham. As they marched they destroyed everything and everyone in their path. With the northern leaders in hiding in the hills, the Conqueror's armies fell upon the peasants. The inhabitants were massacred, villages burned. The grain from the recent harvest was taken or destroyed, as were the ploughs and tools needed for the planting of the following year's crops. The livestock was butchered. Some of the population, remembering half-forgotten tales of

Danish maurauders, took to the old ways and followed their leaders back to the hills and forests; the clerics returned to Lindisfarne. All around were 'scenes, which at every footstep presented traces of destruction – the County lay waste and desolate'. For those who survived the massacres and the burnings, there was to be no food through the winter of 1069–70. After horses, dogs and cats had been eaten, even perhaps human carcasses, some peasants sold themselves into slavery. Many just starved to death. Symeon tells us that 'The roads of the north were littered with decaying bodies that spread disease. Between York and Durham there was not an inhabited town, only lairs of wild animals and robbers, greatly to terrify travellers.' Fordyce adds:

> Such were the effects of the progress of the Normans throughout England, that for nine years the land in this portion of the kingdom remained untilled, and was infested with robbers and beasts of prey. The remnant of the inhabitants who had escaped the sword, died in the fields, overwhelmed by want and misery.

War, death, famine and disease; it must indeed have seemed to those surviving in misery that the Four Horsemen of the Apocalypse had visited Durham and had levied a terrible tribute. Some historians have numbered the dead in the northern counties in hundreds of thousands. Indeed, it is no doubt significant that when, in 1086, King William commissioned the Domesday Book, the great survey of England and its people, his commissioners recorded details only as far north as the River Tees. Beyond that point little remained to be documented. To William the Conqueror, all resistance was now totally crushed; he had at last solved his political and military problems in the north. An anonymous chronicler wrote: 'The whole area was reduced by fire and sword to a horrible desert, smoking with blood and ashes.' And as Thierry recorded: 'It was the end of rebellion according to the Normans, of Liberty according to the English.'

With his northern lands finally under control, William pushed on to the Scottish border to seek fealty from King Malcolm. On his return in 1072, he came to Durham. The position of the city was, he considered, ideal for the building of a strong, permanent fortification.

> The King on his northern expedition observed how proper a situation Durham was by nature of being made a barrier against the invasion of the Scots. So also to keep in awe the inhabitants north of the Tyne, having become the common receptacle of all those abandoned and dissolute wretches of the land, and the followers of those who were discontented with Government and ready on any occasion to take arms.

William decided therefore to make Durham the centre of administrative and military affairs in the north of his kingdom. Fortification and consolidation would now begin. He gave orders to Waltheof the Earl of Bamburgh to begin construction of what eventually became the great castle that towers over the city today, which, once built and garrisoned, would protect the King's realm in the north from 'tumults and insurrections', and hold it safe as a strategic buffer zone between the King in the south and the marauding Scots, stamping Norman authority finally and irreversibly upon the north of England. Laurence, a monk and Prior of Durham between 1149 and 1153, observed of the Conqueror's castle of his day:

> And whereas the strong site everywhere defends the unyielding City, yet art also with a wall defends and adorns it. A strong wall everywhere girds its lofty cress, a wall in scarcely any need of garrison; it is broad and strong, it is capped by lofty battlements with threatening towers at intervals. But the native rock served as its solid foundation, resting on which the skilful structure is still more conspicuous, and thus, strong both in situation and by art, it fears neither the blow of the battering ram, nor the force of the catapult, whichever it be.

It is interesting to consider the state of mind of the King once all rebellion had been crushed. He had come from overseas at the head of an army bent on conquest. He had driven all before him from the south coast of England to the Scottish borders, and with a few thousand knights had seized a country with a population of over a million. The native English had been subjected to fire, sword and starvation and all had finally bowed before the mighty conqueror. William's belief in his own invincibility must have known no bounds. And it was perhaps because of this arrogance that a legend grew, out of a story of what happened when William finally challenged the sanctity of St Cuthbert himself.

When in Durham, probably on the same occasion that he ordered the building of the castle, William made it known that stories of the power of the great northern saint and of the incorrupt state of his body, had reached his ear. He did not believe them, and insisted on inspecting the entombed body of the saint himself. The clerics argued against it and tried to persuade William not to do so. However, recognising the temperament and reputation of the King, as Symeon puts it 'several Bishops and Abbots then present assented to his will, and thought it proper that the King's pleasure should be complied with'. However, as the clerics delayed William grew angry and suspicious, and he solemnly vowed that if he was deceived, and the incorrupt body of the saint was 'merely a tale to work upon the superstition of the vulgar', he would put to death 'all those of superior rank throughout the city who had presumed to impose upon him'. No doubt upon hearing those words the monks prayed devoutly to St Cuthbert for their deliverance. The King commanded the tomb be opened. It was All Saints' Day 1072. The story continues that during the opening of the tomb William 'found himself smitten by a sudden burning fever, which distracted him in an intolerable manner'. Seized with terror at the thought of being struck down by the wrath of the saint for his insolence, the King rushed out of the church, leaving untasted a grand banquet which had been prepared for him. He instantly mounted his horse and sped from the city. Tradition has it that he fled down what is today Dun Cow Lane and out through a gate in the city wall where Bow Lane now stands, to a ford in the river, crossing the river and climbing the opposite bank, 'never abating the speed of his horse till he arrived on the banks of the Tees', about 30 miles south of Durham. The gate in the wall associated with the story became known as Kingsgate. Kingsgate Bridge, linking the peninsula with New Elvet, towers today over the scene of William's flight. The Conqueror had finally met his match. Of course the story of the dread King's flight and the indication of 'God's displeasure' at the attempt to disturb the sacred remains overawed the people of Durham and contributed greatly to the veneration paid at the saint's shrine.

William the Conqueror died as a result of a freak accident at Rouen in Normandy, at dawn on 9 September 1087. He was 60 years old. His Norman legacy was to live on in Durham. The site of his castle, and of course the great Norman cathedral which William never lived to see, is now a World Heritage Site, one of only a handful in Britain. To qualify for this status a site must 'have a value in illustrating a part of history'. It is said that as he lay dying, for only the second time in his life – the first being at the moment of his crowning as King of England, when 'he wept and shook uncontrollably' – William showed signs of guilt and remorse for the deaths of many thousands of people for which he was responsible. An Anglo-Norman historian named Ordericus Vitalis claimed to have recorded William's deathbed confession:

> I have persecuted the natives of England beyond all reason. Whether gentle or simple I have cruelly oppressed them . . . I fell on the English of the northern shires like a ravening lion. I commandeered their horses and corn, with all their implements and chattels. In this way I took revenge on multitudes by subjecting them to the calamity of a cruel famine, and so became the barbarous murderer of many thousands, both young and old, of that fine race of people. Having gained the throne of the kingdom by so many crimes, I dare not leave it to anyone but God.

Part Two

Chapter Four

The Pirate Saint

'When the curfew's toll is stealing slowly o'er the dew bent lea; when
the matin chimes are pealing, ever, ever, prayeth he.'

Outside the small stone dwelling, the February air was chill and dank. The
River Wear, swollen with the winter rains, swept noisily by a few yards away,
its cold, muddy torrent undercutting the steep, high, wooded banks opposite.
Inside, a small fire gave life to flickering shadows which danced across the
earthen floor and played upon the walls. The old man lay dying. He watched
through misted eyes as the shadows capered around the room, picked out in
the orange glow of the fire, the light of which illuminated the dark corners of
his home as if they were the hidden recesses of the old man's mind, revealing
to him memories half forgotten.

He watched as the shadows acted out scenes upon the walls like ghosts of
people long gone who had returned to say their final farewells to Godric, the
Holy Man. He tried to remember; where was Reginald? Would that he were
here! His was the task of recording the story of the old man's life and neither
the life nor the story had yet reached an end. But now, after 105 long years,
most of which had been spent in extreme austerity and self-denial, the last
essence of Godric's earthly being was finally fading and would soon be carried
far from this ancient place, borne away on the wind and in the rushing of the
river.

Suddenly the old man was aware of someone outside; a familiar voice
hailed him as footsteps squelched through the mud and gingerly picked a way
to his door. He was reminded of the time many years ago when strange
footsteps outside had heralded less welcome company. In the year 1138 King
David I of Scotland had led his army south to Durham and some of his
soldiers fell upon Godric with robbery on their minds. He could not

remember what, apart from his cow, they had taken. But he did remember the blows and the beating he received from the 'half naked pagan men'.

A shadow fell across the door, a familiar figure entered. Ah! Reginald at last. Reginald had news. The story of Godric's life was now complete and here before him was Reginald's account of it. Godric smiled faintly as he remembered how he had at first disparaged the idea of any record being made of his life, and had said to Reginald, his would-be biographer, 'You wish to write of my life? Know then that Godric's life is such as this: Godric, at first a gross rustic, an unclean liver, a usurer, a cheat, a perjurer, a flatterer, a wanderer, pilfering and greedy; now a dead flea, a decayed dog, a vile worm, not a hermit but a gad-about in mind; a devourer of alms, dainty over good things, greedy and negligent, lazy and snoring, ambitious and prodigal, one who is not worthy to serve others, and yet every day beats and scolds those who serve him: this and worse than this, you may write of Godric.'

He recalled that after his tirade he had been silent and indignant, Reginald had departed with a look of confusion, and Godric had again been left to himself and to his God. After some considerable persuasion, however, the old man had eventually relented. And now, as he weakened, he signalled Reginald to bank up the fire, sit close by him, and tell the story. His friend opened the volume and started to read. As Reginald's words began to describe places and people long forgotten, Godric closed his eyes and let his thoughts fly back, back through the long years to his youth. Suddenly, as if in a vision, he saw a wild place, a coastline strangely familiar, and a figure: a young man sitting on a sand bar watching the sea thunder in, casting its spell upon him, whispering to him of far-off places, calling him, ever calling him. Godric recognised the youth as himself and knew then that it was beyond the sea and down many long roads that the young man's destiny would ultimately lie. Through the half-heard dream sounds of the surf on the shore – or was it the wind in the trees, or the river outside? – the old man heard Reginald's steady voice speaking words telling of Godric's early years, whence he came, and of the many paths down which he had walked that had eventually led him to a life devoted to austerity, to prayer and to God.

His younger days had been spent in the uncertain years. Born at the time of the Conquest, his youth had gone by during a dangerous time of instability and oppression in England, of rebellion and of despotic Norman warlords. He had been born in Norfolk, between the Wash and the Fens in the village called Walpole. His father, Aeilward, and mother, Aedwen, were of Anglo-Saxon stock and in early post-Conquest England to be of that race was to be considered of lower class, subservient to the Norman masters. In his early years Godric had been a pedlar, travelling around Lincolnshire selling his wares and making some kind of meagre living. Never content, he had always felt the urge to travel, the need to fulfil his destiny; but he did not know then where his destiny lay nor where his journeying would eventually lead him.

In his twenties his yearning to travel had taken him on a pilgrimage to Rome and there the seeds of his future life were sown. But on his return he finally answered the call of the sea. He bought shares in two ships and traded around the North Sea, in Scotland, in Denmark, and in Flanders. He had become captain of his own vessel; 'A crafty steersman he was, a wise weather prophet, a shipman stout in body and in heart.'

However, life at sea was hard and violent, piracy and murder were the norm; Godric was no stranger to either. Human life was cheap and a man had constantly to protect his goods, his ship and his life, and do whatever was necessary so to do. Godric's reputation as a mariner and adventurer had soon grown, and spread to distant shores. In 1101 he had sailed to the Mediterranean, wishing to make a pilgrimage to Jerusalem; and it had been he, Godric, who the following year had been the 'Guderic, a pirate from the Kingdom of England' that had given passage on his ship from Arsuf to Jaffa to Baldwin I, Crusader King of Jerusalem. He had returned to England via Spain where he had become the first Englishman to make the long pilgrimage to the shrine of St James at Santiago de Compostela. The call of his God was beginning to grow stronger. After his arrival back in England he had become steward to a rich Anglo-Norman lord with large estates in Godric's native Norfolk.

In his dreaming, the old man remembered his time there, and how he had stood against his master on hearing of the behaviour of his Norman household; riding out, stealing sheep from the Saxon peasants, butchering the animals and passing off the meat as freshly hunted venison, pocketing a high price. He remembered well that 'like most Normans, they ate, drank, roistered and rioted'.

He heard a voice speaking to him; yes, it was Reginald's, but no, the voice had changed, now it was his former master's, speaking words Godric had heard long ago: 'Let the lads rob the English villains; for what other end did their grandfathers conquer this land?' After this incident Godric had left his employment, and again he began to wander. His religious calling was now becoming of prime importance to him. He made further pilgrimages, to St Giles in Provence and to Rome. Later he returned once more to Rome, taking with him Aedwen, his mother. Godric had trodden the path of the prilgrim to Rome, he had been to Jerusalem and visited the holy places, but now an inner sense was beginning to guide him to a different way of life. In his time at sea he had visited the Holy Island of Lindisfarne, and had heard told the tale of St Cuthbert. Godric had landed on Inner Farne to see for himself where the great saint had spent his dying days. And it had been after this visit that the first yearnings for a life of solitude had been stirred in Godric's soul. Now, years later, those early yearnings had become a burning desire. So it had come about that in the year 1105 Godric had sold all his possessions and sought out the life of the recluse.

At first he had wandered as far as Carlisle where he had lived for some time alone in a forest. Eventually travelling across country he arrived in Wolsingham in the Wear Valley. There he had made the acquaintance of, and drawn inspiration from, Aelric, a solitary who lived in the woods nearby. For two years, until the old hermit's death on 5 October 1107, Godric had remained with Aelric. After the death of his companion, he wished to make one last pilgrimage to the Holy Sepulchre, and it was at this time that Godric had received a vision. In it he was told that on his return from the Holy Land St Cuthbert would find for him a hermitage at a place called Finchale, a place which at that time was unknown to him. So it was that Godric forsook the forests of Wolsingham and once again left his native land to travel east to Jerusalem.

Godric remembered a river, a wide river in a land far away; and thus once again, in his dreams, he beheld the River Jordan. He recalled reaching the great river, bathing there his travel-sore feet and casting away his shoes. Having anointed his feet in the waters of the Jordan, he would walk barefoot for the rest of his life. For many months he had worked in a leper hospital and lived simply in the desert, the same desert in which John the Baptist had lived and preached. He remembered too the holy men, the hermits living solitary lives in desert caves, a way of life that Godric now desperately wished to lead. Eventually he set out from Jerusalem and trod the long road back to England. It was the start of his final journey, seeking out his own hermitage at the place St Cuthbert had promised to reveal to him. The place called Finchale.

On his return, Godric used the skills of his old trade as a pedlar to pay his passage north. He had first settled at a deserted hermitage at Eskdale near Whitby. There he remained for about a year until finally he found his way to Durham. When he first arrived Godric had taken a job as sacrist at the Church of St Giles, and though now in his forties, he attended school with the choir. So it was that Godric had become attached to the monastery of Durham.

It had been during a period of intense activity; the new Norman cathedral was under construction. Teams of craftsmen and artisans that had already spent 15 or more years of their lives on the great project, bustled and busied. Another quarter of a century would pass before the grand design of Bishop William of St Carileph and his architects would reach completion. Within the massive walls of the partly completed edifice, countless stonemasons wielded their chisels. Rough hands that crafted with the skill of an artist wielding a brush; their cries and the music of their chisels, steel ringing upon stone, mingled with the music of the monkish chants from the nearby monastery. Ever upward they worked. The nave was almost completed, the mighty columns that would eventually hold aloft the great vaulted ceiling were being put in place. Each section arrived already cut and finished, ready to be placed by skilled hands on top of the last.

Troops of soldiers issued back and forth from the castle, itself being gradually transformed from timber stronghold to stone fortress. The Prince Bishop's courtiers, arrayed in colurful attire, would ride out for sport, down the narrow streets and out into the nearby parks and forests to hunt and hawk. Long, patient lines of pilgrims made their way to the shrine of St Cuthbert. slowly winding their way between the never-ending traffic of oxen, pulling carts laden with stone. Cut stone and rough, hewn from the earth nearby, the raw material destined to be fashioned into an architectural wonder and a glory to God.

Soon Godric gained renown among his fellows. He showed a gift for clairvoyance and prophecy. He lived his life in great simplicity, and rumour of his humility and holiness had soon spread within the monastery and without, to the people of the city and of the countryside. Becoming aware of the piety of the man, many came to seek him out, for it was told that miraculous healings had been brought about by God through the hands and the prayers of Godric. But still the sins of his past lay as a burden on his soul and he began to look out from the Durham monastery; as yet he could still not see the end of his road. Eventually, however, Godric's dream in the woods at Wolsingham would become a reality, as it was while in the company of the monks of St Cuthbert that the site of Finchale was finally revealed to him.

The site was within the Bishop of Durham's hunting park, on the Bishop's land. However, recognising the esteem in which Godric was increasingly being held, the Bishop, Ranulph Flambard, granted to the Prior and convent of Durham 'the hermitage of Finchale, with its land and fisheries and all other things adjacent thereto, which I have granted to their Brother Godric, with their consent, to be held of them during his life'.

It was indeed an ancient place, situated on a bend of the River Wear about three miles to the north of Durham. It had in the old days been a site of some importance. Great Saxon councils, the Witans, had been held at the place called 'Wincanhale'. It had been the venue for church synods in the years 792 and 810; the scene of the death in 765 of Ethelward, King of Northumbria. Now it was a lonely spot. Surrounded by deep woods, overlooked by forbidding cliffs, it was the haunt of wolves and was infested by snakes. An unfriendly and unforgiving place indeed for Godric finally to find his rest. And so it was, in the year 1110, that 'the first Henry was on the throne of England, when the Norfolk mariner cast anchor at Finchale'.

Godric settled at first at a spot about a mile from the site where in future years the Priory would stand. At St Godric's Garth, as his little hermitage became known, he would be 'the companion of serpents and poisonous asps'.

After five years he had moved along the river to the spot known as Finchale, and there he 'built his cell of thatch, dedicating it to the Virgin Mary'.

And so the story had come full circle. Reginald's words now told of Godric's life at the place where the old man lay dying. How long had Reginald read? Was it hours; it could have been days. All was confusion in the old man's mind, drifting back from blessed dream to cold reality. But he still heard, and the voice he heard was a comfort to him. Reginald began to tell of 60 years of incredible harshness and self-denial that had been Godric's self-imposed penance. A penance for the deeds of the olden days, of his youth. He had been '16 years a seaman, with a seaman's temptations'. And in this lonely place, solitude, devotion to God, and the power of prayer would aid the river to wash away the sins of his past.

Godric had begun a way of life of almost unbelievable austerity. At first surviving on roots from the ground and berries from the trees, he either refused offerings of food or received them with thanks and fed them to the birds. He had gouged out of the riverbed a hollow which would be filled naturally by the flow of the River Wear and in it he would stand, up to his neck in the cold water, both summer and winter, praying through the night. As time passed his personal regime had become more, not less, severe, purging himself of what he saw as the sins of his early days. 'His jerkin was of iron . . . a strange coat, whose stuffe had the ironmonger for the draper, and a smith for the taylour.' He wore a hair shirt covered by a metal breastplate, three of which he had worn out before his death. He baked his own bread, sprinkling ashes from the fire into the dough. The loaves he then left to go stale before he would eat them. No bed had he on which to rest. Lying on the cold earth he used a stone as a pillow. Godric's zealous devotion to God and to prayer became widely known. His reputation both as holy man and clairvoyant had grown. Pilgrims began to visit him at Finchale, for they knew that his were also the hands of the healer. Eventually the procession of pilgrims had become so great that about the year 1150 a new chapel, dedicated to St John the Baptist, was built. The situation was encouraged by the monastery at Durham: 'They were glad to have a "wonder working man" as one of them.'

Visitors gained admission to Godric's hermitage only by carrying a wooden cross which first had to be given them by the Prior of Durham. Through time his fame had spread. The miracles continued; the visions, the premonitions growing in number, the prayer never ending. People began to realise that Godric was becoming even closer to his God.

When he first settled at Finchale his family had followed him and lived nearby. Tragedy, however, followed close behind. Aedwen, his aged mother, had died shortly after coming to Finchale; his brother had been killed, drowned in the River Wear. Burchewen, his sister, had returned to Durham to join the Sisters of the Convent where her life would eventually end. Godric was destined to live on and grow old. At his hermitage he was to 'work miracles and obtain much renown'.

He was granted visions. The Virgin Mary and Mary Magdalene had appeared to him in his cell. He had seen souls ascending to heaven including the soul of his own sister Burchewen, whom he saw singing to him accompanied by a choir of angels. He had written music and hymns and his reputation had grown.

Like other saintly men, Godric had shown an affinity with animals. Often when finding injured creatures or those dying from cold in the winter time, he would take them back to his cell and tend them till they were well enough to return to the forest. Once a stag had been hunted through the woods by the Prince Bishop's party; exhausted, it had taken refuge in Godric's hermitage. The huntsmen asked Godric if he had seen the stag go by or if he knew to where it could have fled. Godric replied cryptically, 'God knows where it is.' The huntsmen, glancing uneasily at each other, excused themselves and apologised to the holy man for disturbing him.

The pilgrims continued to arrive seeking of Godric his healings, his teachings and his prayers. Some wished a vision or a telling of events yet to come. His name had come to the attention of men of rank and influence and he had corresponded with and received as guests senior Churchmen including Ailred, Abbot of Rievaulx, and William De St Barbe, Bishop of Durham.

The years went by and Godric's fame spread far, even beyond the shores of England. Pope Alexander III had written to Godric. The Pontiff had commended him on his devotion and his way of life and had asked the old man to 'pray for him, and the whole Church'.

Towards the end of Godric's life a feud had developed in England between King Henry II and Thomas à Becket, Archbishop of Canterbury. Becket, formerly the King's Chancellor and lifelong friend, had defied Henry over the question of the jurisdiction of both civil and ecclesiastical courts. The King considered that clerics accused of criminal acts should be subject to the King's law and tried in the civil courts and not by the Church's own courts, a privilege which had been held by the Church through Royal Assent. Henry had installed Becket as Archbishop of Canterbury, expecting his friend to pressure the Church establishment into acceding to the King's will. Becket instead sided with the Church, stating that the King was attempting to take away rights granted to the Church by Henry's predecessor. Each held the intractable view that the other was interfering in areas outside their lawful jurisdiction. A rift developed between the two which quickly widened and deepened. During this time of trouble Becket had sent messages to Godric at Finchale, and the old hermit had replied to the Archbishop, offering him support in his struggle against the mighty Henry Plantagenet. Tragically, as a result of hasty words spoken by the King in temper, Thomas à Becket was slain whilst kneeling in prayer on the steps of the High Altar of Canterbury Cathedral. Godric had foreseen the coming of this brutal event; however, he was destined never to hear of its passing.

The old man suddenly heard the quietness. Reginald's tale was told. Godric motioned to him to bring forward his work: 'Reginald brought the book to the Saint and, falling on his knees, begged him to bless it in the name of God and for the benefit of the faithful. Godric blessed the book and bade Reginald conceal it till his death.'

This would now be soon; the book was ended, the life was about to end. Godric's years of devotion were drawing to a close. A harsh life and long, his body so broken by the severity of his living that for the final eight years he had been unable much to move, his voice unable to be heard. But he did hear. He heard birdsong outside, and a soft sweet breeze which made the fresh green leaves dance on the trees. Through the long telling of the tale, winter had passed into spring and spring would soon welcome in summer, but it would be a summer that Godric would never see.

Thus, on 21 May in the year 1170, Godric's last breath escaped his lips, the rigours of his earthly life finally at an end, and he went at last to meet his God.

Godric had lived long. He had been born at the time of one mighty king, William the Conqueror, and had died in the reign of another, Henry II. Between his birth and his death, England had seen war and civil strife. The turbulent reigns of four kings had ended before finally a new stability had come about through the emergence of a nation united. Through much of this time the 'Norfolk mariner' had devoted his solitary life to God. He was looked upon as a saint by all those who sought his teachings and his prayer. A quiet man whose fiercesome appearance, 'flashing grey eyes under bushy black brows, thick bearded and of great breadth of chest and strength of arm', was an appearance which belied his manner. He was a man 'eager to listen and slow to speak; always serious, and sympathetic to those in trouble'.

He was buried in his own chapel of St John. The tomb in which he was laid can still be seen today. In the year 1196, Finchale became a cell of Durham and the beginnings of a Priory came about, on and around the site of St Godric's hermitage. It is the ruins of that Priory which still stand at Finchale.

The Church of St Godric can be seen to the western side of Durham City. Standing on a lofty site his church looks over the city and out across the peninsula to the cathedral, the final resting place of St Cuthbert. A fitting place, perhaps, as it was partly from the tale of Cuthbert that was drawn the inpsiration for the life, the teachings and the devotion to God of St Godric, the pirate saint.

Chapter Five

Of Brave and Bowld Sir John

'One Sunday mornin' Lambton went a fishin' in the Wear/And catched a fish upon his heuk, he thowt looked varry queer.'

So begins C.M. Leumane's popular 'Tyne Pantomime Song'. Written in 1867, it tells the story of the most notorious of Durham's legendary beasts, and of how 'Brave and Bowld' Sir John Lambton returned from the Crusades and slayed the monster, ridding the people 'on byeth sides o' the Wear' of the terror that was 'The Famous Lambton Worm'. The story of 'young Lambton' and the worm has been an enduring one and, unlike many other folk tales which are invariably embroidered upon, it has come down through the centuries relatively unchanged. Even though slight variations have occurred through the telling and retelling of the tale, mainly through poem, ballad and song, the essence of the story, passed down through the writing of earnest chroniclers of such tales, has remained remarkably consistent.

Young John Lambton, heir to Lambton Estate, was, we are told, a ne'er-do-well, a wayward and wild youth who cared little for others, being selfish in nature, and brought trouble upon his father and his family. One day – the song of course says one Sunday, but other writers have suggested it was in fact Easter Day – instead of going with his father to church, he went fishing in the Wear, for 'the sweet strains of worship had no charm for him'. As the matin bell tolled, young John set off for the river. He fished a long time with no luck and grew impatient and angry. He cursed the fish, he cursed the river, he cursed his luck and he cursed the day, Easter Day. Suddenly a pull on his line, a strong pull, a sizeable fish, but when John examined his catch he saw it was neither salmon nor trout but a small worm or eel of 'most unseemly and disgusting appearance'. With a shiver of revulsion, John tore the worm from his hook and threw it down a nearby well. Just at that a stranger appeared, an old man, who asked John, 'What sport?' 'Well truly,' John replied, 'I think I've caught the devil.' He told the old man of his mysterious catch. The stranger went to the well, looked down deep into the clear water, and saw the worm writhing on the bottom. He flashed John a piercing sideways glance, and as he turned to walk away he gave a queer laugh and said, almost under his breath, that this worm 'tokened no good'.

Life went on, John grew older and eventually, we are told, repented of his rebellious youth and changed his ways. He 'bathed in a bath of holy water, took the sign of the cross, and joined the Crusades'. Seven years he was away, and while he was away the evil thing that he had let loose grew and grew. It moved out of the well and coiled itself round a rocky crag in the middle of the river. There it stayed by day, at night retreating to a nearby hill, the Worm Hill. Surtees records that 'Worm Hill stands not within the domain of Lambton, but on the north bank of the Wear in North Biddick, a mile and a half from "old" Lambton Hall. The worm well lies betwixt the hill and the Wear.' Stephenson, in his book *The Lambton Worm – a Legendary Tale*, tells us that 'the old hall stood on the southern bank of the Wear on the brow of a hill, nearly opposite Lambton Castle'. As the worm grew, it took to moving around the nearby countryside, devouring livestock and terrorising the inhabitants. It became a ravaging monster 'committing every species of injury on the cattle and peasantry, the neighbourhood lay waste and barren'. The early fourteenth-century *Romance of Syr Dygore* describes the worm as 'a dragon great and grymme, full of fire, and also of venymme; with a wide throte and tuskes grete'. And Brocket tells of 'a serpent of great magnitude and of terrific description; a hideous monster in the shape of a worm or dragon'.

The Lord Lambton was frail and bent with age, he could not take arms against the beast. Seven others had tried and failed. By some devilry, when the worm was cut to pieces by sword or axe the pieces rejoined and the monster became whole again. The Lambton Estate was being laid low by the beast, people lived in 'mortal fear'. Seeking new feeding grounds the worm crossed the river and headed for the old hall itself. A trough of milk was set out daily as an offering. The beast would come, drain the trough filled with the milk of 'nine kye', nine of the finest oxen on the estate, and return to the river or the hill. The old lord desperately needed a champion, a great warrior who could rid him of this curse, the curse that his son John had unleashed on that Easter Day, seven years before. But John was now Sir John, he had 'gone to the wars in a far distant land, to wage war against the infidels'. He had grown strong in stature, stout of heart, mighty in battle, and his courage was great.

'Thus on the plains of Palestine, he gained a mighty name/And full of
 honour and renown, to the home of his childhood came.'

The evil he had unleashed before was apparent to him on his return. His father's joy at his son's return was made bitter by the tale he had to tell of the dreadful circumstances of the estate, and of the fear and destruction of the worm. Sir John made a solemn vow to rid the people once and for all of the curse. He would destroy the worm that he had let loose in former days. His father told him that some dark magic was about the worm that enabled it to rejoin when cut by a blade. Other brave men had tried to kill it, all had failed. 'No knight nor vassal this worm can kill, but various it hath slain/No Lord of the dale, nor Lord of the hill, its fury can sustain.'

Sir John decided to consult a 'wise woman'. If the tales were true then force of arms and skill in battle were not to be enough to destroy the worm. He needed the counsel of someone skilled in another, more ancient craft. The wise woman he consulted seems to have been almost as daunting a sight as the worm itself, a bent, gnarled old woman 'with matted locks and piercing eyes, and a rugged screaming voice'. She gave Sir John the advice he needed, she told him how he could kill the worm. He must forge a special suit of armour with razor-sharp spearheads embedded in it. He must engage the beast in battle in the middle of the River Wear and allow it to coil itself around him. The worm would therefore cut itself to pieces on the blades and the Wear would carry the pieces away, so denying the monster a chance to rejoin itself. The advice, however, had a price. The wise woman told Sir John that after the death of the worm he must kill the first living thing that he saw. A small price to pay, he thought. But it was a price the Lambton family would continue to pay over the next nine generations.

Plans were made, the suit of armour forged and Sir John prepared himself for battle. This was to be no ordinary combat. Other forces, apart from mere muscle and sinew, would decide the day. Sir John knew the ferocity of his opponent and the size of his task. The worm had seen challengers come before and brave men had perished in its crushing coils and its tearing jaws. As we are told in *Syr Dygore*, 'Many a man he had shent, and many a horse he had rent.'

And so as mass was said in the family chapel, allegedly the chapel of Brigford, 'Brave and Bowld Sir John', having fasted and made due penance, set out to do battle with the beast. As he rode towards the river the sky began to darken ominously and a drenching blanket of drizzling rain began to fall. The murmur of his passing started rooks from the treetops and sent them wheeling noisily up into the still air, breaking the brooding silence of the forest. The dull clump of his horse's hoofs seemed somehow muffled, and as the sky grew dark as night and thunder rumbled in the distance it seemed the very countryside itself was watching, waiting with morbid anticipation for the mortal combat that was to come. Leaving behind his horse, the knight journeyed on, drawing ever nearer to the river, and the beast. At last, with a sudden gusting wind lashing the chill rain into his face, Sir John arrived at his journey's end. The darkness had deepened and enveloped both the lapping water and the dark, wooded riverbanks. It seemed everything, man, beast, water and woods, was indistinct in the gloom. All that could be heard was the hiss of the rain on the river and the sighing of the wind in the trees.

Suddenly a flash of brazen white light, a deafening crash of thunder; lightning struck a gnarled old oak tree near the river and rent it in two halves.

'Then lo! the beam of lightning's gleam, illuminates the darkness all.'

In the eerie glare Sir John at last saw his quarry, coiled around its rocky haven in the middle of the rushing river. Sir John marked the beast, and the beast marked him.

'In monstrous coil the worm there lay, i'th'midst of Wear's old stream/A reptile huge might strike dismay, in stoutest heart e'er seen.'

Clutching his sword and offering up his soul to providence, Sir John waded out into the torrent and joined battle with the worm. Again and again he struck the monster about the head with his sword, his blows having no more effect than would insect bites, his blade glancing off the thick hide, serving merely to 'vex' the beast. Again and again the worm lunged at him with gaping cavernous jaws. Time after time Sir John hewed at the monster, blow after savage blow until his body ached and his heart pumped as if it would burst. His strength began to wane. He could wield his sword no more. The worm thrashed and roared. The river boiled around him. The thunder cracked above as if the very sky were splitting asunder and the stinging rain blinded his eyes. The worm moved in for the kill.

'Tho' his heart was stout, it quivered no doubt, his very life-blood run cold/As around, around, the wild worm wound, in many a grappling fold.'

As the worm 'wound itself with great fury' around Sir John's body, his legs, his arms, he knew that the end was near. Round and round it coiled, tighter and tighter until the razor-sharp spearheads embedded in Sir John's armour began to do their bloody work. The blades bit deep into the flesh of the monster, in agony it writhed. The more it writhed the deeper the blades bit; the worm in its rage was cutting itself to pieces. Seizing the advantage, Sir John gathered the last vestiges of his strength to wield his sword once more. With one supreme effort he hacked at the neck of the dying beast until the hideous head was severed from its body. The pieces were carried away by the river, swollen and rushing with the rain, thus the worm was unable to rejoin and was finally and totally destroyed.

Sir John watched as one by one the pieces of the worm were washed away by the stream. He staggered wearily back to the riverbank and collapsed with exhaustion, his body aching, his head reeling. He remembered the words of the wise woman and the price he now had to pay. He recalled he must kill the first living thing he saw or the heirs of Lambton would be cursed for nine generations, never to die a peaceful death.

'What thing soever he first doth meer, that he shall quickly slay/Or down to thy ninth heir one shall ne'er die a-bed by night or day.'

He put his plan into action. Fearing some family, friend or wanderer in the woods may blunder into his sight, he had arranged with his father that on a signal of victory, a single blow upon his hunting horn, Sir John's favourite hound his father would let slip, and when the hound found its master its sacrifice would forestall the witch's curse. Sir John blew a great blast on his horn; his father, listening in the woods, let loose the dog, but in his joy he also ran to his son. The dog ran off into the thick undergrowth and could not find a way through to its master. The old man, forgetting the pains of his bones, hurried to the river, and was the first living thing his son saw. It was a grievous sight to Sir John such a terrible price as this surely could not be exacted. Suddenly his hound darted out from the forest, Sir John knew what he must do, and with great 'grief and reluctance' he plunged his sword into the heart of his faithful companion. This he thought would be sacrifice enough. It was not to be. The price required had not been paid and from that day onwards the heirs of Lambton were cursed never to die peacefully in their beds.

'Yet true the sacrifice prophesied, down to the ninth male heir/Not one of whom in bed there died, this truth can all declare.

'So now God rest their names all, and prosper long that line/No deed before was e'er achieved, like this in olden time.'

It is not known precisely from when the story dates. George Allan, writing in 1824, tells us that the Lambton family were seated at Lambton as early as the twelfth century; *Syr Dygore* is dated as early fourteenth century. The years of the Crusades are well known but exactly which crusade Sir John is meant to have joined is not recorded. If the date of the tale is unsure, what then of its origins. W. Stephenson concluded of the story, whether 'matter of fact or from whence it emanated, it is impossible to account and must forever remain in impenetrable darkness'. But in every legend it is said there is a kernel of truth, and down the years it seems to have been a popular pastime to put forward possible explanations for the origins of the story. Indeed it seems we have been left with a choice of explanations as to the story and history of 'The Famous Lambton Worm'.

Was the figure of the worm, as has been suggested, merely symbolic of the misdeeds the heir of Lambton had committed when young, before his conversion and his mission to the Holy Lands? Was it the result of some evil which he himself had sown in his youth finally put to rights by him on his return, and the worm merely a fanciful invention of the family or the local people, bequeathing the story for ever to legend? Perhaps!

Sir Cuthbert Sharpe, writing in the early 1800s, suggested in his book *The Worme of Lambton* that the worm may have been representational of an invading army or warband, possibly Scottish, well disciplined and trained in the arts of battle. Perhaps the legend has its origins with an army which encamped permanently on the Lambton Estate and demanded tribute, much in the style of Danish invaders long before. Such an army would certainly feed off the land, take cattle and sheep for food and raid for plunder. The old Lord of Lambton, being frail and advanced in years, may have been unable to rid himself of them, but perhaps successive attempts were made by the local nobility and militia to disperse and defeat this army. During battle the mysterious rejoining of the worm was simply a regrouping of forces, standard military procedure. An army encamped would seek a defensive position. What better than a hill, a shield wall 'coiling' up and around it which, when the warband was on the march in single file battle order over the undulating hillsides and winding its way through thick forest, would give the appearance of a gigantic worm. Sir John returned from the Crusades an experienced soldier, familiar with military strategy; did he ride at the head of his own force and engage the invaders, perhaps joining battle or even ambushing the enemy as it crossed the River Wear, the stream making it difficult for their ranks to regroup once split? Can we then imagine a skirmish or even a full-scale battle across the River Wear near Lambton Castle? Too fanciful!

Possibly a more simple, though less colourful, explanation is that Sir John was credited with slaying the wrong animal. The Norse word 'orme' is a generic term for serpents, dragons and mythic worms. Perhaps the legend has grown out of a simple misunderstanding or incorrect translation of the story. It is thought probable that the heavily wooded and sparsely populated countryside of the time was infested with wild boars, animals which were invariably large and highly dangerous. The ancient name for the wild boar is the 'brawn'. Corruptions of the word can still be heard, in place names around Durham: Brancepeth, for example, originates from Brawn's Path. Could then the monstrous Lambton 'orme' have actually been the monstrous Lambton 'brawn', and was this the basis around which the more fanciful elements of the story were later woven? We will probably never know!

Of course there is, some would say, another explanation: that the story is true. Robert Surtees, whose great work *The History and Antiquities of the County Palatine of Durham* was published between 1816 and 1840, records that in his younger days he visited the Estate of Lambton and there was on display a piece of some tough skin-like substance resembling bull's hide. He was assured that this was part of the skin of the Lambton worm itself. Fordyce tells us that on 13 May 1810 Surtees wrote to his friend Sir Walter Scott. Scott, apparently, was inclined to be attracted to legendary tales. Similarly Surtees was an enthusiastic chronicler of such stories, 'cherishing them, for delight of the imagination'. Surtees wrote:

I have been lately near the supposed haunts of the Lambton worm, and

I really feel much inclined to adopt your idea, that animals of this description may have been formerly nourished to a much larger size in our woods and waters . . . The country around Lambton seems particularly favourable for the production of such a creature. The banks of the river have been, time immemorial, a thick tangled forest; and part of the adjoining flats are low and marshy, and full of willows and brush wood.

The curse of the wise woman was also observed by generations of 'curse watcher's. The son of the hero of the legend apparently drowned near Brigford Chapel where his father had made his solemn vows. Sir William Lambton, a Royalist, was killed at Marston Moor during the Civil War, and his son, William, died at Wakefield at the head of a troop of dragoons in 1643. General Lambton, not being able to die in bed, had to be taken out of it before his agonies could be terminated. Henry Lambton MP was observed with great curiosity by the old people of the neighbourhood. The curse was due at last to end with his death. He died apparently of a heart attack, in his carriage, whilst crossing the new bridge over the Wear at Lambton on 26 June 1761. If the curse is retraced from this Henry Lambton back for exactly nine generations, it would reach one, Sir John Lambton, Knight of Rhodes. The various recorders of this story have invariably mentioned a curious entry in an old Lambton family pedigree, once in the possession of the family of Middleton, of Offerton. The entry reads: 'Johan Lambeton that slewe ye worme was Knight of Rhodes and Lord of Lambeton and Wood Apilton.'

The educated and well-read observer of today would, no doubt, scoff at and pour scorn on such childish imaginings. But as J. Watson points out in his nineteenth-century Ballad of the Lambton Worm:

> . . . For knowledge to their view has spread,
> Her rich and varied store;
> They learn and read and pay no heed,
> To legendary lore.

> And pure religion hath o'er them shed,
> A holier, heavenly ray;
> And dragons and witches, and mail-clad Knights,
> Are vanished away . . .

Chapter Six

Battle on the Red Hills

'This battel by us was called the Battel of Nevil's-Cross, and was the most fatal and bloody to the Scots.'

–T. Cox

Once a year, in observance of an ancient tradition, the choir of Durham Cathedral used to climb the 325 steps to the top of the great central tower. There they sang anthems of praise and thanksgiving. They sang facing to the north, to the south and to the east. They did not turn their faces to the west.

For it was out of the west on an October day in the year 1346 that a Scottish army under the command of King David Bruce came upon Durham, and the community of St Cuthbert was threatened with death and destruction. The Scots were met on the high ground to the west of the city by an English army commanded by the northern nobles Ralph Neville, Henry Percy and Thomas Rokeby. The story is told that on that day as the ensuing battle raged nearby, the monks of Durham ascended the cathedral tower and prayed for an English victory. Such was their fear, however, they dared not look out to observe the changing fortunes of the fray. They would not look towards the west.

The English King, Edward III, was in France. On 26 August of that year he had inflicted a crushing defeat on the French forces at the Battle of Crécy, His conquering armies marched on through Montrevil and Etaples to Boulogne, passed through the Forest of Hardelot, and opened the Siege of Calais. The French King, Philip VI, was in desperate need of help. His fighting forces were broken and he needed something; an armed ally, a calculated political manoeuvre, some unlooked-for twist of fate, anything to lift the siege and rid him of the English invader. The Scottish King, David Bruce, had long considered an invasion of England. He desired to make his name in a campaign more successful than previous expeditions, and he knew advantage could be taken of Edward's absence.

Indeed, David Bruce's ambitions towards England were not lost on Philip. Emissaries were sent from the French King to Scotland. They offered King David aid, money, weapons and men as an inducement to invade his neighbour. Philip knew if his heralds were successful and the Scottish King took the bait, as he did, Edward's own realm would be in danger and the English King would be forced to return to defend it. Thus the Siege of Calais would be lifted, and France would once more be freed from the aggressor.

The threat from the north had already been considered by those left in England, not least the King's wife, Philippa of Hainault. It was apparent that an army was needed in the north of England to meet any potential Scottish invasion. On 20 August 1346 the Queen had issued a 'Proclamation of Array' charging the Archbishop of York, William De La Zouch, together with the northern nobles Ralph Neville and Henry Percy with command of the English forces. Preparations were made for conflict.

David Bruce was in confident mood. He was only 23 years old, a young king 'stout and right jolly, and desirous to see fighting'. His time, he reckoned, had come. He held a 'parliament' at Perth where, predictably, it was decided to invade. The Scottish army rode south across the border then turned east, and in early October marched across Cumbria, ransacking Lanercost Priory on their way. They entered Northumberland and sacked Hexham. There they halted and prepared the town to act as a depository for their provisions and their plunder. From Hexham, King David's forces moved south towards Durham, eventually encamping at the Prior's hunting lodge and park of Beaurepaire near Bearpark, three miles from the city. From here foraging parties were sent out to pillage and plunder the surrounding countryside. A summary tax was levied on everyone that crossed their path, 'a penny for every head and a penny for every foot'. Three pennies were demanded from every peasant; those who refused to pay were put to the sword. So confident were the Scots of meeting little or no resistance that on the night of 15 October no guards were posted at their camp. It seems they were totally unaware of the massed English forces camped only a few short miles away.

The English army had been mustered in the grounds of the Prince Bishop's Palace at Bishop Auckland. As dawn broke on 16 October the English struck camp and began to move out, off down the old road to Merrington, part of the ancient Roman highway of Dere Street along which the legions had tramped on their way from York to Hadrian's Wall a thousand years before. The English had intelligence of the Scottish position, and Merrington, perched high on a ridge, would be an excellent vantage point from which to observe the enemy.

Indeed it was an exceptional morning for reconnaissance. Looking out through the crisp, clear October air, the English leaders could easily mark the Scottish host as it mustered on the hills to the west of Durham, six miles distant. There was some indecision in the English camp: should they remain where they were, in an excellent defensive position, and await the onslaught of the enemy forces, or should they advance to engage the foe at Durham. To an extent the decision was past taking. On sighting the enemy the standard bearers and heralds moved off. They rode the ridge as far as 'Fery on the Hill'; the English army followed. The wheels of war had started to turn. Battle was about to be joined.

The vanguard of the English army reached Ferryhill and came across a Scottish foraging party, about 500 horsemen commanded by the Earl of Douglas. The Scots, taken completely unawares, were in danger of being cut off and destroyed. They retreated as best they could, north towards Durham and their main force. The English with the advantages of surprise and superior numbers fell upon them. The retreat was harried along the North Road, down from Ferryhill and up on to what was the heathland, which we know as Thinford today. The Scots fought desperately as the clamour of battle intensified. The fiercest fighting took place between Thinford and the area where the Coach and Horses Inn now stands. There the majority of the Scots fell and the retreat became a rout. The invaders were ridden down and cut to pieces. Of the 500 of Douglas's horsemen over 300 were killed in the brief action, and the *Chronicle De Lanercost* singles out one Northumbrian knight, Robert Ogle, who it is claimed killed many Scots with his own hands. To this day the area where this bloody opening skirmish took place can be seen marked on any map as 'Butcher Race'. It was the opening clash of arms, the prelude to the Great Battle of Durham.

The Scots that survived Butcher Race fled back along the North Road with the English still in pursuit. They rode down to Croxdale, and crossed the River Wear at Sunderland Bridge. There the English outriders were halted. Those Scots who were left made their way back to the King to warn of the approach; Douglas was among them. He urged the King not to engage the English army in his present position, but to retreat to nearby high ground and seek a strategically more advantageous site. David Bruce did not heed him. The English, however, held back at the River Wear and encamped near to what is now the small village of Hett, just to the east of Sunderland Bridge. There they spent the night. In the morning they struck camp, crossed the river and marched towards Durham. The Scots, arranged in line of battle, awaited the coming of the English: 'The time had come when doomed men must needs fall. Then clamour arose, bitter was the rush of battle.'

Accounts of the numbers involved in the battle vary greatly but there were probably between 15,000 and 20,000 Scots, including the French reinforcements sent by Philip. The English forces probably numbered between 12,000 and 15,000, a slightly smaller force but better armed and better trained. The Scottish fighting force was made up mainly of poorly equipped feudal levies; the English army, it has been suggested, included a detachment of about 5,000 battle-hardened veterans of King Edward's forces from France. Also, significantly, and ultimately for the Scottish decisively, the English line included a large number of archers. Massed ranks of longbowmen were the secret weapon of the day; used effectively, they could alone turn the tide of a battle. Winston Churchill tells us:

> The power of the longbow and the skill of the bowmen had developed to a point where even the finest mail was no certain protection. At 250 yards the arrow hail produced effects never reached again by infantry missiles at such a range until the American Civil War.

In the lull before the battle, as the English approached, heralds were sent out by Henry Percy to try to persuade King David to turn and go home. The King refused to listen. A story is told that the Prior of Durham, carrying out instructions he had received in a dream the previous night, sent forth monks from the cathedral to a place near to the battlefield, the Maiden's Bower, there to strike a spear into the earth and from the shaft fly as a banner the Holy Corporax cloth, the same cloth St Cuthbert had used to cover the chalice during the Eucharist. There the monks would remain in prayer until the outcome of the day was known. There is a legend that a small number of Scots came across the monks, who appeared to be in such earnest and intense prayer and meditation that the soldiers, fearing some divine retribution, spared their lives. It may have been from the Maiden's Bower that two 'Black Monks' came before the Scottish King to plead for peace. But King David would have none of it. He had 'inherited the bravery, though not the wisdom of his father, Robert Bruce'. The scene was set: it was mid-morning on Tuesday, 17 October 1346, and the opening moves of the play were about to be made.

The English advanced in four divisions, three abreast, one in reserve. They marched north along the road, past what we know today as Neville's Cross and over the modern railway cutting. They took positions on Crossgate Moor: the right wing under Henry Percy comprised the spearmen of Northumberland; the centre and main force, men of Durham. Led by their commander-in-chief Ralph Neville, his son, and the Archbishop of York, the men of the bishopric would directly confront the Scottish King. The English left wing, comprising mainly archers from south of the Tees and Lancashire, were under the command of Sir Thomas Rokeby. They took their position probably on the high ground where today Toll House Road meets the North

Road, around the area of the Pot and Glass public house, overlooking the steep rising ground to the west and the Scottish right flank below on the low ground around Arbour House. The reserve, mainly cavalry and spearmen, held back. In this force rode Robert Ogle, hero of Butcher Race, and one John Copeland, a Northumberland knight who would achieve his own fame before the day was ended. Each of the English divisions was flanked by archers, the longbowmen who had proved so effective at Crécy, and who would be so again under a future king at Agincourt.

The Scots moved on to Durham Moor, arrayed in three divisions: the right, under the Earl of Moray and William Douglas, opposed Rokeby's archers; the King and his royal household led the centre against Ralph Neville; and the Scottish left division, commanded by the High Steward, was in position on the open ground where school playing fields can be seen today. The Scottish host moved slowly southwards, the October sun shining in their eyes. Down the small incline from Durham Moor, towards Crossgate Moor they charged, and around the site of the Durham Johnson School the two armies clashed.

The Scots' right wing attacked Rokeby's division. They charged recklessly into the blinding sun, the undulating and steeply rising ground making their charge difficult. They quickly tired. They struggled up the incline from Arbour House. They looked up towards the enemy and were dismayed. A shadow fell over the sun and spread across their upturned faces. A dense cloud of arrows rose into the air and hurtled, with murderous precision, down into the ranks of the attackers. Skipping off shield and mail, shower after deadly shower fell on to the advance. Many darts found their mark. The charge was halted. The bowmen continued their barrage and the Scots were driven back: 'A shower of steel fell incessantly upon them, and they were slaughtered in great numbers.' Choosing his moment, Rokeby charged what was left of the Scottish advance, which gave way and was routed. The Earl of Moray was killed, Douglas was captured, and the English archers turned their longbows on the now unprotected right flank of King David's division.

The other fighting had been pitched. The Scottish left had dismounted and fought the English hand to hand, with sword and battle axe wreaking a bloody havoc on both the English and Scottish lines. But for a time the lines held. Gradually, however, the English right, Percy's Northumbrians, became hard pressed by the High Steward's forces on the open ground. Little by little they were pushed back. The Scots commanders, sensing a breakthrough, charged their men forward in a frenzy. In their raging they paid no heed to a dull rumble in the air which suddenly became a crashing thunder all around them, and the screams and snorting of charging horses filled their ears as the English reserve smashed against the Scotitsh line like a tidal wave, and all was swept before it. The Northumbrian spearmen rallied and counter-attacked.

The High Steward's division, now in disarray, was driven back. They were dismayed and exposed and feared both thrust of lance and sting of dart but still they 'dealt many severe strokes with hard and sharp axes'. The High Steward, however, did not share the same resolve. Whether he had in mind the survival of what was left of his men or merely his own survival, he was the first to give the order to abandon the field.

King David was now exposed on both flanks, the English archers were free to hit wherever the most severe damage could be wrought, and the remains of all the English army fell upon the Scottish King's own division. In his romance novel *Marmion* (1808), Sir Walter Scott described the scene:

> The English shafts in volleys hail'd, in headlong charge their horse assail'd; front flank and rear, the squadrons sweep to break the Scottish circle deep, that fought around their King. But yet, though thick the shafts as snow, though charging knights like whirlwinds go, though bill men ply their ghastly blow, unbroken was the ring . . .

The end was in sight, but the fiercest struggle was yet to be seen. The Scottish nobles fought with a fury around their lord. He was, after all, the only son of the heroic Robert the Bruce, 'the great deliverer of his country'. The final fighting was long, bitter and bloody. The antiquarian and chronicler John Stow recorded in his *Annals*: 'The residue of the Scots continuing faithfully with their King, stood about him like a round tower, keeping him in the middle, who so continued till there were scarce forty of them left alive, out of which not one of them could escape.' But King David did escape. Somehow, through the frenzied and confused butchery of the last throes of the struggle, he was spirited through the battle lines and found freedom. At least for a little while.

Most of the Scottish royal household and nobility had been slain. The English searched, but King David was not amongst the dead. The hour was now well past noon, and after more than three hours of intense fighting the hard-won English victory was heralded by a single trumpet blast. The triumphant army cheered and the monks on the nearby cathedral tower, singing the Te Deum and ascribing the victory to God and Holy St Cuthbert, 'filled the air with the sounds of their acclamations, crying out and praising God and weeping tears of great joy'.

The English now pursued the surviving Scots who tried to make good their escape, either on foot or on horseback. Many were taken prisoner, many more were killed. The immediate retreat was pursued as far as Findon Hill near Sacriston. Those who fled on horseback were pursued and cut down as far away as Prudhoe and Corbridge in Northumberland. The Scottish dead that lay on the field were robbed of their arms and possessions. The Prior of

Durham, riding out on to the battlefield, observed: 'The most powerful of the Scottish nobles lay dead and despoiled of their arms, and stripped bare on Beaurepaire Moor.'

John Copeland, a knight of Wooler in Northumberland, was riding some way from the battlefield when he crossed a small, one-arched bridge over the River Browney. As he glanced down into the water he caught in the reflection a glimpse of a mail-clad figure cowering underneath. It was the Scottish King. Copeland dismounted and challenged David Bruce. The King, wounded by arrows in the leg and face, was weak with loss of blood, but even as Copeland struck the sword from the King's hand David fought back, smashing out two of Copeland's teeth with his mail-clad fist before finally being overpowered. Aldin Grange Bridge, probably of fifteenth-century origin, stands today about midway between Crossgate Moor and Bearpark on the site of the earlier bridge where John Copeland claimed his royal prize. It is said that Copeland chose eight companions and, putting the wounded King on horseback, rode off with him into Northumberland to Ogle Castle, the newly erected stronghold of Sir Robert Ogle, there to hold him securely until he could be transferred to Bamburgh where the fate of David Bruce King of Scotland would be decided. Of course, the King of Scotland was a great prize for ransom, but he was only worth a ransom if he remained alive, and David II was grievously wounded. So it was that Masters William Bolton and Hugh Kilvington, 'barber surgeons', were sent for from York and given the task of extracting the arrows from the King, and healing his wounds. This successfully achieved, they were paid six pounds for their services.

After the battle Ralph, Lord Neville, and the leaders of the English made their solemn way to the cathedral, there to offer up thanks for the victory. Such acclaim and distinction did Neville – a man 'who fought so hard that traces of his blows struck to the enemy' – receive for his role as commander-in-chief of the English army that upon his death he was afforded the highest honour of being the first layman in over 250 years since its foundation to be buried within the walls of the cathedral. His tomb and that of his son remain there still. Early the following year, David Bruce was removed from Bamburgh and taken to the Tower of London, where he was confined, pending payment of a huge ransom, for 11 years. We are told that to add insult to injury, during all that time he was made by King Edward to pay for his own keep. He was allowed over the years that followed occasionally to visit Scotland on business, being at all times confined in the northern strongholds at Berwick and Newcastle. Always he was under the charge of his old captor John Copeland, who because of his exploits in battle and his capture of the King had had bestowed upon him by King Edward great gifts of land and many honours.

Historians have been divided over the final death toll of the battle. Some chroniclers have suggested that the Scottish dead amounted to no more than

1,000. This number may seem rather small considering the size of the armies involved and the intensity of the fighting, but it must be remembered that records of the time usually included only the deaths of men of rank, members of the royal family, the nobility, knights and esquires. Perhaps, then, it was only the number of dead amongst the Scottish hierarchy that amounted to about 1,000 and, as has been written, 'of the common people who fell, we have no account whatsoever'. The fourteenth-century secular priest and historian Jean Froissart put the number of Scottish dead at 15,000; of the English he wrote only that they 'lost many of their men'. This figure may be an exaggerated one, but there is no doubt that the massive scale of the Scottish defeat at Neville's Cross was decisive, the Scottish threat was destroyed for a generation, and for many years the people of northern England would be free from war.

Shortly after the battle a cross was erected near the site, in commemoration of the English victory. We are told that:

> On the west side of the City of Durham, where two roads pass each other, a most notable, famous, and goodly cross of stone work was erected to the honour of God, for the victory there obtained in the field of battle and known by the name of Nevil's Cross and built at the sole cost of the Lord Ralph Nevill, one of the most excellent and chief persons in the said battle. Also in token and remembrance of the Battle of Durham, and to the perpetual memory and honour of the said Lord Nevill and his posterity for ever, it was termed by the title and name of Nevil's Cross, as above said, and so did remain till the year 1589, when, in the night time, the same was broken down and defaced by some lewd, contemptuous and wicked persons . . .

The monument stands today, just to the east of the busy Neville's Cross traffic lights, almost unnoticed amongst the hustle and bustle of everyday life. However, the importance of the battle, its size and significance, has been acknowledged by its inclusion in English Heritage's National Battlefields Register. Following the destruction of the original monument the base of the cross was all that remained intact, and on it was placed an old milestone, a humble offering indeed to serve as an everlasting memorial to the deeds of that day.

And it has been said, though not by me, that if, when the time is right, you walk nine times around the memorial and put your ear to the ground, you will hear the rumble of distant hoofs, the cries of spectral hosts, and the far-off clash of armour; the echoes of a battle fought one bright, clear October day long ago when the sky was filled with English arrows and the hills of Durham ran red with Scottish blood.

Chapter Seven

The Sons of Cecily Neville

'In her good she was not elated, in her evil days she was not
cast down.'

Cecily Neville, the 'Rose of Raby Castle', was born in the year 1415, the youngest of the 21 children of Ralph Neville, First Earl of Westmorland, and his second wife Joan Beaufort. She was to become one of the most remarkable women of the fifteenth century, a noblewoman who would give birth to two future kings of England, a wife and mother who would see her husband and each of her four grown sons meet violent and untimely deaths. She was to live through a time of intrigue, of feudal strife, of claim and counter-claim to the greatest prize of all: the crown of England. The Wars of the Roses would end before Cecily's death, but during the course of the long years of that conflict she would witness the tragedy of her family killed in battle, or executed, or murdered. She would become a woman 'whose life was indissolubly linked with the chief actors in the savage battles, ruthless executions and shameless treasons which stamp the struggle between the rival houses of York and Lancaster'.

The young girl born at Raby was indeed of noble lineage. Her great-grandfather was Ralph Neville, hero of the Battle of Neville's Cross, who had been entombed in Durham Cathedral in 1367. Her mother, Joan Beaufort, was sister to King Henry IV and daughter of the mighty John of Gaunt, Duke of Lancaster; the wealthiest landowner in England, he was the most powerful man in the land during the minority of Richard II, virtually ruling the kingdom as head of the Council of Regency. The Neville family had themselves become rich and powerful during the fourteenth century. Holding vast areas of land in the north of England they had become influential in the running of the state and, together with the Percys of Northumberland, ruled as feudal overlords in the northernmost part of the King's realm, heeding little the King's authority.

In her youth Cecily became known for her vitality and high spirits and as she grew into womanhood she became renowned for her great beauty. It was said that her room adjacent to the Keep in Raby Castle had windows secured with iron bars, her father having them fixed in place to prevent the youthful Cecily secretly leaving the castle and perhaps meeting with someone of whom the Earl did not approve. She was educated with her future husband, Richard Duke of York, who was a ward of Ralph Neville, and when they eventually married the scene was set for a family tragedy of epic proportions. For Richard Plantagenet, Duke of York, would become Lord Protector, Steward of the Realm during King Henry VI's prolonged periods of insanity, and he would be proclaimed by Parliament heir apparent to the throne of England.

When Henry V, warrior king and hero of Agincourt, died prematurely in 1422, his infant son, only nine months old, was declared King Henry VI. The child king would be crowned when only eight years old in 1429, and during the period of his infancy the country was effectively ruled by the 'Continuing Council' of ministers. Richard, Duke of York had always been a loyal subject of the King; an able and efficient administrator and accomplished soldier, Richard's lineage and indeed his claim to the throne was as strong as the King's own. He was, after all, the great-grandson of the mighty Edward III. Henry VI grew into manhood but he was of a gentle nature, totally unsuited to his position. He was a simple man, devout and sensitive. He suffered from bouts of madness which made his reign subject to speculation and doubt. Richard was appointed Regent during the King's first bout of madness, but when the King eventually regained his sanity, Richard's power was lessened. He was, however, eventually named as Henry's successor.

Cecily was fully supportive of her husband's claims. He was of noble blood, he was backed by Parliament and he had the support of a large section of the English population. Cecily herself began to act imperiously, as a queen in waiting; she had an innate sense of pride of her own lineage: 'Such was her pride of race that she never allowed any to forget the blood of the haughty Nevilles and imperious Beauforts flowed in her veins.' She received guests in regal style, assuming 'all the state and dignity of a reigning monarch', giving audiences in her 'throne room' as if she were already by right Queen of England. Cecily bore Richard nine sons and four daughters. Five of their sons would die as children. The surviving boys grew into manhood, but their destinies would ultimately be caught and twisted by the webs of treachery and betrayal which symbolised those years, and which would bring grief to the House of Cecily Neville. Of those four sons Edward, Edmund, George and Richard, one would be slain prematurely, one would be arrested and executed for treason against his own brother, and two would become kings of England.

Cecily was certainly an ambitious woman but she was also, despite her great beauty and indomitable pride, devout almost to the point of piety, described by Walpole as 'a princess of spotless character'. An ancient account gives an interesting insight into her domestic life. Rising at seven in the morning she had mass performed by her chaplain several times throughout the day. She would read endlessly from the holy books. In the afternoon she would give audiences and attend to household business. Supper was at five in the afternoon and it was only after supper that Cecily would

> disposeth herself to be famyliar with her gentlewoman to the seeking
> of honest myrthe, and, one hower before her going to bed she taketh
> a cuppe of wynne, and after that goeth to the privy closette and taketh
> her leave of God for all nighte, makinge an end of prayers for that
> daye, and by eighte of the clocke is in bedde.

She became renowned for her devotion both to her God and to her husband, but throughout her years she never lost sight of the crown: 'Her life was dominated by two supreme ideas: the care of her soul, and the furtherance of her ambitious hopes for herself and her family.'

In April 1445, Henry VI married Margaret of Anjou, niece of the King of France. She took an almost instant dislike to Richard, Duke of York, the King's one-time Protector and Chief Councillor; she distrusted his motives. By 1450 unrest was growing throughout the country. The King still had no heir, and because of his mental illness he was becoming more and more incapable of ruling his realm. The possessions in France, fought for and gained by his heroic father, were gradually being lost. Two years later Richard's patience was at an end, and he made his first move as the lawfully nominated heir apparent.

He gathered an army round him and marched on London, but on reaching his destination unchallenged he dispersed his forces and sought parley with the King and Queen. A compromise situation was reached and Richard was appointed Constable of Calais, a position he would hold for over a year. In 1453 there took place two events the effects of which would finally plunge England into the inevitability of a bitter civil conflict. Further defeats in France finally sent the King mad. So severe was his illness he could not speak, he could not recognise anyone, not even his wife. Richard was sent for. He returned and was re-established as Protector with the support of both Houses of Parliament. Surely his time had come, surely he would now be named King, and Cecily would become his Queen. However, despite the King's apparent imbecility, on 14 October of that year his wife, to the surprise of everyone, produced a son and heir; Richard's claim to the throne was suddenly and unexpectedly at an end. The next year the King just as suddenly regained his sanity. Richard now knew that if the crown was ever to be his, he would have to take it by force.

The first skirmish on 22 May 1455, at St Albans, heralded in what would become the Wars of the Roses. Over thirty years of treachery and bloodshed would follow, involving most of the rich and powerful families in the kingdom. Civil strife had degenerated into civil war. After five years of increasing hostilities between the rival houses of York for Richard, and Lancaster for the King, all-out war was raging. But Richard was soon to reach the end of his role in the unfolding tragedy, and a time of hope for Cecily Neville would be replaced by a time of sorrow.

The day of 30 December 1460 was a fateful one for Richard and for Cecily, for on that day was fought the Battle of Wakefield, and the outcome of that battle would finally mark an end to the cause of Richard, Duke of York. The battle lost, his forces crushed, Richard was taken alive on the battlefield. Summary justice was swiftly delivered by his enemies. The story tells that, dragged to an ant hill, Richard was seated upon a makeshift 'throne' and crowned with a garland of knotted grass. There, with cries of 'hail king without a kingdom, hail prince without a people', he was taunted and humiliated. The defeated Richard, having been robbed of his pride, was then mercilessly robbed of his life. Executed on the field, his head was cut from his body and was delivered to Margaret of Anjou. It is said that Margaret crowned it with a paper crown, and that she ordered it to be mounted on a pike on Micklegate Bar in York and displayed for all to see.

Cecily's husband was dead. Her brother Richard, the Earl of Salisbury, was killed the same day, falling in the thick of the fighting. Cruellest of all, her young son Edmund, Earl of Rutland, was captured during the battle. Showing defiance to the last to the enemies of his father, the 17-year-old was cruelly murdered by Lord Clifford. In one day Cecily had lost husband, son and brother. What personal agony such a tragedy brought her can only be guessed at. Hopes for her family's accession to the throne of England for the moment lay dashed and broken on the field at Wakefield. Soon, however, fate was again to intervene.

The Yorkist cause was taken up by Richard and Cecily's eldest son, Edward. On Palm Sunday, 29 March 1461, only months after his father's death, he was to achieve at the age of 18 years what his father had never been able to. Edward's army was victorious at the bloody Battle of Townton, ten miles east of Leeds. The great battle, fought in a blizzard, cost 6,000 Yorkist lives and 10,000 men of the King's army fell slain upon the field. By right of victory, Edward, son of the late Richard Plantagenet, Duke of York and Cecily Neville, the Rose of Raby, was declared Edward IV, King of England. The pitiable figure of the deposed Henry VI was imprisoned in the Tower; his Queen, Margaret of Anjou, returned to France with her young son. Cecily, as mother of the new bachelor King, would at last become the first lady in the land, at least for a while.

Three years later, after a brief period of relative stability, the King very much enjoying 'the good life', Edward took a wife. His choice of bride, however, was to bring about further discontent and unrest. Elizabeth Woodville, a widow with two children, was the daughter of 'a simple squire of ordinary descent'. Cecily, crushed at the prospect of losing her position as 'First Lady', deplored Edward's choice of bride. A previously married woman with children was no fit choice as Queen of England. Cecily implored Edward to rethink his decision; he replied: 'She is indeed a woman and hath children, and by God's blessed lady, I who am a bachelor have some too, madam my mother, I pray you be content.'

But Cecily was not content, and neither were others influential in the realm, notably the King's cousin Richard Neville, Earl of Warwick, the most powerful nobleman in the land. So it was that after the wedding Cecily became increasingly privy to the thoughts, plans and aspirations of her youngest son, Richard, Duke of Gloucester. The Earl of Warwick, aware of the simmering discontent of the King's other brother, George, Duke of Clarence, began to make plans. Rebellion was once again in the air. The Duke of Clarence realised that even without a direct heir the claims of the two sons of Elizabeth Woodville would precede his own claim to the throne as brother and heir to Edward. Clarence threw in his lot with Warwick, and together they took up arms against the King. They were successful. Edward was captured and imprisoned in Middleham Castle. Edward, though, still had plans of his own. He assured Warwick that he would mend his ways and he signed pardons for all those who had taken up arms against him. Warwick released him. In March 1470, on the pretence of suppressing a Lancastrian rebellion, Edward gathered his forces and turned against Warwick and his traitor brother, George, Duke of Clarence. Both fled to France, seeking help from King Louis XI. They returned with another army in the September of that year. Now it was Edward's turn to flee, to Burgundy, to the court of his brother-in-law, Charles the Bold. Here he would wait while another force was assembled. Meanwhile in England Warwick released Henry VI from the Tower and ruled the realm through the puppet King.

Edward returned. Landing in March 1471 he marched inland and proclaimed himself King again. The decisive blow was about to be struck. On 14 April 1471 the rival forces met at Barnet. Edward was victorious. During the battle the Earl of Warwick was caught and battered to death. On that day Margaret of Anjou, wife of Henry VI, landed with her son, the rival Prince of Wales. For their cause, strong Lancastrian forces were gathered near the Welsh border. Once again battle was joined, this time at Tewkesbury; once again Edward was victorious. Margaret was captured. Initially held for ransom, 11 years later she was to die in poverty in Anjou. Her son was slain in the battle. With the heir of Henry VI dead, the Lancastrian line seemed ended. On the night of 21 May Richard, Duke of Gloucester, proceeded to London, there to supervise the execution of the pitiful figure of Henry VI who for 50 years had been rightful Lancastrian King of England.

Before the Battle of Barnet Edward's brother George, Duke of Clarence, had begged forgiveness for his previous act of treachery. Edward granted it, but never trusted his brother again. The Duke of Clarence continued to flout the King's authority, defying the royal courts. In January 1478 Edward's patience finally ran out. Fearing his brother was again plotting against him, Edward called Parliament together to condemn the Duke of Clarence. He was charged with treason and imprisoned in the Tower. It is unclear exactly how he died, but it has been suggested that 'imprisoned by the hand of one brother, he was murdered by the hand of another'; popular tradition, and William Shakespeare, maintains that the greedy and unfortunate Duke was finally 'drowned in a butt of malmsey wine'.

When Edward IV died suddenly and somewhat mysteriously in April 1483 aged 40 years, Cecily Neville was left with only one son, Richard, Duke of Gloucester. Edward and his Queen had left two sons: heir to the throne Edward, Prince of Wales, the presumptive Edward V, and his younger brother, Richard, Duke of York. Richard their uncle, however, had his own designs on the throne, and the child King Edward V would never wear the crown of England.

In 1461 Edward IV had conferred on Richard the title Duke of Gloucester. Born in 1452 he had still been a child when hostilities had begun. At nine years of age he was sent to Middleham Castle and the household of his cousin Richard Neville, Earl of Warwick, known to history as the 'Kingmaker'. Richard later married Neville's young daughter Anne, and by so doing inherited the large Neville estates in Durham. The young Duke of Gloucester was still only 19 when the Kingmaker was killed at the Battle of Barnet. King Edward sent Richard to York; from here he would rule the north country through the 'Council of the North'. He is remembered in the north of England as a just and more than capable administrator, governing as Duke of Gloucester for 12 years. Richard maintained close links both with Durham and with Barnard Castle, of which he was Lord between 1477 and his death in 1485. His emblem, the white boar, is still today depicted in the town's coat of arms. It is said that he enjoyed hunting on the Neville estates around Brancepeth Castle and both he and his wife were members of the Fraternity of St Cuthbert at Durham Cathedral.

Following the sudden death of his elder brother, King Edward IV, in 1483, Richard was named as Lord Protector to Edward, the infant heir and presumptive Edward V. At this time it seems that the baser ambitions of

Richard were aroused. Shortly afterwards he revealed evidence, genuine or manufactured, that prior to his brother Edward's marriage to Elizabeth Woodville – the marriage to which his mother Cecily had been so implacably opposed – Edward had entered into a pre-marriage contract with one Lady Eleanor Butler. It was claimed by Richard that this contract was binding; his claim was accepted, and the King's children were therefore declared bastards. The right of succession to the throne of the young Edward was not recognised. So it was that by decree of Parliament, and by right as heir to his dead brother, Richard was crowned King Richard III on 6 July 1483. For Cecily Neville another, and the last, of her sons was King of England.

Popular history has remembered Richard III as Richard the Crookback, the black caricature of Shakespearian drama, the evil usurper of the throne from the rightful heir, his young nephew. He has been generally assumed to have ordered the imprisonment in the Tower of London, and later the callous murder, of both Edward and his younger brother, Richard, Duke of York, 12 and ten years of age respectively. The mystery of the fate of the 'Princes in the Tower' has never been satisfactorily explained, but history has invariably pointed the finger of shame at Richard.

Richard's short reign ended with his death on Bosworth Field on 22 August 1485, where he fell 'fighting manfully in the thickest press of his enemies', the last King of England to be killed in battle. So ended the Plantagenet dynasty that had ruled England since the twelfth century, and so passed all the sons of 'the Rose of Raby'. After Richard's fall at Bosworth, Cecily saw the crown go to 'an illegitimate stem of the Lancastrian line', Henry Tudor, who would be crowned King Henry VII. After Richard's death Cecily withdrew further into her private life. However, even though in 1480 she had taken the strict vows of the Benedictines, she still used the Arms of England and France quartered, implying that she was by right Queen.

Cecily died in 1495, at Berkhamsted. She had lived 35 years as a widow, and out of her family of 13 children only one had survived her and nearly all her relatives were dead, either killed in battle or executed for treason. 'She had lived to see three princes of her body crowned and four murdered.' 'The time was a stormy one, and in consequence of the greatness of her connections she endured grievous misfortunes.' Her last request was that she be buried with her husband at Fotheringay Castle in Northamptonshire. Their tombs were destroyed during the Reformation, but Elizabeth I, after a visit to Fotheringay, ordered that her ancestors be reburied in the church, and suitable monuments erected to their memory.

With the marriage of Elizabeth, Cecily's eldest granddaughter, to King Henry VII, the Houses of York and Lancaster were finally united, and the Tudor dynasty begun. So it was that the Rose of Raby's place in the lineage of the royal houses of Britain, and indeed Europe, was established, for Margaret

Tudor, daughter of Elizabeth and Henry VII and great-granddaughter of Cecily, was the grandmother of Mary Queen of Scots, in turn the mother of James I, and from his granddaughter Sophia, Electress of Hanover, all successive sovereigns are descended. A seventeenth-century manuscript tells us:

> From Lady Cecily Nevill, Duchess of York, are lineally descended seven Kings of England, three Queens of England, four Princes of Wales, four Kings of Scotland, two Queens of Scotland, one Queen of Spain, and one Queen of Bohemia; as also, one Prince Elector Palatine of the Rhine. The aforesaid Lady Cecily Nevill died in the 11th year of Henry VII, 1495, having lived to see three Princes of her body crowned, and four murdered. She was the youngest daughter of Ralph, Lord Nevill of Raby, first Earl of Westmorland, and Earl Marshal of England, and of his wife Lady Joan Beaufort, daughter of John of Gaunt, Duke of Lancaster and Acquitane, and King of Castile and Leon, and the sister of King Henry the Fourth of England, and to Lady Philippa, Queen of Portugal, and to Lady Katherine, Queen of Spaine, from whom descended all the late Emperors of Germany, the Kings of Spain, the House of Austria, and most of the Princes throughout Christendom now living.

Part Three

Chapter Eight

The Rising of the North

'To arms without delay! To York, and then to London.'

When, early in the sixteenth century, King Henry VIII sundered relations with the Pope and declared himself spiritual as well as temporal head of the nation, his action heralded in what would become an age during which the storm of religious revolt and persecution ravaged England, as it had already done in Europe. It was a time when scheming and ambitious ministers of state would bend monarchs to their will, and when religious hysteria would sow the seeds of lasting hatred and bitterness. The upheaval which resulted would leave England forever changed, a time of distrust and of fear, of betrayal and of cruelty, a time 'when rogues prospered, and honest men suffered'.

In 1537 the first open rebellion against Henry VIII's 'new order' took place. The 'Pilgrimage of Grace', as it became known, was led not by a soldier but by a country gentleman who had been at one time in the service of the Earl of Northumberland, Robert Aske. He was a man of high integrity but with a soul too trusting for the times in which he lived. There had developed in the northern lands a general discontent over the disestablishment of the Catholic Church and the increasing interference in affairs of state by Henry's self-seeking ministers. In 1536, discontent gave way to open rebellion. A popular revolt soon took hold throughout Lincolnshire and Yorkshire and, on 16 October 1536, Robert Aske, marching behind the banner of St Cuthbert, occupied York. On the twenty-first of that month his forces captured Pontefract Castle. Aske announced his intention to march on London, there to lay his people's grievances before the King and his ministers, to demand the expulsion of King's counsellors of low birth, and to obtain the restitution of the Catholic Church.

From Pontefract the 'Pilgrimage of Grace' marched with 40,000 men to Doncaster. The King, however, did not challenge the rebels in open combat; instead he sent messages to Aske, recognising their grievances and promising a special Parliament in York to hear them in full. Aske, believing his objectives had been achieved, dispersed his forces. He was received by Henry in London, where he secured a further promise of free elections from the King. The King's word, however, was false. In April 1537, after doing personal service to Henry, Aske was arrested, tried before a commission and sentenced to death for high treason. In the July of that year he died on the scaffold, a deceived and disillusioned man; altogether 216 people were executed for treason following the 'Pilgrimage of Grace'. So it was that to prevent further such uprisings a medieval governing council was re-established and given greater powers by the King. The 'Council of the North' would now govern in the north of England and would administer directly the decrees of the monarch and of his ministers.

Throughout the kingship of Henry's young son, Edward VI, and the subsequent reigns of Mary Tudor and Elizabeth, religious zealotry swung first towards extreme Protestantism and then back to the Church of Rome, returning to the Protestant code in the court of Elizabeth. Favourites of one royal court would become victims of the next and the numbers of religious martyrs both Catholic and Protestant, from the humblest of priests to the most powerful archbishops, began to grow. Attitudes hardened. In the north of England the power of the great medieval, feudal and Catholic families of Neville and Percy, the Earls of Westmorland and of Northumberland, was gradually eroded by the growing Protestantism of the state and the increasing domination of the monarch and the high ministers, governing directly through the 'Council of the North'. To the northern nobles it seemed that unless the situation was halted, or even reversed, their ancient Houses were doomed to a gradual and inglorious demise.

On 13 November 1569, in the eleventh year of the reign of Elizabeth I, a great assembly was held at Raby Castle. The nobles of the north had gathered with their retainers to discuss a matter of grave import. A decision had to be made on that day, the far-reaching consequences of which could not be seen, but could indeed be guessed at. For the one item on the agenda that day was high treason: armed insurrection against the Queen and her ministers, the first move in a plot to place Mary Queen of Scots on the throne of England and to restore the Roman religion to the land.

The Council met in the Great Baron's Hall at Raby, where in feudal times the mighty Nevilles, Earls of Westmorland, had 'held court' to their subjects, as Wordsworth tells us in his *White Doe of Rylstone*. '700 knights, retainers all of Neville, at their master's call had sate together in Raby's hall.' But now the power of the northern nobles, of Percy and Neville, Northumberland and

Westmorland, was diminished. Their strength of arms was weak, as was their strength of will. The assembly dithered. They knew that if once they took up arms against the Queen they would inevitably achieve either victory or death. Neville and Percy were already suspected by the Queen's ministers of plotting together, and they had been summoned for a third time to appear before the Queen and the Earl of Sussex, 'all excuses and pretences apart', to explain their actions and their motives. The time had come to make the final, fateful decision. The assembly wavered, fearing the consequences of defeat.

It is said that they were goaded into their final decision by the wife of Charles Neville, who was also sister to the Duke of Norfolk. Urging them to strike against the Queen for the dignity of their illustrious lineage, and for the honour of their heirs, she brought them from near abandonment of the plan to final agreement to declare themselves and to take up arms. At length the northern nobles issued a proclamation, stating their intentions to all. The decision was made, now there could be no going back; the fate of the conspirators and of the ancient House of Neville was sealed.

The proclamation issued to the people, in which the rebels swore their allegiance to Elizabeth, claimed that it was not against the person of the Queen that their anger was directed, but against the 'diverse, disordered and evil persons, about the Queen's majesty, who have sought by their subtil and crafty dealing to advance themselves'. They concluded: 'We therefore have gathered ourselves together to resist by force; and by the help of God and you, good people, to see redress of things amiss.' Signed by Neville, Percy and nine others, it was hoped that the proclamation would once more rally northerners to their old feudal lords and that their crusade would gain strength as they marched at the head of a general Catholic uprising of all England. Their plan was already known to, and encouraged by, Mary Queen of Scots. Her ministers had obtained a promise of troops and arms from the Duke of Alva, Spanish Governor of the Low Countries. The Courts of France and Spain also encouraged the plan but Neville and Percy were all too aware that they were already under suspicion; if they were to move, they must do quickly. Rumours of the rebellion, however, had already reached the ears of Queen Elizabeth.

On the night of 14 November, Thomas Percy's sleep was troubled. Suddenly at midnight he was woken up by his servants who had received a report, later proved to be false, that their lord was about to be arrested by officers of the Queen. He assumed his situation to be desperate, and at once gathered to him all the men and arms that he could muster and made his way to the Neville estates. He came to Brancepeth Castle 'where he found a great number of people'. Charles Neville had wasted no time. He too had gathered together what forces he could. So it was that the standards of Charles Neville, Sixth Earl of Westmorland, and Thomas Percy, Seventh Earl of Northumberland, were raised at Brancepeth with the cry, 'To arms without delay! To York and then to London'. And so the reluctant rebels, unprepared of plan and ill-equipped of men and arms, set out from Brancepeth Castle with but 1,500 supporters. As they marched away more joined them until their tiny force was swelled to about 4,000 foot and 1,600 horse. Soon they passed through the gates of Durham, made their way up the narrow streets, and entered the cathedral. The 'Rising of the North' had begun.

The rumours that had reached Queen Elizabeth were now proved true; her northern nobles were indeed in open revolt. She was enraged:

> the newes unto London came in all the speede that ever might be, and word is brought to our Royall Queene of the rising in the north countrie. Her grace she turned her round about, and like a Royall Queene swore, 'I will ordayne them such a breakfast as never was seen in the north before'.

It was not out of character, apparently, for Elizabeth to fly into violent tempers, swearing at her ministers, even her bishops; if greatly annoyed she was also prone to 'boxing their ears'. Mary Queen of Scots was immediately taken and secured in the heavily fortified town of Coventry, far from the reach of the rebels. The Duke of Norfolk, the would-be husband of Mary, following a successful rebellion, was imprisoned in the Tower of London.

In Durham, the rebels set to work in the cathedral. The communion table was thrown down, English bibles and prayer books were burned and two new altars were erected. Then, on St Andrew's Day, 30 November 1569, the Catholic mass was heard again in Durham Cathedral. Here the rebels remained for almost two weeks, as again they dithered over the direction they should next take. Finally they began their march south. The number of supporters and camp followers increased, but critically their march did not bring about the general uprising of ordinary Catholics that the leaders of the Rising had hoped for. Nonetheless the march south continued, to Darlington and beyond, to Richmond, Ripon, Boroughbridge. A detachment was sent to Hartlepool to make preparations and await the arrival of the promised Spanish reinforcements; the wait was to be in vain.

By the time the rebels reached Clifford Moor near Wetherby, the rising was nearly 13,000 strong. But their leadership, reluctant rebels at the outset, were now unsure as to how they should proceed; much of their force, little of which was made up of professional soldiers, was undisciplined and out of control. They required payment from Neville and Percy which they in turn were unable to provide; they had not provisions for a sustained campaign nor had they means of acquiring any. It was true that they had as yet met no resistance, but neither had they inspired the hoped-for countrywide Catholic uprising. They reconsidered their position and retreated to besiege Barnard Castle.

Sir George Bowes, staunchly loyal to the Queen, had been expecting the rebels. With Barnard Castle well garrisoned and prepared for a siege he easily held out for ten days, time enough to hold the rebels until the day when Neville and Percy received intelligence that they had now become the hunted. The Earl of Sussex, Lord President of the Council of the North, was hastening from York with 7,000 troops. The Earl of Warwick was close behind him with a larger force. On hearing this news the rebels abandoned Barnard Castle and struck out north, to Hexham. The Earl of Warwick pressed on with the pursuit, continuing his march north with 12,000 men.

On reaching the border country, the forces of Charles Neville and Thomas Percy were disbanded and the leaders themselves sought refuge with Scottish lords whom they thought were sympathetic to their cause. So it was that without the support of the Catholic uprising they had sought to induce, without the strength of the promised forces from Europe, and in the face of the stronger, better-trained and better-equipped armies of the Queen, the ill-prepared, ill-fated 'Rising of the North' was ended without a major battle being fought. Retribution, however, would be merciless.

For a while both Neville and Percy remained in hiding in relative safety, but these were treacherous times and secret deals were eventually struck with the Queen's officers. Thomas Percy was eventually betrayed, sold in May 1572 to Queen Elizabeth 'for a certain price agreed upon'. Neville had fared slightly better. Remaining safely in hiding at Ferniehurst near Jedburgh until the autumn of 1570, arrangements had been made for him to take ship from Aberdeen across the North Sea to Flanders, a journey from which his earthly body would never return. Of their followers, the would-be rebels, those that were caught or implicated were held under martial law. They would receive no trial. By order of the Earl of Sussex, 66 were executed in Durham City alone; more met their deaths at York and London. It was the proud claim of Sir George Bowes that 'for 60 miles in length and 20 in breadth, between Newcastle and Wetherby, there was hardly a town or village where he had not executed at least one of the inhabitants'. It has been estimated that in all about 800 died as a result of their involvement in the 'Rising of the North': 'they cruelly bereaved of life; and many a childe made fatherless, and widowed many a tender wife'.

Percy died on the scaffold in York on 22 August 1572, as his father had done after his involvement in the 'Pilgrimage of Grace'. Charles Neville, Sixth Earl of Westmorland, had escaped successfully to Flanders, where he remained in exile for the rest of his life surviving on a meagre allowance granted to him by the King of Spain. As he grew old, resigned to his destiny, he reflected on his life. The once mighty House of Neville was now fallen and in ruins; he knew he must accept only whatever bitter and unlooked-for end Fate had decided for him, 'and that which should accompany old age; honour, love, obedience, troop of friends, I must not look to have'. He died in Flanders, a lonely man, on 16 November 1601. The tale has since been told that during the hours of darkness his ghost journeys back across the sea, back to Raby, there to wander in sorrow and longing around the ancient seat of the House of Neville until dawn's light decrees that he must fly back to his lonely Flanders grave.

His lands and property were forfeited to the Queen. Charles Neville's daughters, however, lived on, and Margaret, who had been only five years old at the time of the rebellion, has a prominent part to play in the next chapter of the story. The downfall of the Nevilles was, however, complete. The strength and influence that their once great martial lords had gradually built up and wielded for more than two centuries, enabling them to become one of the most powerul families in England, were gone. The defeat of the Rising sounded the final death knell of feudalism, even in the remote north. The direct rule of the Queen and her ministers would now be dispensed by the 'Council of the North'. The legislation it was to administer would become more and more repellent to the northern population. Turbulent times still lay ahead, even after the defeat of the 'Rising of the North'.

Chapter Nine

The Execution of John Boste

'Behold, the heart of a traitor!
No! the heart of a servant of God.'

The prisoner was dragged away from the Assizes Court out on to Palace Green under the towering gaze of the cathedral. As guards tried to force shut the door behind him, spectators from inside the courtroom, in their eagerness to follow the unfolding drama, pushed and heaved against them. Gradually, as inch by inch the door was closed, the last of the rabble squeezed through and spilled out, swearing and fighting, into the sunshine. The door clanged shut and the clamour and din from inside suddenly subsided. A low cart waited outside, gaolers bade the prisoner climb on to it. Then the middle-aged, crippled and broken man was secured and manacled in readiness for his journey to the gallows.

Guilty was he of crimes against the state; guilty was he of treason against the person of Queen Elizabeth; sentence would be carried out at once. Now the prisoner must pay the ultimate price for his crimes. Some of those who had gathered around ran off through the streets to tell of the court's sentence. For here was an important prisoner indeed, a dangerous felon who had evaded capture for ten years, and there were many who would gladly see him take his last journey. As messages were despatched to the executioner bidding him to make preparations, the horses moved slowly off, dragging the cart and the condemned man behind them.

The words of the courtroom still rang in his ears. The accusations, the confession, the condemnations, this and the cheers as sentence was passed all rolled around in his consciousness. He knew the barbaric fate that awaited him that fine July evening, but he was at peace; at peace with himself, at peace with God. He had nothing to fear from the executioner or from the transient agonies of the gallows. The man to be put to death was neither murderer nor common thief; no crime against another had he committed. His only wrong was to have an unshakeable conviction in his faith and his beliefs. For the prisoner about to die was John Boste, a Roman Catholic missionary priest whose treasonable offence was to preach his doctrine and administer the Roman Catholic mass to his followers. To do so, however, in Elizabethan England was to commit an act of treason, and any caught practising such rites would inevitably pay a terrible price of torture and death.

With the failure of the 'Rising of the North', overt Catholic rebellion was, for the time, ended. However, it had left the authorities and the Queen's ministers in a constant state of paranoia about possible plots against Elizabeth and threats to the Protestant state. With the threat of the Spanish Armada in 1588 all anti-Catholic suspicions had seemed justified. However, already by that time suspicion had turned to persecution, a persecution which would reach its peak in the early 1590s.

Sir Francis Walsingham, a 'strong-minded Puritan' and fanatical protector of Elizabeth's Protestant England, had in 1573 been appointed Joint Secretary to the Privy Council. He had, years before, been responsible for the development of a network of spies to root out plots against the Queen; it had been he who had brought the evidence finally damning Mary Queen of Scots to execution in 1583. After the defeat of the Armada, this 'shrewd contriver in the Elizabethan web of plot and counter-plot' turned the emphasis of the work of his spies to the tracking down of Catholics active in England, especially the growing number of Catholic missionary priests arriving from the Douai Seminary College in Flanders, and setting up secret ministries throughout the land. It was Walsingham's spies that had exposed one of these priests, John Ballard, who had been implicated in a plot to kill Queen Elizabeth. His capture would later have dire consequences for John Boste.

William Cecil was Elizabeth's Principal Secretary of State and one, if not the closest, of her advisers. Cecil, however, was far more inclined towards the Puritans than was the Queen. It had probably been he who had finally despatched the death warrant of Mary Queen of Scots. And with the justification of the Pope's excommunication of Elizabeth in 1570, he defended on political grounds the increasing severity of legislation towards Catholics. It was to Cecil that all information and intelligence about plots, traitors and enemies of the State would ultimately be channelled.

Henry Hastings, Earl of Huntingdon, was of noble birth: Plantagenet blood ran through his veins. He was cousin to the Queen, his wife a lady-in-waiting in the Queen's Court, and as Lord President of the Council of the North he was the Queen's anointed. From his appointment in 1572 his was the task of eradicating Catholicism in this part of the Queen's realm. The Council, a body of fifteenth-century origin, the function of which had been to administer legal and domestic legislation in the northern counties, had been modified by Henry VIII following the 'Pilgrimage of Grace'. Under the direction of Huntingdon it began to administer an increasing amount of religious legislation hostile to northern Catholics. With the threats of the Catholic Mary Queen of Scots and the onset of the Spanish Armada, it became a time 'when Protestantism and patriotism seemed inseparably linked'. As indeed did Catholicism and treachery. With Huntingdon as President, the powers of the Council of the North had been built up. Its first object was to 'reduce the north to order'. The enforcement of religious legislation made the Council unpopular, but with Huntingdon, 'a precise Puritan', the Court had a President to whom 'public opinion' mattered little. He was also a man with the highest royal connections and he worked well with William Cecil, Principal Secretary of State.

As the Catholic missionary priests began to arrive from the Continent – 'a time when it seemed the forces of the Antichrist, in the persons of the missionary priests, were assembling against the children of light, and the triumph of northern Protestantism was far from assured' (Gilby) – Catholic persecution in England had intensified. Huntingdon and his agents began their work in earnest. The Lord President was to the authorities a 'solid and conscientious worker', to the northern Catholics a hated tyrant, bent on their destruction. Soon the dungeons of Durham and York began to fill with arrested Catholics. Many would never see trial, but would die incarcerated, riddled with infection and disease.

Large crowds now gathered and lined Durham's narrow streets, basking in the late afternoon sunshine. The prisoner was dragged down from Palace Green and out through the Great North Gate which bestrode North Bailey. It had been in the stinking cells of the Northern Gate Prison, the Gaol Gate, that Boste had been held while awaiting his trial. Some of the crowd pushed forward, craning their necks for a glimpse of the prisoner. The horsemaster snapped his whip over the sweating animals. As the cart was dragged roughly by, the crowd jeered and spat. Some cried 'Traitor!' as the procession passed by, 'Death to the traitor!' Traitor. Broken though his body was, that word still stung him like a dart. Whatever he had been, he had always protested his innocence of that charge.

He prayed, and between his prayers he mused to himself, and he remembered. He remembered his time at the Catholic seminary college. The college, which had been founded at Douai in Flanders and had been forced by religious and political upheavals throughout Europe to relocate across the French border at Rheims. He remembered also the day 12 years ago when he had been raised to the priesthood. John Boste had been an Oxford academic theologian and teacher, originally ordained in 1572 into the Protestant ministry, but eventually reverting to the Roman Catholic faith. This was forbidden in the great English universities, so Boste had committed the illegal act of travelling to Rheims to study and be ordained there as a missionary priest of the Catholic Church, a priest whose mission it was to return undercover to England, there secretly to practise the Catholic mass and administer the Sacrament to the faithful. Boste recalled being ordained as deacon along with 18 others, seven of whom had since died on the scaffold. He had known then the fate that awaited him on his return to England if ever he was arrested. For the simple act of saying mass was an act of treachery, punishable by death.

On 11 April 1581, he did return. Landing secretly at Hartlepool he had quickly made his way south, first to East Anglia to be sheltered by Catholic sympathisers in a network of 'safe houses'. On then to London and, by necessity, a false identity. Becoming one John Hartley, Boste had played the part of a servant in the house of the conforming Catholic family of Lord Montague. Under this cover he had set about his mission. But John Boste was a man of the north country. He had been born in the small village of Dufton near Appleby in what was then Westmorland; his mother had lived in Durham City. Soon relatives, old friends and sympathetic contacts from the north made themselves known. There was still strong support for the Catholic cause in the north of England, even after the failure of the Rising. So it was to the north country that John Boste returned, to the jurisdiction of Huntingdon, Lord President of the Council. And it would be here that his fate would eventually be sealed. For some time he preached in secret in the remote places of Cumberland and Westmorland. His renown as a gifted priest had soon spread among Catholics, many of whom were in permanent hiding, even living rough, during this time of rabid persecution. Now as he lay manacled and in pain, he remembered well the wild places and the frightened people.

Into the Market Place now. The crowd had grown. Some followed the horses, others stood by the roadside. Many cursed and mocked the prisoner, some stood quietly by, impassive, expressionless, in great torment of mind. John Boste turned his head to view the scene. The old Market Place where in 1570 Thomas Plumtree, Principal Chaplain to Thomas Percy, Earl of Northumberland, during the Rising and condemned as a 'dangerous and treasonable rebel', had been hanged, drawn and quartered to become the first Catholic martyr in the reign of Elizabeth Tudor. His would not be the only blood to stain the streets of Durham. Now it was John Boste's turn to suffer his martyrdom.

Having eventually made his way across country, Boste had established his mission in Durham. His teachings and his influence soon had a marked effect. Catholic faithful and Catholic sympathisers were spread thinly over the whole county. Activities were generally based around the properties of the families of Catholic nobles who, after the defeat of the Rising had been either executed, exiled or imprisoned. and it was around these families that John Boste had based his mission. He had been a frequent visitor to the Hylton family of Hylton Castle at Sunderland. But he centred his secret activities around Brancepeth Castle and the Deerness Valley, the estate of the Nevilles. The ancient family of Neville had at times over the preceding centuries been one of the most powerful and influential families in England, but Charles Neville, the Sixth Earl of Westmorland, co-conspirator in the Rising, had been exiled and the ancient family estates had been forfeited to the Queen. Only his daughter, Lady Margaret Neville, now remained at Brancepeth. and it was Lady Margaret who gave John Boste aid, shelter and what protection she could.

As the years went by John Boste's secret ministry gathered strength and momentum. With his teachings and the power of his prayers the Catholic faith was being rallied and Boste's mission became the first genuinely effective one in the north of England. However, entrenched Catholic sympathy, especially centred on the old nobility, was considered by the authorities a very real threat to the Queen's Protestant state in the north. The name of John Boste came to the attention of the Earl of Huntingdon. It was Boste, it seemed, that had been the prime mover in the resurgence of Catholicism in the north since the defeat of the Rising, and if the faith of the people could not be totally eradicated, then their priests must be. They would be ruthlessly tracked down and brought to trial. All of these missionary priests were considered dangerous, and John Boste was prominent among their numbers.

As the grim procession now left the Market Place and paraded slowly down Silver Street, some in the crowd pressed forward and with hushed, hurried words, implored the prisoner to bless them, only to be dragged away by the militia and swiftly arrested. John Boste looked on helplessly; he was minded of his own arrest and of the trap that had been sprung to ensnare him.

For some time the spy Francis Egglesfield, a former Catholic, had been working his way around the county. His method was simple: to pose as a practising Catholic, establish himself in the company of a prominent Catholic family, and by these means eventually to ingratiate himself to such an extent as to become trusted and privy to information about the future whereabouts of the itinerant missionary priests, especially, he hoped, the future whereabouts of John Boste. Practising Catholics would be, by necessity, guarded and suspicious of strangers, their world filled with spies and with betrayal. But Francis Egglesfield was very good at his job. Dates and times of visits by the priests were spread by an underground network of worshippers. The location also would only be revealed to those who were trusted. A secret mass could be said anywhere, but they were usually carried out in the 'safe houses' that were scattered around the county.

Eventually Egglesfield had made the acquaintance of Lady Margaret Neville and the surviving members of the Brancepeth Estate. Gradually and skilfully, in the manner of his profession, he had ingratiated himself and become a trusted member of their circle. The Waterhouse was a dwelling which stood within the old Neville Estate, to the north of Brancepeth, about two miles from modern-day Esh Winning. The house was owned by the wealthy Catholic family of Thomas Claxton, though Claxton himself was at the time imprisoned. News came that it was to the Waterhouse that Father Boste himself would come to say the mass and administer the Sacrament. The date was to be 10 September 1593. The news spread quickly through the circle, and it soon came to the ear of Francis Egglesfield. The spy wasted no time in reporting his success to the Pursuivant, Sir William Bowes, who passed on the good news to Huntingdon, Lord President of the Council. Plans were set in motion, arrangements were made, the trap was about to be sprung.

The fateful day arrived. The faithful made their way through the woods and the fields to the Waterhouse. Lady Margaret Neville was there with her maid, Adeline Claxton; Grace, the wife of Thomas Claxton, with her young family; Thomas Robinson, a servant of Lady Catherine Gray, Lady Margaret's sister; and of course Francis Egglesfield. John Boste arrived oblivious to the fate that awaited him that day. After mass had been said, the small congregation left the building. Suddenly Egglesfield turned and asked Father Boste for a blessing. Boste duly blessed the man who had betrayed him. The action was a prearranged signal to the secretly watching militia, the signal which said: this is John Boste, this is your man! The soldiers charged out of the woods and encircled the building. Boste quickly turned and disappeared. The house was surrounded but Boste could not be found. They burst into the Waterhouse and ransacked the building. Still they could not find their prisoner. A sudden cry and the soldiers turned their heads. There, standing in the doorway, framed against the light, was Egglesfield. He pointed to the chimney breast and told the soldiers to break it down. This they did, and found Father John Boste hiding in a priest hole behind the masonry of the fireplace. Egglesfield had indeed done a thorough job, he had learned all their secrets. All in the group were arrested. The women were taken back to Brancepeth Castle, Robinson to York; John Boste was taken to Durham where he was bound in chains in the North Gate Prison. He would be examined the following day, but it would be ten months before his trial would begin.

The Earl of Huntingdon was at Darlington when the message of John Boste's capture reached him. The news pleased him greatly, and he was 'so elated at such a capture, he hastened to the scene of the forthcoming legal operations'. The next morning he sat at Durham as Lord President of the Council of the North, and John Boste was brought before him. The examination of the prisoner began. Had Boste left the country and illegally taken instruction at the Catholic College at Rheims? Had he been ordained a Catholic priest? Had he been in contact with Catholic lords in England and Scotland, the same Scottish lords who had actively pursued the claim to the throne of Mary Queen of Scots? Had he practised the Catholic mass and preached the Catholic faith, contrary to Her Majesty's laws, her crown and dignity? All of these charges were treasonable; John Boste answered 'Yes' to each of them. In his defence he said that for the past five years he had been active only in the bishopric, occasionally in Yorkshire and Northumberland. He added that in all his time since returning to England, 'if I said not mass every day it was against my will'. A report was made of Boste's confession at that first examination on 11 September 1593:

> [Boste] confesseth that within these five last years, he hath bin a moneth to gether in Yorksheir. He confesseth that he hathe saied masse, but when or how manie, he will not confesse he had saied. Yet he confesseth, that if he said not everie daie a masse, it was against his will. He also saieth he is an Englishman born at Dufton in Westmerland. Vera Copia. John Boste. H. Huntyngdon.

The prisoner was led away, but he was not to stay at Durham. Secret despatches were exchanged between Durham and London. Huntingdon received orders from the highest level that Boste had to be sent to the Tower of London for 'further examination'.

The westering sun now blinded his eyes as John Boste was dragged, manacled to the hurdle, out of the city for the last time across Framwellgate Bridge with a large crowd of people now following. He recalled that none had followed when he had left the city as a prisoner nine months earlier. He had been taken first to York and then, on 3 October 1593, had begun the long journey under armed guard to London and to the Tower.

Richard Topcliffe was at the height of his powers. With the skill he had acquired over the years in his own particular art, he was a valued asset to the authorities of Elizabethan England. To others the name was hated; evil was he, the very devil incarnate. For Richard Topcliffe was chief interrogator at the Tower of London. Black was the name of Topcliffe, the arch torturer. John Boste was examined 15 times, questioned relentlessly about his activities, his alleged involvement in plots against the Queen. The authorities wished to know about his associates, other missionary priests who were still at large, and the secret network of Catholic sympathisers and safe houses which existed to protect them. Boste revealed nothing, maintaining that he was only a priest of God. Reaching out to the souls of the faithful was all of his mission. Of matters temporal, of plots, politics and intrigue he knew nothing, they had not been of his concern. After some time Boste was handed over to Topcliffe.

Four times he was stretched on the rack. He was hung from the wrists by manacles chained to the ceiling. His body would be so broken and crippled after the attentions of Topcliffe that John Boste would never walk upright or unaided again. But he did not give way to his agonies, and through all his pain never once did he betray those who had aided him, sheltered him and supported him.

So celebrated a prisoner had he become that Queen Elizabeth herself wished to see him. Boste was brought to Windsor and questioned personally by William Cecil, the Queen's Secretary and Lord Treasurer. Perhaps the Queen looked on from some hidden place. Perhaps she wished merely to view the prisoner. Who really was this man? Traitor or champion of the north, fanatic or saint? She would have the report of Huntingdon, her cousin, and his account of the activities of John Boste; she had also the word of Topcliffe who had described him as 'that most resolute of traitors'. Boste said nothing more, adding only that he lamented 'the lack of popish priests in England' and declaring his loyalty to the Queen in matters temporal, but in matters spiritual upholding the Pope's right to depose her as a heretic.

As it became obvious that John Boste would reveal no more under torture it was decided to return him for trial, and execution, to Durham. The area where he had been most active and had a most loyal following, there would the example of his execution have the most effect. So it was that to the north country he was returned, retracing his earlier southward journey and again halting first at York. 'On the 16 July 1594, John Boste and one George Errington, were sent pinioned to Durham from York Castle.' George Errington was a layman who had been active in the secret movement of priests. He was to die two years later at York. A contemporary chronicler observed of Boste: 'When he went to Durham, he had been racked to sore, that when he sat on his knees (as for the most part he ever was) he was all in a heap, as if he had been all in pieces . . .'

But John Boste now felt beyond pain. He was aware that the horses were moving more slowly, that the snap of the whip came more often as the procession climbed the slope up out of Millburngate and towards the site of the execution. People still lined the way, many 'ladies of good standing' looked on and wept as the doomed man was paraded by them. Boste watched the faces, the faces stared back; many faces. It seemed to him that the whole range of human expression could be seen on those faces as he passed. He saw hate, anger and fear. He also saw sympathy, sorrow and shame. It seemed he saw the state of England in a thousand faces as he was dragged towards his death. He remembered too the cold, set faces in the courtroom. The faces of Huntingdon and the Council.

The trial had opened on Monday, 22 July 1594. John Boste was brought before the court the next day. He again pleaded guilty to previous charges, he again delivered his confession for the record, but he was not allowed to address the court. Huntingdon, however, had new evidence. John Ballard was another missionary priest who had contacted Boste at a wedding ceremony. Ballard had been involved in a plot to kill the Queen. This was to have been the first move in the 'Spanish Enterprise' against Protestant England. Huntingdon claimed that at this wedding ceremony Ballard had informed Boste of the impending Spanish Armada, information which Boste had kept secret. Boste replied to the court that yes, Ballard was known to him from his days at the seminary college, and yes, the men had met at the wedding. Ballard had told of the invasion but Boste had replied: 'You and I are made priests, it is our function to invade souls, and not to meddle with temporal invasions, they do not belong to us.' Boste replied to Huntingdon: 'It would be foolish to disclose every rumour one heard.' Father John Boste then delivered his confession:

> I am a priest of the Holy Catholic Church; and I came, though unworthy, according to St Paul, to preach the gospel of Jesus Christ, whereof I am not ashamed, and to administer the sacraments to my beloved countrymen . . . all this I needs confess, and I am not ashamed of it, but do greatly rejoice that I have done so.

The Court retired to consider its sentence.

The horses were halted, the procession stopped, they had reached the scene of the execution. It had been near here four years earlier that the missionary priests John Holiday, John Hogge, Edmund Duke and Richard Hill had met their deaths, executed at the place of the common gallows. 'A brook near the gallows, at the time of the execution ceased to flow, and has remained dry ever since, and is thence called "Dryburne" to this day.'

The prisoner was dragged from his funeral carriage. He was come at last to the very shadow of the gallows, and the air of death was around him. Though many people viewed the scene there was a strange silence. No bird sung in the midsummer air and a chill breeze blew. John Boste shivered in the breeze, and at the memory of the words in the courtroom, the pronouncement of his sentence, which would now be carried out:

> You will be carried either upon a sled or upon a hurdle to the place of execution. There you will be hanged by the neck, presently you shall be cut down and your members shall be cut from you and cast in the fire even in your sight, your bowels shall be pulled out of your body and cast likewise into the fire. Your head shall be cut off, your body quartered and the parts of your body shall be disposed as officers shall see occasion.

The chill breeze blew again. The executioner made ready. John Boste began to climb up to the scaffold and, on reaching the platform, he made the sign of the cross. He recited the Angelus and was allowed one brief statement to the watching crowd. He referred to his alleged offences against the Queen, saying: 'I never offended her, I take it upon my death, I never went about to offend her. I wish to God that my blood may be in satisfaction for her sins.' As the noose was put over his head, he viewed the faces in the crowd. Some he recognised, many wept openly. One face was that of friend and fellow seminary priest Christopher Robinson, and it was Robinson's account of the ghastly events of that day that would bear lasting witness to the martyrdom of John Boste, ghastly events which would eventually take place again at Robinson's own execution. According to Robinson, Boste was cut down from the gallows semi-conscious and as the butchery began with the executioner plunging his knife into John Boste's body, the priest was heard to say: 'God forgive you. Go on, go on. Lay not this sin to their charge.'

With that, mercifully, he died. The executioner carried on with the full grotesque exercise. When he cut Boste's heart from his body, he held it up to the crowd and said: 'Behold, the heart of a traitor!' A voice replied: 'No! The heart of a servant of God.'

The martyr was dead. His limbs were displayed on the castle walls. His head was mounted on a pole on Framwellgate Bridge. There they stayed as an example and a warning until, in the night time, some unknown person took down the head and carried it away.

Lady Margaret Neville escaped execution by conforming to the new religion, only to revert back to Catholicism in 1598. John Boste's pursuer, Henry Hastings, Third Earl of Huntingdon, Lord President of the Council of the North, was to die childless after a two-week illness at the King's manor in York the following year. He was 59 years old. William Cecil, Elizabeth's chief minister and oldest adviser, died in 1598. Spymaster Sir Francis Walsingham had died in 1590.

Queen Elizabeth herself ruled on until her death in 1603. But the Elizabethan age was already coming to an end, an age which has come to be regarded by some as the flowering of England and of Englishness, a period which saw the nation's development into a player on the world stage. The defeat of the Armada, the great voyages of Drake, Raleigh and Frobisher, these had all been contemporary with the missions of the seminary priests. The year of John Boste's death, 1594, saw the publication of one of William Shakespeare's first works. This was the gloss from which later historians have reflected the glories of the Elizabethan years. but it was a time, indeed a century, in which England saw constant internal strife, religious and political paranoia, persecution, treachery and brutality. It would be only another half century before internal conflict would arise again, when the monarch would turn from the people and the English Civil War would tear country, communities and families apart.

Schoolchildren today run carefree on the site where, 400 years ago, John Boste met his cruel fate. There is no marker to indicate the exact site of his death, but the scene of the execution is the area of land which now forms the grounds of St Leonard's School, near to County Hall. From his death and for almost 400 years the Blessed John Boste was revered as a Roman Catholic martyr. On 25 October 1970, Pope Paul VI canonised John Boste as one of the 40 English and Welsh martyrs. Of the 40, St John Boste was the only one to have been martyred north of York, and as such reserves a special place in Durham's sometimes bloody history.

Chapter Ten

The King, the Covenanters and Oliver Cromwell

'It was in Scotland that the torch was lighted which began the vast conflagration.'

– Churchill

When, in 1625, Charles I acceded to the throne of England, he did so with the unshakeable conviction that his destiny was to rule over his people by 'Divine Right'. His royal duty, he considered, was of the highest kind. He believed that he was the Lord's anointed, God's deputy on earth, and as such he was answerable not to his subjects, certainly not to Parliament, only to God, and that he must hold faithfully that sacred office until death, when the rigours and responsibilities of earthly kingship would be left behind and his earthly crown would be exchanged for a heavenly one.

The shy, aloof young monarch was married by proxy on 1 May of the same year to Henrietta Maria, the beautiful and vivacious youngest daughter of King Henry IV of France. Over the next 15 years their royal court would become the envy of Europe. It exemplified sophistication, elegance, grace and good taste. The royal household surrounded themselves with, and enjoyed, all that was finest. Inigo Jones, one of the greatest of all English architects, built for them; Rubens painted for them; Van Dyck faithfully recorded their elegant likenesses for future generations. But as the years went by the ostentation of the royal court began to create growing unrest amongst the King's subjects, and resentment within the Puritan movement and within Parliament.

The King, existing as he did in his own private world of style and gracious living, surrounded and flattered by a royal court of an estimated 2,000 courtiers all living at his expense, was isolated from the groundswell of discontent throughout his land. He was alienated from his own people. As for Parliament, he had slight regard. To Charles, Parliament served two functions:

as a court of law and, more importantly, as a body to grant taxation: 'Parliaments are altogether in my power for their calling, sitting, and dissolution. Therefore as I find the fruits of them to be good or evil, they are to continue, or not to be.' Parliament, Charles considered, was merely his instrument, existing and functioning by his own good will. Parliamentarians of course did not share in this conviction. For their part, they did not deny the King's prerogative powers, but they would not consent to his claim of a sovereign right to take any action he deemed necessary, regardless of the will of Parliament. Tension between the two began to grow, Parliament eventually refusing to raise more taxes to finance what they saw as endless, meaningless wars in Europe and a profligate and barely solvent royal household. In March 1629, Charles took the ultimate step of dissolving Parliament. He hoped he would never have to call another; he would rule by royal decree.

An insight into the sanitised, cosseted world of pomp, ceremony and ostentation within which the King lived may be gained from an account by Dr Cosin, then a Prebendary of the Cathedral, of the King's first visit to Durham. The occasion arose in 1633 during Charles's journey north to Edinburgh and his coronation on the throne of Scotland. After breaking his journey as a guest of Sir Henry Vane the Elder at Raby Castle, the King travelled on to the Bishop of Durham's Palace at Auckland Castle. J.J. Dodd, writing in 1897, described in his book *The History of the Urban District of Spennymoor* the splendour of the King's company on that journey as 'one of the finest sights ever beheld by the people of the locality . . . a brilliant, imposing cavalcade, attended by a large retinue of the nobility'.

The next Saturday, 1 June, the King and his entourage were met by the High Sheriff, William Belasyse, and escorted to Durham Cathedral where he arrived at five o'clock in the afternoon. Dr Cosin's account begins: 'Our most illustrious and most gracious King Charles, whom to see is to love'. It goes on to describe in detail the devotions paid by the King to the Church, and by the dignitaries of the Church to the King. He was met at the north door of the cathedral by the Dean, Dr Hunt. A carpet had been laid specially for the occasion. On his entrance the King knelt on 'a faldstool with a costly cover, provided with cushions of purple velvet and began to say the Lord's Prayer in a low voice, while a canopy of silk and gold, supported on eight gilded staves, was held over him by eight Prebendaries of the church'. The King was then led, still under the sumptuous canopy, to a seat near the front, then after a speech of welcome by the Dean they proceeded down the nave, 'the choir in good order going before, and the canopy held over the king while "Te deum" was sung accompanied by the organ and the musical instruments'. Then, on a seat specially prepared for him between the Bishop's throne and the High Altar, Charles Stuart, King of England, heard prayers and anthems in Durham Cathedral.

After the ceremony the procession visited St Cuthbert's tomb, where the King was presented with 'a most costly cope of red velvet, embroidered throughout with silk and gold'. Following the presentation, still under the canopy, he visited the Galilee Chapel and the tomb of the Venerable Bede, and after confirming his assent to the 'rights, privileges and property of this ancient church, the King took his leave of the Dean and Prebendaries as they all knelt at the north door'.

The next day the King, 'accompanied by a numerous and splendid retinue', attended morning prayer in the cathedral, after which he was led to the Deanery where the Bishop 'entertained the King and his train at a most magnificent banquet, and also bestowed on his majesty's servants, liberal gratuities'. By ancient custom the finery acquired by the Dean and Chapter for use during the King's visit was given to the King's servants. The carpet, the expensive stool cover and cushions were given to the King's master of horse; the magnificent gilded canopy went to the King's footmen; all of these items had then to be bought back by the Dean and Chapter if they were to be retained by the Church. The cost to the Bishop for entertaining the King was £1,500 a day.

The day of the King's departure arrived, but not before he had sent a letter to the Dean and Chapter in which he mentioned certain things which during his visit he had observed. There were certain 'meane tenements' in the churchyard and adjoining the church wall which he thought 'most unfitting for that place, and altogether unbeseeminge the magnificence of so goodly a fabricke'. He left instructions that after his departure the tenements together with the occupants be removed. With that, Charles I departed Durham Cathedral at ten o'clock in the morning on Monday, 3 June 1633. It would be six years before he returned, and the circumstances under which his next visit would take place would be vastly different.

As the direct rule of Charles I continued throughout the 1630s, his arbitrary methods of imposing taxation further antagonised Parliamentarians. The King's justice was swift and severe: anyone refusing to pay the King's taxes was arrested by the King's officers and summarily jailed. The King's methods were becoming, it seemed, increasingly despotic. The King himself was becoming deeply unpopular with his subjects, and he was despised by many influential Parliamentarians. The situation came to a head when, in 1635, Charles reintroduced and extended the Elizabethan 'Ship Tax', whereby all counties of England would now be forced to pay ostensibly for the upkeep of the navy, whereas before only those counties with a coastline were obliged to contribute. The country was enraged. The first voices of open dissent to the King's prerogative powers were heard. Two years later, with the country simmering with discontent, King Charles I made the mistake which would eventually cost him his crown and his life.

His introduction and imposition of the new Anglican Prayer Book on the Scottish Presbyterian Church would have a backlash that started with riots and ended on 28 February 1638 with the signing at Greyfriars churchyard in Edinburgh of 'The Covenant'. The Covenant of the Scottish Presbyterians was, as they saw it, a solemn bond of the whole nation of Scotland, a document enshrining and demonstrating their religious independence from the English King. The 'Covenanters', as they became known, were deeply suspicious of the King's motives, fearing he was attempting to impose upon them moves which would eventually lead towards links with the Church of Rome. The King *was* head of the Anglican Church, but was not his wife a Catholic? Militant Presbyterians whipped up popular anger into hysteria; some of the Covenanters cut their veins and used their blood as ink to sign their names on the document. Hostility and anger grew, and Scottish thoughts duly turned away from solely religious independence to a more fundamental form of independence, that of the Scottish nation.

The King moved to quell the malcontents. He ordered the dissolution of the Scottish General Assembly. They ignored him, openly defying his authority. The Scots began to gather their armies together. The King's position was becoming perilous. He had no option but to parley with the Scots, he had not the resources to war against them. He resolved to journey north. Already a well-trained, experienced Scottish army, 20,000 strong and commanded by the brilliant Field Marshal Alexander Leslie, was massed on the border at Berwick. Flying their banner exclaiming 'For Christ's own and the Covenant', they looked south and waited for the coming of the King.

This, then, was the occasion of Charles's second visit to Durham. On 29 April 1639, he was again received and 'sumptuously entertained' at Raby Castle by Sir Henry Vane, Treasurer to the King's Household and Secretary to the Privy Council. He then proceeded to Durham where he remained while forces of horse and foot were raised, in readiness for the march to the border. At Berwick the rival forces stood opposite each other. The King, fearing his position, made considerable concessions and gave assurances to the Covenanters regarding their independence. Eventually the Scots were appeased and the 'Pacification of Berwick' halted for a while the onset of hostilities. But to the King it was merely a vital breathing space to allow him to gather, in some order, his own forces and prepare for what now seemed to be the inevitable conflict.

Over the next year the Covenanters exploited the King's weak position and wrung more and more concessions from him. Charles could not afford a war, his royal funds were impoverished; to fight he would need to raise, through taxation, large amounts of money. However, to do this he would now need the support of Parliament, the same Parliament that he had personally, 11 years previously in a climate of great bitterness and ill feeling, dissolved.

Parliament was duly summoned and met on 13 April 1640. Old grievances quickly returned. Parliamentary rhetoric was vehemently hostile to the King. He dismissed the 'Short Parliament' on 5 May. Seeing an opportunity, the Scots moved south as far as the Tyne. There they were met by a vastly inferior Royalist force.

On 28 August 1640 a Scottish army of 20,000 foot and 2,500 horse looked out across the Tyne at the King's force of 3,000 foot and 1,500 horse, commanded by Lord Conway. When hostilities eventually began Scottish cannon, positioned in Newburn Village, pounded the English defences. The King's men fell back. When, at low tide, the river became fordable, a few hundred Scots cavalry and musketmen under a Major Ballantyne charged across. The Royalist force fled. Described as an 'infamous and irreparable rout', a contemporary chronicler wrote that 'Never had so many ran from so few with less ado'. The King's men fled south to Durham where they commandeered weapons, horses, food, anything of use, before fleeing south again to Northallerton. The Scots marched on Newcastle which they took and there made an appeal for aid to English Parliamentarians and the Puritan movement, after which they proceeded to take control of all of Northumberland and Durham.

The reaction of the people of the north was mixed. Though the northern aristocratic families were for the King, it was said of the 'common folk' that in the public houses of Durham toasts were drunk to the health of the Scottish Covenanters. Many, however, perhaps mindful of the tales of Scottish invasions of ancient days, were more cautious, and fled in the face of the oncoming Scots. Rushworth described the scene:

> As far as the City of Durham, it became a most depopulated place; not
> one shop for four days after the fight open; not one house in ten that
> had either man, woman, or child in it; not one bit of bread to be got
> for money for the King's army had eat and drank all in their march to
> Yorkshire; the country people durst not come to market, which made
> that City in a sad condition for want of food.

And it was into that 'sad' city that on 30 August 1640 the army of the Scots Covenanters marched, there to demand payment from an impoverished population. The following month the inhabitants of the city petitioned the King 'to relieve them from the heavy distressing levies of the Scots'. But the King, like the city, was impoverished, and in the north the Scottish army would remain for the time being, in the ascendant.

Charles again summoned Parliament. The 'Long Parliament', as it became known, was installed on 3 November 1640, the final and fateful Parliament of the reign of Charles I. There began an uncomfortable truce with the Scots: Charles was forced to make more and more concessions, but when agreement was finally reached to hand over to the Scottish army a retrospective 'sustenance' of £850 a day, the Covenanters were temporarily satisfied and, in 1641, they returned to their homeland. The relationship between King and Parliament grew worse. Charles's plans to raise taxes to subsidise the military came under increasing attack by members in the House. The positions of those supporting Parliament and those supporting the King began to polarise and harden. After a further year of continued attacks on the King's sovereignty, Charles's patience snapped and he signed warrants for the arrest of five of his most vociferous opponents in Parliament. On 4 January 1642, the King rode with three or four hundred of his mounted swordsmen, his 'Cavaliers', to the House of Commons to arrest them for high treason. But as the King entered the House of Commons, the only monarch ever to do so, he observed, 'I see the birds have flown'. Tipped off by an informant in the King's household, the five members had made good their escape. The King had no option but a humiliating, and for him fatal, about-face. In response to the King's inflammatory action, London, already against him and for Parliament, rose up. Charles was forced now to accept the inevitable. He would leave the capital and retreat first to Newmarket, then to Nottingham Castle, where he would raise his standard and command all that were still loyal to rally to him.

The first battle of the English Civil War was fought on 23 October 1642 at Edgehill in Warwickshire. Neither side could claim a victory, but as a sad foretaste of the tragedies to come during the Civil War, on that day two fathers fought for the King and their two sons for Parliament. The early exchanges of the war went reasonably well for the King. In November 1642, the Earl of Newcastle formed the counties of Northumberland, Durham, Cumberland and Westmorland into an 'Association for the King's Service', his men of Northumbria eventually becoming the famous 'Whitecoats' regiment who were to gain renown for their bravely, fighting spirit and loyalty to the King. So it was that the north fell once again under the control of Royalist forces. But they were still in the main volunteer armies, and the tide would eventually turn when confronted by Cromwell's dreaded 'Ironsides'.

On 25 September 1643, secret negotiations between Parliament and the Scots resulted in the signing of a treaty between the two: they would become allies in the fight against the 'tyrant' King. Another Scottish army, again commanded by Leslie, crossed the border during a snowstorm in January 1644, and fell upon Newcastle. However, finding that this time the city was well defended most of the Scottish army continued south into Durham. On 28 February, at Medomsley, a Scottish force of 20,000 men crossed the nearby River Derwent on a bridge made of tree trunks; the next day their camp lay within a mile of Chester-le-Street. They crossed the River Wear near Lumley

Castle and sporadic fighting began. On 24 March a Scottish detachment was defeated at Boldon by Royalist commander William Cavendish. Running battles and skirmishes against the Earl of Newcastle's forces ensued, but there was not one decisive engagement.

However, a document dated 18 August 1646 and rather grandly entitled 'A Perfect List of all the Victories Obtained (through the blessing of God), by the Parliaments Forces' gives an indication that the battle in the north was beginning to slip away from the King. We are told that 'In the moneth of Aprill, 1644, Our religious Bretheren of Scotland took Durham with al the ammunition; In the moneth of May, 1644, Lumley Castle taken by our Bretheren of Scotland, with al the ammunition'.

In June 1644, a request to the Earl of Newcastle to make haste with all his forces to York resulted in a sudden dash south by the Royalists. The Scots pursued them. Passing through Quarrington Hill and Ferryhill the Scottish army eventually came upon them at Darlington where again the armies skirmished. The Royalists pressed on and after another skirmish with the Scots at Northallerton, they joined the forces of the King and the cavalry of Prince Rupert on the high ground about four miles from York, a place known as Marston Moor. At Marston Moor the Earl of Newcastle's 'Whitecoats' and the massed forces of foot and horse of the King and Prince Rupert would clash head on with the Parliamentary armies under General Fairfax and the Scots under Leslie. The Royalists were routed. The Royalist cavalry, the King's 'Cavaliers', eventually fled the field in the face of a relentless onslaught from the enemy. Newcastle's 'Whitecoats', the men of Northumbria, died where they stood. According to one chronicler, out of 1,000 men 'all save some 30 were cut down to a man'. The commander of the Parliamentary 'Eastern Association', a brilliant captain of horse and an increasingly influential voice within the Parliamentary movement, Oliver Cromwell, said of the day: 'God made them as stubble unto our swords.'

To the King, the defeat at Marston Moor meant that the Royalist north was now lost. It meant a turning in the tide of the war, against him. Indeed it marked the beginning of the end for Charles. His armies would eventually be decisively defeated at Naseby in 1645. The King himself would be taken prisoner by a Scottish force at Newark the following year. He would spend two years in captivity, for a time incarcerated by the Scots at Newcastle. From there, in 1647, he would make his final visit to Durham as a prisoner on his way south to his eventual trial and execution. The Battle of Marston Moor also marked the beginning of the rise to ultimate power of Oliver Cromwell.

In the meantime the storm of war continued to blow across a ravaged and embittered country. Though in the north the winds of that storm for a while blew less strong, there remained those who actively supported their cause, if not by joining the respective armies then by using some other influence or

ABOVE: Lonely Lindisfarne
Castle on Holy Island.

RIGHT: Lindisfarne Harbour,
peaceful today but Vikings
landed here in AD 793.

'Cuthbert's Isle' - St Cuthbert's first retreat as a hermit.

Staindrop Church. It is said that Cnut the Great ordered an extension to the Church.

In the shadow of the Cathedral - the original shape of William's Castle can be seen from above.

Kingsgate Bridge today towers over the scene of William the Conqueror's flight.

Ruins at Finchale - the stone cross in the foreground marks the tomb of St Godric.

The Church of St Godric looks across to the Cathedral.

Finchale in winter.

Monument to the Battle of Neville's Cross.

The western towers of the Cathedral looking towards the battlefield.

Ruined Barnard Castle rises over the River Tees.

RIGHT: Brancepeth Castle - from its gates marched 'The Rising of the North'.

skill or particular talent, or simply by voicing their opinions for all to hear. Sir Henry Vane the Younger of Raby, whose father, a King's officer, had twice in recent years entertained Charles, was an ardent Republican; indeed, it had been he who had been sent to negotiate the signing of the treaty with the Scots which brought them into the war on Parliament's side. Sir Henry moved freely within the most influential circles, was made Speaker of the House of Commons and was a friend of Cromwell. Throughout the Civil War he continued to champion the cause of the Republic. However, one Francis Walker of Barnard Castle had, apparently, views diametrically opposed to those of Sir Henry. Walker publicly stated that:

> The Parliament are rogues, rebels and traitors – God confound them and the devil confound them; I wish the Parliament house blown up with gunpowder as it should have been once, I hope to see them all hanged, one against another within a short time. Parliament seek to be the King themselves, and they would have the King to be worse than you and I, and that he could not say whether the horse he rode on was his own.

For this passionate, if perhaps ill-considered outburst, Walker was arrested and sent for trial on 3 January 1644 at the Durham Sessions.

Life in the north seems to have returned to a reasonable state of normality. 'Witches' were executed in Durham Market Place. Indeed the Civil War years were the years of the great witch hunts over much of eastern England, when the notorious 'Witchfinder' Matthew Hopkins carried out his cruel and bloody work. During the course of the war more than 80 people were executed in Suffolk alone, condemned by Matthew Hopkins. Whitelock states that, 'In 1649, 14 men and women were burned alive at a small village near Berwick; the entire population of the village being only 14 families.'

By 1648, the rising captain of horse at Marston Moor had become Lieutenant-Colonel Oliver Cromwell. The King's cause was lost. A final twist in the tale, however, was still to come about. The 'Moderate' party of the Scottish Church sought to reinstate Charles as King, at least of Scotland. The focus of the troubles therefore returned north and by order of Parliament Cromwell was sent to Scotland to re-establish Parliamentary authority there. As he and his 'New Model Army' marched north through Durham to Gateshead and Newcastle, people gathered, as one apprentice boy named Ambrose Barnes reported, 'the sooner to see him who was the hope and expectation of the age, and that famed host he led, whose doings were the theme of every tongue'. Young Barnes spoke of the 'New Model Army' in adulatory terms, extolling their apparently saintly qualities. They were, he said:

not like other armies, composed of mercenaries of rude, profligate manners, but of sober, judicious, serious volunteers, it being Cromwell's maxim to enlist none but such; many of them being gentlemen of good families and fortunes, all of them of honest callings and trades who, knowing the cause they had espoused, ventured their all for it, and were trained to the discipline of religion as well as of arms, both officers and soldiers making up so many pious Christians to be found this side of heaven.

Cromwell and his band of 'so many pious Christians' marched on into Scotland, eventually reaching Edinburgh without being challenged. Parliament's authority being thus reaffirmed over the Scottish 'Moderates', he began, on 16 August 1648, his return journey south. On 20 October he reached Durham City where he lodged in the castle and was entertained by his friend the Governor of Newcastle, Sir Arthur Haselrig. Haselrig six years earlier had been one of the 'birds' that had flown from the House of Commons, before the arrival of the King.

During Cromwell's march to Scotland, violence had again broken out in England. In the north, those forces still loyal to King Charles went into action once more. Raby Castle, home of the Vanes, was besieged by Royalists. The Staindrop parish register records that on 27 August 1648, one 'William Joplin, a soldier, slain at the siege of Raby Castle, was buried in the church . . . many soldiers slain before Raby Castle witch were buried in the park and not registered'.

All Royalist efforts were to be in vain; Cromwell returned from Scotland with his growing authority unchallenged. A Mr Sanderson of Egleston recorded in his diary Cromwell's arrival and welcome at Barnard Castle, following his stay at Durham:

> Lieutenant General Oliver Cromwell entered Barnard Castle on Tuesday, 24 October 1648. Anthony Martindale, Mathew Stoddard, Cuthbert Raine, Robert Hutton, Francis Hutchinson, William Hutton, Morgan Rowlandson, Thomas Heslop, Samuel Martindale, George Dale, John Lively and William Wharton, went out to meet him and rode before him to the lodgings.

It must be assumed that Cromwell's vociferous Barnard Castle critic, Francis Walker, was either unwilling or perhaps unable to voice his very definite opinions about the Parliament on this occasion.

Blaygraves House, now a restaurant, is reputedly the oldest surviving house in Barnard Castle. Allegedly once the property of King Richard III, a story tells that the house was given by him when still Duke of Gloucester and

Lord of Barnard Castle to one Miles Forrest as a reward for his alleged part in the murder of Richard's nephews, the 'Princes in the Tower'. This then was to be Cromwell's lodgings during his visit. After offering words of greeting, his welcoming party turned and escorted him to his quarters where, we are told by Mr Sanderson, the mighty Oliver Cromwell, later to become Captain General of the Parliamentary armies and 'by the grace of God, Lord Protector' was offered 'burnt wine and shortcakes'. When next he returned north, the Civil War would finally be over, the King executed, but Cromwell's 'New Model Army' would have to face yet another threat, and once more that threat would come from north of the border.

After the execution of King Charles I, the Moderate party in Scotland acknowledged his son Charles II as their King, and armed forces were gathered to support their claim. Again Cromwell was given the task of riding north to crush the Royalists. On 14 July 1650 Cromwell, by now Captain General of the Parliamentary army, arrived once more in Durham. Met again by Sir Arthur Haselrig, Cromwell was made guest of honour at a 'sumptuous banquet' at a house allegedly now part of the Royal County Hotel, after which a fast was kept to implore God's blessing on the coming campaign, a campaign for which Cromwell drew five companies from the Durham garrison to serve as reinforcements in his army. Both Cromwell's campaign and the cause of the Scots Moderates ended at the Battle of Dunbar on 3 September 1650. Parliament's armies under Cromwell achieved a crushing victory, many Scots were killed and 5,000 were taken prisoner. The following day Cromwell gave orders that they should be taken south. Many of the defeated, half-starved wretches, died on the march. A letter written from Newcastle by Arthur Haselrig to the Council of State on 31 October 1650 stated:

> When they came to Morpeth, the prisoners, being put into a large walled garden, they ate up raw cabbages, leaves, and roots . . . which cabbage (they having fasted, as they themselves said, near eight days), poisoned their bodies; for as they were coming hence to Newcastle, some died by the wayside . . . when I sent them to Durham, about 140 were sick, and not able to march. Three died that night, and some fell down on their march from Newcastle to Durham and died. On entering the great Cathedral Church, there were counted to be no more than 3,000.

The Scots were imprisoned in the cathedral over the winter of 1650. Half starved and freezing they set fire to what they could to stay alive. The remains of the original medieval woodwork, the organ and the choir stalls were broken up and burned. The tombs of Ralph Neville and his son John were partially destroyed. Thus the Scots took their revenge upon the conquerors of their forefathers at the Battle of Neville's Cross. Of the Scots prisoners, many did not survive the winter. Those that were 'lucky' enough to do so were transported, as slave labour, to the new American colonies or to the West Indies. Most of them were to die there of yellow fever.

The period of the Protectorate saw the cathedral returned to the state of ruin and decay, despoliation and neglect that had been begun immediately after the Reformation. On 2 May 1649 the castle, the ancient seat of the Prince Bishops of Durham, the only northern fortress never to be taken by the invading Scottish armies of old, was confiscated and sold to the Lord Mayor of London for £1,267. 10d. Cromwell was indeed no benefactor to the ancient city, but the Lord Protector did leave Durham one notable thing. After Dunbar and his visits to Durham, Cromwell petitioned Parliament in 1650 requesting that a college or school be established in the now abandoned Dean and Chapter houses. Parliament eventually approved the request and in 1657 Cromwell, as Lord Protector, signed a Writ of Privy Seal founding a University of Durham. His foresightedness was not, however, universally acknowledged. Petitions against the founding of the new university came from both Oxford and Cambridge and its immediate establishment was delayed. The matter was not settled before Cromwell's death, and after the restoration of the monarchy his idea was forgotten and the Church property returned. It was to be almost another 200 years before England's third oldest university would finally be founded.

King Charles I went to his death on 30 January 1649. Beheaded on the scaffold in Whitehall, his severed head was held up and shown to the assembled crowd. Described by some as the 'tyrant, traitor and murderer, Charles Stuart', considered by others as a royal martyr, Charles was never popular with his subjects; he was haughty, aloof, alienated from the people. Nevertheless it was with great trepidation that he was executed. When it came to the end, the English, 'ever fond of a King', blanched at the thought of executing one, an execution which some have described as a 'cruel necessity', others as more a sacrifice than an execution. Charles's family and his supporters were forced into exile and England became a republic.

The King's loyal general in the north, the Earl of Newcastle, had fled abroad following the defeat at Marston Moor. After the annihilation of his 'Whitecoats', this able ally took no further part in the war, much to the loss of the King. Of the Vanes of Raby, Sir Henry the Elder tried unsuccessfully to avert the execution of the King. His efforts were to be of no avail and he withdrew from public life to Raby. He died in 1656. His son, Sir Henry the Younger, had always been a fervent believer in the cause of Parliament. One-time leader of the House of Commons and described as an 'Intellectual Revolutionary', he believed in liberty, freedom of thought, and of religion.

His early friendship with Cromwell soured after the execution of the King. Though an ardent Republican, he was no supporter of the army. He began to regard Cromwell increasingly as an ambitious military despot; in turn Cromwell regarded Vane as a scheming intellectual trying to benefit from gains which had, after all, been accomplished by the army ('The Lord deliver me from Sir Henry Vane'). After Cromwell's death and the restoration of the monarchy, Vane remained a committed Republican. Nonetheless he was promised an amnesty by Charles II, no doubt in recognition of his own and his father's attempts to prevent the execution of Charles I. However, when he continued publicly to promote Parliamentary sovereignty, the King's promise proved false. Sir Henry Vane was arrested and executed as a traitor.

In 1653 Oliver Cromwell, Captain General of the army, leading light in the war against the King, took the title Lord Protector. He became the most powerful man in the land and the figurehead of the Republic. However, when offered the crown of England, Cromwell, sometimes strong and ruthless, at other times almost a reluctant and apologetic leader, refused. He died on 3 September 1658, the eighth anniversary of the Battle of Dunbar. Tyrant or visionary, dictator or man of destiny, Oliver Cromwell's great years had passed in the storm of a civil war; it was fitting perhaps that death finally came to him as a storm raged in the skies above.

Cromwell had named his son, Richard, as successor, but he was totally unsuited to take up the awesome responsibilities bequeathed him by his father. Until Cromwell's death Richard, 'Tumbledown Dick', had lived the life of a country gentleman; he had not been prepared for power. He held no influence within the army, therefore could not be guaranteed their support. Within two years he had lost control and he simply returned to private life. He left England for France, where he would remain until his eventual return in 1680. Then, on 12 July 1712, Richard Cromwell, son and heir to the mighty Oliver Cromwell, Lord Protector, died and with him went the memories, the dreams, the aspirations of England's first and so far only experiment with Republicanism. In 1660, the 'Thousand Year Monarchy' was restored. Charles II was crowned King; it was eight days later that the news reached Durham.

Chapter Eleven

Murder at 'Cutty Throat' Farm

'Reader, remember, sleeping we were slain . . .'

A diary entry for Thursday, 25 January 1683, begins: 'A sad and cruel murder . . .' What follows in the diary is a brief description of a brutal murder which took place not far from Ferryhill on that dark winter's night. The diary entry is merely descriptive in the style of its day. But the murder and the events that followed have, over the years, melted into the realms of local legend. Every region has its murders and murderers, but the helplessness of the young victims in this case has given to the following story an extra degree of horror and tragedy.

The old horse snorted uneasily as it plodded along in the darkness, blowing plumes of hot moist air into the cold January night. The stillness was broken only by the steady, muffled clump of its hoofs on the rough, rutted, earth road, and the slow rhythmic creaking of the cart wheel. The night was quiet and peaceful and there was nothing to betray the terrible events that had just taken place at Brass Farm between Ferryhill and Merrington. It had been a pleasant evening, John and Margaret Brass had been visiting friends for a Christmas season celebration. As they rode quietly home they talked together of their hopes for the new year of 1683, of the plans they had made for their elder daughter's forthcoming wedding.

Suddenly, something caused them to stiffen and sit bolt upright in their seats. Dogs at nearby farms began to howl. Owls screeched wildly in the trees. Their horse, terrified, reared up and refused to go any further. John and Margaret were startled, frightened, breathless. What lurking danger, they wondered, were they about to meet, out on the lonely road. John Brass struggled to control the horse, expecting at any moment to be assailed by ruffians or robbers, common enough in these parts. They heard footsteps running straight towards them. Suddenly a figure appeared out of the darkness and stood motionless in the road ahead. To John and Margaret's initial relief, they realised it was neither ruffian nor robber. It was the familiar figure of Andrew Mills, the young lad who worked for John Brass at the farm. But Mills did not stop to exchange courtesies and small talk with his employer. He stared out from the shadows and, recognising Brass, turned tail and disappeared into the night.

Alarmed at Mills's strange behaviour and now knowing instinctively that something was very wrong, John and Margaret Brass made all haste back to their farm. Mills had been there with their three children all evening, and they feared something dreadful must have happened. The harrowing scene that greeted them was destined to become part of local legend, and a play written about the events of that fateful January night in 1683 was still to draw packed houses at the Spennymoor Theatre over 200 years later.

Andrew Mills was a young boy, not yet 20 years old. He had worked for John Brass for some time and had always seemed, indeed was, quiet and mild-mannered. He was of low intelligence and was childlike for his age, but there was nothing at all odd in his personality. Certainly nothing to suggest to anyone that he was capable of the acts of brutality he committed on the night of Thursday, 25 January 1683, at Brass Farm, soon to become known locally as 'Cutty Throat' Farm.

The younger children, John and Elizabeth, had gone to their beds when Mills, for reasons which were never established, suddenly went berserk. Jane being 20 years old was the elder daughter and was shortly to be married. She became alarmed when she noticed that something about Mills's behaviour was wrong. He became agitated; he quickly angered for no reason that Jane could judge. She became frightened. Mills's anger turned into a blind rage, as he seemed to lose control of his own senses. Suddenly he picked up an axe and swung at her. She struggled violently with him as the younger children slept in the next room. Jane somehow managed to ward off Mills's vicious blows, escape into the bedroom, and bolt the door between herself with the sleeping children and Mills. She had earned but a brief respite, for now the crazed man beat upon the door. The children woke, screaming. He hurled himself time after time against the door until, little by little, it began to give. A final crash and the wooden bolt shattered. In desperation Jane used her own arm as a makeshift bolt, thrusting it through the door staples and wedging it tightly, trying desperately to keep Mills at bay. But his assault was now so frenzied that she could no longer hold him back, her strength drained by the unrelenting onslaught. Mills finally smashed in the door, in doing so breaking Jane's arm and sending her flying across the room. He then proceeded with his bloody work. Taking his axe, he brutally murdered Jane and her younger brother, John. Mills then turned his attention to little Elizabeth.

'After he had kil'd the sone and the eldest daughter, being above twenty yeares of age, a little lass her sister, about ye age of eleven yeares, being in bed alone.'

She was in bed, terrified and alone. She was only 11 years of age and she had just witnessed the whole savage spectacle. Mills approached. Elizabeth pleaded desperately with him. She wept hysterically. Pathetically she offered him food, sweets and toys. At his trial it was said that because of his childlike ways, Mills had formed a particularly strong relationship with Elizabeth. Perhaps because of this or perhaps because of her pleadings, Mills stopped in his tracks. It suddenly seemed that Elizabeth was to be spared. He turned, as if in a daze, and shuffled slowly away from the scene of the carnage, leaving Elizabeth alive and sobbing helplessly. In his confession Mills claimed that as he walked from the bedroom, Elizabeth's cries still ringing in his ears, something evil stood in the shadows outside. The devil, in the form of a hideous creature, 'with fiery eyes and eagle's wings', commanded him: 'Go back though hateful wretch, resume thy cursed work. I long to view more blood, spare not the young one's life. Kill all, kill all.' Mills turned and walked slowly back to Elizabeth: 'He drag'd her out of bed and kil'd her alsoe.'

After cutting the throats of his three innocent victims, it is said that for some time Mills just sat amongst the bodies of the children. Then, realising the enormity of his crime, he bolted and ran off up the dark road, straight to his meeting with the parents of his victims, John and Margaret Brass. When the bodies were discovered, the distraught parents immediately thought of their encounter with Mills and of his curious behaviour. The alarm was raised, but there was to be no great manhunt, no lengthy investigation. Mills was quickly apprehended at Ferryhill. His deranged behaviour and bloodstained clothing had attracted attention. When word of the murders got round, he was arrested by a group of soldiers who, by chance, were marching from Darlington to Durham that very night.

He was tried at Durham. No motive for the killings was ever established. There was a suggestion of jealousy: Jane was to be married, perhaps Mills harboured some secret desire for his employee's elder daughter. If they had been alone and Jane had refused Mills's advances, this may have been the trigger for the sudden explosion of violence. It was all conjecture, nothing could be proved. No evidence of premeditation was shown, and Mills maintained his story of diabolic influence. His account of the events and the nature of his confession were enough to satisfy the authorities that Mills was totally insane. He was duly condemned to death.

Andrew Mills went to the gallows on Wednesday, 15 August 1683. The only contemporary account of the events, recorded in *Jacob Bee's Diary*, states merely that Mills was 'hanged in irons upon a gybett'. It is unclear from this whether Mills was sent alive to the gibbet or executed and then his body hung as a warning to others, a common practice of the time. Both are possible, the latter is more plausible and from other indications more likely. Local folklore, however, will have none of this, and it is from here that the known facts of the case begin to blur into legend.

Tradition maintains that Andrew Mills was hung alive in chains upon the gibbet, the scene of the execution allegedly on the very spot where he had met John and Margaret Brass that fateful night almost seven months earlier. As was the practice of the time the gibbet overlooked the scene of the crime, the gallows standing about a quarter of a mile south of where the Thinford Inn stands today on the Darlington Road, just to the north of Ferryhill. The tale is told that Mills survived for some considerable time, a sweetheart feeding him milk through the bars of his iron cage. It is said that when he starved, a 'penny loaf' was suspended on a string in front of his face, but just out of his reach, so as to add torment to his pain. People living locally moved away, unable to bear Mills's cries, not to return until after his death. Legend has it that Andrew Mills finally expired 'with a shriek that was heard for miles around'. The gibbet remained. To the local people the site of the agonies of Andrew Mills became an eerie and evil place; in the dark rumour of a storm, or when the night winds wailed, none would pass that spot.

Andrew Mills's Stob, as the gibbet became known, remained on the spot for many years. The noted nineteenth-century explorer and naturalist Charles Waterton, author of, among other works, *Wanderings in South America* and *Natural History Essays*, attended school at Tudhoe. The *Monthly Chronicle* tells us that just before his death in 1865 Waterton recounted some of his childhood memories; he writes:

> Betwixt Tudhoe and Ferryhill there stood an oaken post, very strong and some nine feet high. This was its appearance in my days, but formerly it must have been much higher. It was known to all the country around by the name of Andrew Mills's Stob.
>
> We often went to see it, and one afternoon whilst we were looking at it an old woman came up, took a knife from her pocket, and then pared off a chip which she carefully folded up in a bit of paper. She said it was good for curing toothache.
>
> I suspect that the remains of this oaken post must have long since mouldered away. I have not been there for these last seventy years, and probably if I went thither I should not be able to find the site of this formerly notorious gibbet.

The remains of the gibbet did in fact survive until the 1830s when the site was enclosed, levelled and ploughed up. What happened to the remains of the wretched Andrew Mills is not recorded.

The Brass children were buried in Merrington churchyard. A memorial was erected on which was carved a lengthy inscription which tells of Andrew Mills being 'executed and hung in chains', a pointer perhaps to the truth about his death. However, a curious feature of the inscription is that the word 'executed' has obviously been deliberately worn away. A local story maintains that this was done by Andrew Mills's father. Shocked and ashamed at the terrible crimes his son had committed, yet still retaining some vestige of fatherly love for his own child, he went every day to the churchyard and, little by little, scraped away the word 'executed' with the metal tip of his walking stick. A poignant story. Unfortunately, as the memorial was not erected until over 100 years later, in 1789, the story cannot be true. A more probable culprit was, apparently, an eccentric local innkeeper who continually argued with anyone who would listen that Mills could not have been executed and hung alive in chains as well. And, 'as everyone knew' Mills had been gibbeted alive, the innkeeper took it upon himself to remove the word 'executed', which was obviously incorrect.

The sad tale of the 'Merrington Murders' serves to illustrate that actual events can eventually become merely the basis of a good story which is kept alive down the years and which, through time, is varied, embroidered upon and distorted until it becomes difficult to distinguish historical fact from local legend. That having been said, however, the facts do remain that the murders at John Brass's farm did happen, the children were killed, and Andrew Mills did die on the gallows.

Go up to Merrington church today. The memorial to the murdered Brass children has survived the years. Now weathered but with the inscription still just readable, it remains as a tangible link, bearing witness to the tragic events that took place at 'Cutty Throat' Farm on a dark January night over 300 years ago:

> Reader, remember, sleeping
> we were slain;
> and here we sleep till we must
> rise again.
> Who so sheddeth man's blood, by man shall
> his blood be shed.
> Though shalt do no murder.

Part Four

Chapter Twelve

The Wear Men, the Tyne Men, and the Old Man of the Sea

'A rather elaborate design of water communication.'

A leaden statue of Neptune stands once more in Durham's old Market Place. The monument to the god of the sea must to some seem rather incongruous, situated as it is in a city which can hardly be described as coastal, let alone having any obvious connection with the sea. Monument to lost dreams or mere folly, the story of the Neptune statue has been a minor epic in itself, as indeed was the story of the reason for its presentation to the city. The statue represents a scheme, indeed several schemes, introduced throughout the eighteenth century, to make the River Wear navigable between Durham and the growing port of Sunderland, to link the ancient city with the open sea. If but one of those schemes had been successful, it must surely have made Durham the strangest 'port' in the land.

The first meeting of the Commons Committee, convened to debate 'The Sunderland Bill', sat at ten o'clock in the morning on 28 March 1717. Charles Sanderson, Attorney-at-Law of the Inner Temple, was in attendance at that meeting representing one of the 'interested parties', and he recorded the discussion. Proposals contained in the Bill involved making the River Wear navigable from Shincliffe Bridge just outside Durham City to Sunderland. This would involve dredging and the removal of shoals and sand between Durham and Chester-le-Street; from there the incorporation of a series of locks, dams and sluices would 'canalise' the river as far as Sunderland. It was the hope of the 'Wear Men' – the cartel of rich landowners and businessmen headed by the Earl of Scarborough, the Hedworths, the Lambtons and the Conyers – that factories could be established along the banks of the river. A navigable river, at least for smaller vessels of up to 20 tons, would allow quick, easy and therefore cheap traffic for their produce. Similarly, such a waterway would provide a cheaper means of access for many necessary materials: lead and coals, lime, stone and timber, butter and tallows. To cope with the inevitably increased traffic of goods it was further proposed that the harbour of Sunderland be considerably improved.

The growth in the size and importance of Sunderland as a coal trading port had been brought about by the invention and development of colliery wagon ways, enabling the mines along the River Wear at Washington, Lumley, Rainton and Chester-le-Street to be exploited to the full. However, further growth in Sunderland would be seriously prejudicial to the coal trade on the Tyne; indeed it had been the swift rise of Sunderland as a major coal port in the early eighteenth century that had caused grave concern for the 'Tyne Men', as it may be appropriate to call the wealthy coal traders distributing from Tyneside, and had even provoked the opposition of the Bishop of Durham. The Tory Member for Saltash spoke for the Bishop at that first meeting in March 1717, and claimed that the Bishop 'was the conservator of the Wear, and that his rights and privileges might not be taken away unheard'. Heard they were; nonetheless the Wear Men had their day: they obtained the Enabling Act for their scheme. All they needed now was investment.

The scheme, however, by its very nature involved the use of an enormous amount of manual labour and was therefore expensive, for the powered machinery of the kind needed for such a task as this had not yet been developed. With underinvestment in an over-ambitious scheme, the proposals withered on the vine and died. The plan was never put into effect. However, as an issue 'The Wear Navigation' rumbled on throughout the eighteenth century. What would be termed today as a 'political football' remained at the very centre of political and electioneering rhetoric, indeed it became a staple of local politics. Local Members of Parliament were even at times moved to speak on the subject in the Commons. In 1749, local landowner and MP for Gibside and Streatlam, George Bowes, made his one recorded speech in the House on the very subject.

Another scheme was moved in 1754, but it was basically the same as the earlier proposal and never got off the ground. However, the controversy raged on and once again figured prominently in local politics, this time in the city elections of 1760. As the Bishop had done previously, the Dean and Chapter entered the fray. Also as the Bishop had done, they opposed the idea. They claimed that the increased working of the collieries resulting from completion of the project would be in direct violation of a contract already made with the Church. Furthermore, they asserted that the plans would be prejudicial to 'the trade of ye City, by supporting a chimerical, impracticable scheme to make the River navigable to ye City and carrying goods by water at a dearer rate than they could have them by land from Chester-le-Street'.

Of all the schemes put foward, that which came closest to operation was that mooted in 1796. A far more ambitious project, the idea was to connect the River Wear with both the North and Irish Seas, with further links to many of the larger northern cities. A canal was to be cut from the River Tyne and linked with the Wear at Chester-le-Street. Plans and estimates were drawn up, and it is said that the scheme 'charmed the more enterprising men of the north'. But for all the forward planning it never came to fruition, for by then other considerations determined that the plan was a virtual non-starter. Although the years between 1795 and 1805 could be said to be the peak period of canal building in this country, within a quarter of a century the railways were to be born. The power of steam was to replace 'a rather elaborate design of water communication'.

So it was then that no dredging of the River Wear was ever undertaken, no locks were every built; in spite of the plans and the controversy that surrounded an issue which dominated the politics of eighteenth-century Durham, three schemes spanning 80 years, and Bills laid before Parliament, not one trench was dug. Durham was destined, after all, never to become a port. All the city had to show for almost a century of hopes and fears, of aspirations and arguments, was a seven-foot-high leaden statue of 'The Old Man of the Sea'.

Neptune was presented to the city by George Bowes in 1729 as a symbol of the aspirations of some at least to connect Durham with the open sea. It was thought, no doubt because of his watery connections, that Neptune should stand in the Market Place on the Pant covering the well head which had, since the middle of the fifteenth century, been the main public supply of water for the city. It seems that Neptune remained in favour for almost 100 years before several attempts were made to remove him. In the 1860s it was only popular local opinion which saved the old man from oblivion. After already surviving one attempt to have him removed, in 1816, it seemed that when, almost half a century later, a new Pant was designed to stand over the old well head, without Neptune, that the last link with the grand schemes of the previous century would finally be severed. The locals, however, would have none of it, and by popular demand Neptune was saved.

The new century saw a new threat. In 1900 a new Pant was gifted to the city and Neptune's position was again in doubt. However, nothing if not a survivor, he was to remain on the spot, still undefeated. Indeed he was to stay there, unmoved if not undisturbed, until the year 1923 when he was finally taken down, and the pant demolished, to make way for another former Durham curiosity, a police traffic control box. The statue was moved to Wharton Park, above the railway station, overlooking the city. There forgotten and neglected, Neptune began to suffer from the effects of age and exposure to the elements, and from the indignities of vandals. In 1979 it seemed that the old man had been dealt his final blow when, one stormy night, the Lord of the Oceans was struck by lightning and the partially destroyed statue was finally, after 250 years, removed from public view.

However, all was not lost for George Bowes's gift to the city. In 1986 an appeal was set up by the 'City of Durham Trust' to have the statue restored. The appeal was a great success and a complete restoration of the statue was carried out. Returned to his former glory Neptune returned to public view, in a Claypath shop window. A Neptune celebration was held in the town hall. The main attraction of the social evening, attended by civic leaders and members of the church, was to be old Neptune himself who, it was thought, would stand proudly in the foyer of the town hall. Arrangements were made, invitations sent out, and preparations were completed for the historic evening. Unfortunately, shortly before the event, when council officers inspected Neptune's proposed location for the evening they pointed out that if the seven-foot-high lead statue were placed on the venerable floorboards at the spot suggested the Lord of the Oceans would disappear, suddenly and rather dramatically, down into the bowels of the town hall. This of course was a great disappointment to all concerned. Nonetheless the party went ahead without its star guest, toasts were drunk to absent friends, and it is said the evening was a great success.

Neptune continued to lounge in the shop window until a permanent location for him could be agreed upon. Several sites were suggested throughout the city, including a man-made island in the middle of the river. Eventually, however, the statue was returned to his familiar place of old, back in the Market Place. Gone was the police traffic control box, gone indeed was the traffic, and on 16 May 1991 Neptune returned, resuming his rightful place in the centre of the city. It is, some say, a little unfortunate that visitors to the cathedral and castle do not perhaps get the most endearing view of the old man as they enter the Market Place from Saddler Street, but anyone familiar with that comic view must be tempted to think that the bare backside, exposed now to new generations of townsfolk and tourists, is for one thing an everlasting gesture by 'The Old Man of the Sea' to those persons who in previous times would have had him removed ignominiously from his place of honour, and also perhaps a suitable comment on the ill-prepared schemes that so abjectly failed to turn Durham City into an eighteenth-century port.

Chapter Thirteen

Look Away Dixieland

'Sir, where did you acquire your education, was it at Oxford or at Cambridge?' 'Neither Sir, it was in a pit cabin on Cockfield Fell!'

In 1733 a boy was born in Bishop Auckland whose early years would be spent in relative isolation in the small, remote village of Cockfield. One hundred and thirty years later and thousands of miles from Cockfield, his name would be echoed in a battle song during one of the bloodiest conflicts in history, the American Civil War. The boy was destined to become not a famous military leader nor a great statesman, but a self-taught mathematician, astronomer and surveyor. His name, Jeremiah Dixon. He would, along with Charles Mason, survey and give his name to the Mason–Dixon Line, the border between Maryland and Pennsylvania in the USA, the symbolic dividing line in the civil war between the North and the South, the free and the slave states. Thus was born 'Dixieland', and 'Dixie' would be the anthem favoured by the forces of the Confederacy.

In the early 1730s George Dixon, a Quaker colliery owner from Cockfield, was presented by his wife with two sons. They would eventually grow up to be two of the most ingenious men County Durham has ever produced. Yet so little has been recorded of their lives and achievements that today if they are remembered at all it is only as a vague memory, two shadowy figures from an ill-remembered period in County Durham's history.

The two sons, George and Jeremiah, both received a basic education at the establishment of Mr John Kipling at Barnard Castle. George, born in 1731 and elder brother by two years, 'possessed a genius to rival Jeremiah's', but unlike Jeremiah he was eventually to put down lasting roots in his native country. After an early journey to London, seeking his fortune, when he had worked as a painter of china in the famous Chelsea Pottery, he rarely travelled

113

far from his home in the north. He worked at various coal works, at which it is said he always displayed both extensive knowledge and competent judgement. He was a man of, literally, many talents; indeed his story alone would fill a chapter of this book. As well as being an accomplished painter and engraver, he was renowned in many areas of science. A mathematician and mineralogist, he was also an experimentalist in chemistry, hydraulics and pneumatics. In addition, George was also a more than proficient surveyor. In the process of his work on systems to dispel poisonous gases from coal mines, he succeeded in producing light from coal gas.

As well as their formal education at John Kipling's academy, both boys were encouraged by their father, himself something of a mathematician and amateur astronomer, to study at home and in his colliery workshops. So it was that the main education of the boys began. For Jeremiah it would be the beginning of his more advanced studies of astronomy and of mathematics. The profound ability of Jeremiah Dixon in mathematics soon became apparent and he would eventually come to be spoken of as one of the most ingenious men of his age. But as he later travelled the world in the course of his professional life, the scientific establishment by whom he was employed knew so little about his early background that he was popularly believed to have been born in a coal mine – a belief, it seems, Jeremiah did little to dispel. The young Jeremiah's intellect eventually became known to William Emerson of Hurworth, near Darlington. Emerson, a 'celebrated and strange compound of genius and eccentricity', was to become tutor, friend and mentor to the gifted young Dixon.

The celebrated William Emerson has been described popularly, if not euphemistically, as an 'eccentric'. A colourful character, inclined to unpredictable behaviour, he was indeed a 'truly original genius' whose ability in all disciplines of mathematics set him apart as one of the greatest scholars of his day. Between 1743 and 1776 he produced 13 volumes on the various branches of mathematics, papers on 'Mechanics', 'The Method of Increments' and 'The Doctrine of Fluctions' which were long considered to be the most informed of their kind. This then was to be the level of intellectual discipline into which the young Jeremiah Dixon was introduced. However, if Emerson's mathematical genius was to place his learned contemporaries in awe of him, his appearance and behaviour must have seemed to some distinctly alarming. His dress habits, as well as his genius, were truly original. His usual attire would comprise a home-made shirt, worn back to front, over which was thrown an old sleeveless waistcoat, invariably fastened only at the top and bottom. He also had a penchant for wearing the oldest hat he could find; only a very few served him for all his 81 years. For cold weather he contrived for himself his 'shin covers', pieces of old sacking tied around the knees that would protect his legs from the elements. This unpredictable genius, it seems, cared little for the sartorial correctness of the time. Emerson was also fond of a drink of beer. It was his habit every Monday to visit Darlington market. Once settled in the hospitable surroundings of a popular ale house, it was not unusual for Emerson to stay for some considerable time in the company of his fellow thinkers and drinkers. Indeed his wife would occasionally have to wait until the Wednesday before seeing her husband again.

His coarse and abrupt way of speaking led many of his critics to believe that he couldn't possibly have written those renowned mathematical papers and that someone else must surely have translated them into English. Indeed, if any made so bold as to disagree with him during serious discussion with learned colleagues, he would simply retort with his favourite exclamation, 'Damn thee, thou fule thou'. His speech became even more colourful when confronted with what he considered stupidity; Emerson did not suffer fools gladly: 'The fire and impetuosity of his temper betrayed him, when provoked by "nincompoops", into language far distant from the strictness of mathematical demonstration.' He did not, it seems, care much for accepted standards. A popular tale related of him tells of the time when, one Sunday morning, Emerson caught a young boy stealing fruit from a tree in his garden. Churchgoers looked on in amazement as they passed by on their way to Sunday morning service. There in the garden underneath the tree stood Emerson, brandishing a large axe at the terrified boy. They were even more amazed as they returned home after a lengthy service to see still there in the garden the unfortunate boy seemingly fixed in the treetop, and Emerson still below, waving his axe and threatening to 'hag his legs off' when he came down.

The genius of Emerson was widely recognised, nationally as well as locally. He was offered a Fellowship of the Royal Society. He reacted to the offer by saying: 'It's a damned hard thing to pay so much a year to have initials after my name, when I've burned so many farthing candles in writing my works. – Damn them, and damn their FRS too!' One day, visitors arrived from the University of Cambridge. They had come to request Emerson's assistance with a particular mathematical problem. Emerson looked at the paper and handed it to his friend and former pupil, the local bricklayer John Hunter, who was at the time on Emerson's roof carrying out some repairs. Having no paper on which to write down the solution, Hunter wrote it on the crown of his hat. This he then threw down to Emerson who handed it to the Cambridge scholars. Hesitatingly one of the men asked Emerson if he was confident the solution was correct. Emerson glanced at the hat and merely nodded. For some time the Cambridge men stared incredulously at Hunter's hat. As they continued to attempt to understand the solution, Emerson lost his patience and snapped that if they couldn't work it out they should 'take the damned hat with them and return it when they had discovered the explanation'.

The influence of Emerson undoubtedly developed Jeremiah Dixon's capacity for mathematics. However, an entry in the Quaker minute book for the monthly meeting of 28 October 1760 suggests that possibly Emerson's influence over the young Jeremiah extended in other, less conventional directions; the entry reads: 'Jerry Dixon, son of George and Mary Dixon of Cockfield, disowned for drinking to excess.'

Individual and eccentric though Emerson undoubtedly was, he was one of a number of men of high intellect who resided at that time in County Durham. He and the others – notably Thomas Pigg of Sunderland, and the engraver, instrument maker and mathematician John Bird, of Bishop Auckland – formed an eminent circle into which Jeremiah Dixon was introduced and it was no doubt through the contacts of Emerson and Bird that Dixon was eventually brought to the attention of the Royal Society. Founded in 1660 the Royal Society was, and still is, the UK's National Academy of Sciences, supporting and encouraging research into both the pure and applied sciences. Fellowships of the Society are strictly limited to those who have distinguished themselves in a particular scientific field. In Jeremiah's time, past presidents of the Royal Society included Sir Christopher Wren, Samuel Pepys and Isaac Newton.

There seems to have been some confusion as to whether Jeremiah was ever actually elected as a Fellow of the Royal Society. The truth is that our Jeremiah Dixon never did attain that distinction. Various chroniclers have recorded that he did, but it was undoubtedly because of a bizarre coincidence which was to confuse later researchers that the uncertainty arose, indeed not for the only time in Jeremiah's career. On 18 November in the year 1773 another scientific researcher who lived and worked at the same time, who had been born seven years before and would die three years after Jeremiah and who had also carried out commissions for the Royal Society, was elected as Fellow of that establishment. His name, astonishingly, was Jeremiah Dixon, a merchant's son, of Gledhow, near Leeds in Yorkshire.

Nevertheless, Fellow or not, our Jeremiah Dixon was selected by the Royal Society to travel on their expedition to Bencoolen (Bengkulu) on the island of Sumatra in what is now Indonesia, there to plot the transit of the planet Venus. This was probably the first major government-sponsored astronomical expedition of its kind, and it was a measure of the importance of the subject that the Royal Society obtained funding from the Treasury to finance the expedition. Dixon's companions were to be men with scientific minds of the highest calibre. The *Universal Magazine* for November 1760 reported that Neville Maskelyne, who would eventually become Astronomer Royal, would accompany Robert Waddington to St Helena; Jeremiah Dixon would travel to Sumatra with Charles Mason, Assistant Observer at the Royal Observatory. The Royal Society received the sum of £1,600 from the Treasury to finance both voyages. The importance of the transit of Venus was such that its recording enabled astronomers of the day finally to calculate the distance from the earth to the sun. The Astronomer Royal, Edmund Halley, had previously forecast that a transit would take place in 1761, and so towards the end of 1760 preparations were made for the two voyages.

Jeremiah's expedition to Sumatra set out from Plymouth late in the year, the observers sailing aboard the HMS *Seahorse*, a ship specially commissioned for the journey. Initially, all was not to go smoothly. Four years earlier, in 1756, the so-called Seven Years War against the French had broken out. Ostensibly the conflict was over possession of the disputed North American colonies, but hostilities inevitably spilled over into waters considerably nearer home. Not long out of Plymouth the *Seahorse* was attacked and badly damaged by a French warship. The story is told in Charles Mason's letter to the Council of the Royal Society that '34 leagues S.W. from the Startpoint, the "Seahorse" engaged the "Le Grande" a thirty-four gun frigate'. There followed an 'obstinate dispute of about an hour and a quarter'. Subsequently, after boarding the crippled *Seahorse* to claim his prize, the French captain, having been made aware of the nature of the voyage and the identity of the passengers, allowed the *Seahorse* to continue, saying: 'Gentlemen, France is not at war with science.' However, Charles Mason reported that 11 men had been killed in the engagement, 37 wounded, many, Mason believed, mortally so. The ship was so badly damaged that she had to be returned to Plymouth for urgent repairs. This would make it impossible for Messrs Mason and Dixon to reach Sumatra in time to observe the transit. They had to go elsewhere. When the voyage resumed their destination would not be Indonesia but South Africa and the Cape of Good Hope.

The Cape was reached after a generally uneventful voyage and the *Seahorse* finally dropped anchor in Table Bay on 27 April 1761. After a suitable site was found for the observation of the transit, the instruments were landed on 2 May and the transit was successfully observed by the two astronomers on 5 June. They stayed some time at the site, carrying out various other scientific studies, and it wasn't until the end of September that the instruments were packed away in readiness for the voyage home. But Jeremiah would not sail at first for England; he and his companion were to board a ship for St Helena, where they would rendezvous with Neville Maskelyne and Robert Waddington. They set sail on 3 October reaching St Helena 13 days later, only to find that the observations of Maskelyne and Waddington had been largely unsuccessful due to persistent bad weather. Dixon was to spend several months on St Helena collecting tidal details and drawing maps for the Admiralty before eventually returning to England. For their efforts Jeremiah Dixon and Charles Mason were paid £100 each by the Royal Society.

It is at this point in Jeremiah's career that another uncertain tradition seems to have arisen. There is an enduring story that it was on his return from the Cape of Good Hope that Jeremiah had made the acquaintance of, and become professionally involved with, the great explorer and navigator Captain James Cook. The story tells that the men struck up a personal as well as a professional friendship that was to last until Dixon's death. Certain facts are true. The men were indeed contemporaries, both carried out similar commissions for the Royal Society (Captain Cook observed the transit of Venus from Tahiti on 17 June 1769), and both men were from the north of England: Captain Cook was born in the village of Marton, just to the south of Middlesbrough. The men may well have been known to each other, they may indeed have met at some time and formed a friendship, but the records of the Royal Society seem to show that at no time did the men either voyage or carry out observations or scientific research together. A certain degree of confusion may have arisen from the fact that Captian Cook's first officer on the *Resolution* was one George Dixon RN. During Cook's voyages Dixon had discovered the Queen Charlotte islands and had assisted Cook in his research for the Royal Society. Another Dixon, but again, not Jeremiah. The ship in which Jeremiah sailed from the Cape to St Helena was the *Mercury*, and the captain of that vessel was not, as some have recorded, Captain Cook, but one Captain Harrold.

After the Cape and St Helena, Jeremiah and his colleague Charles Mason returned to England. They did not know it then, but their greatest endeavour was about to begin, an endeavour which would take them thousands of miles in a different direction. For Jeremiah that journey would begin when he received a request to travel the considerably shorter distance to Kiplin Hall near Richmond in North Yorkshire, for Kiplin Hall was the home of Lord Baltimore, and that noble family had been involved in a long-running boundary dispute over the possession of land in the developing provinces of America.

In 1632, at the time of the early settlements of the American colonies, King Charles I had granted to Cecil, the second Lord Baltimore, and to his heirs, the Province of Maryland. Later, in 1681, the Province adjoining Maryland was granted by Royal Charter of King Charles II to William Penn. Pennsylvania would subsequently come to bear his name. However, the grant and charter obtained by William Penn included 'many indefinite and some impossible clauses'. The Delaware Territory had formerly been within the boundaries defined in the original 'Maryland Charter', but was, in 1682, transferred to William Penn by authority of a grant from the Duke of York. A dispute inevitably arose, and claim and counter-claim followed from both parties: 'If all of Pennsylvania's grievances are ruled justified, Maryland will be reduced to a mere strip of land. If all

Maryland's desires are granted then Philadelphia will be in Maryland.'

The dispute was to continue for almost one hundred years. There was a long-lasting lawsuit in the Chancery Court. Years after the death of the original claimants, agreements were still being drawn up and redrafted, only to the final dissatisfaction of one or other of the parties. On 10 May 1732 an agreement was executed between the heirs of William Penn and the great-grandson of Lord Baltimore. This was followed by yet another agreement in 1760, when commissioners were appointed finally to set down a definitive boundary line on which both parties could agree. However, the commissioners had great difficulty in carrying out the demanding work, and so it was decided that independent surveyors be appointed to complete the arduous and difficult task.

It is not known exactly why it was that Jeremiah and his colleague Charles Mason were chosen. Mason's credentials as Assistant Observer at the Royal Observatory would have been obvious to both parties, Jeremiah's perhaps less so. Could it have been that Lord Baltimore, residing as he did in North Yorkshire, had heard of the renowned northern astronomer/surveyor and of his work for the Royal Society? Perhaps. William Penn's family were Quakers, so possibly this was another reason that Dixon, also a Quaker, was acceptable to them, and therefore to both parties. At any rate Messrs Mason and Dixon were appointed to carry out the sensitive work and on 15 November 1763 they arrived in America and prepared to carry out their challenging commission.

The Mason–Dixon line is usually thought of as only dividing north and south. Actually it is the east/west boundary that separates Pennsylvania from Maryland and part of West Virginia, and the north/south boundary is between Maryland and Delaware. The work itself would be difficult and dangerous. The nature of the commission – defining a lengthy and consistent boundary line through largely hostile terrain – would be a new venture for them. Their methods of carrying out the survey, partly by trigonometrical means and partly by astronomical observation, would at the time constitute a great advance in practical surveying. Mason and Dixon's initial notes in the *Philosophical Transactions* of the Royal Society tell us: 'In this work the first thing to be considered was how to continue a right line: and this was done by setting up marks with the assistance of an "equal altitude" or transit instrument, made by Mr John Bird [Jeremiah's friend from Bishop Auckland].' The practicalities of the work involved cutting a consistently straight and accurate line through miles of dense forest. Neville Maskelyne, who had by then become Astronomer Royal, wrote an introduction to Mason and Dixon's work in the *Philosophical Transactions.*

In the course of the work, they traced out and measured some lines lying in and near the true meridian, and extended, in all, somewhat more than 100 miles: and for this purpose, the country in these parts being all overgrown with trees, large openings were cut through the woods in the direction of their lines, which formed the straightest and most regular, as well as most extensive vistos that, perhaps, ever were made.

The lines laid were indeed 'somewhat more than 100 miles'; by the end of the work the cutting through the forest had extended onwards for 245 miles. The work was arduous and uncomfortable, and conditions were generally hostile to the work. Earlier American surveyors had reported numerous hazards and discomforts as they cut deep into the unexplored forest. Indian attacks were not uncommon, rattlesnakes were a constant threat to man and horse, indeed previous surveys had been carried out only in spring and autumn to avoid the summer months when the reptiles were at their most active. All year round they were subjected to the unwanted and constant attentions of 'horseflies, mosquitoes, vermin and other bugs'. However, the difficult and protracted work progressed and the Mason–Dixon line was gradually, mile by gruelling mile, laid down. As they cut into the forest the measurements were made by chain and checked by brass statute yard. The first 132 miles were marked with boundary stones, each fifth stone having engraved on one side the arms of Penn, on the other the arms of Lord Baltimore. Where stones couldn't be erected the line was marked by cairns. Charles Mason describes the scene in the forest: 'The visto cut through the woods in the work was about 8 yards wide, and, in general seen about 2 miles, beautifully terminating to the eye at a point.'

There was on occasion a diversion from the surveying work. A story is told that one day Jeremiah came upon a slave master savagely beating a slave woman with a whip. His sense of morality enraged, he told the slaver: 'Stop, thou must not do that!' 'You be damned, mind your own business, I'll do what I like with my own,' came the reply. 'If thou doesn't desist, I'll thrash thee,' Jeremiah countered. The slave master didn't 'desist' and was therefore 'soundly thrashed' by Jeremiah, who grabbed the man's whip and beat him with it. The whip itself Jeremiah kept as a souvenir. After his death it was in the possession of his sister Hannah. The whip it seems was then handed down through successive generations of her family to one Solomon Chapman of Whitby. As a footnote to this story it may well be, though records are inconclusive, that the same whip of which Jeremiah relieved the unfortunate slave driver is today exhibited in what used to be the Wilberforce Slavery Museum in Hull.

On a more professional level, the lines drawn up by the two surveyors of necessity needed on occasion to be checked. An idea of the laborious nature of the measuring and checking of the line, for mile after mile through unfriendly forest, can be gained from Charles Mason's notes to the Royal Society on how the pair actually achieved it:

> The levels used in this work were, each, 20 feet in length, and 4 feet in height. They were made of pine, an inch thick, and in form of a rectangle; the breadth of the bottom board was 7.5 inches, that of the top = 3 inches, of the ends = 4.5 inches, and the bottom and top were strengthened with boards firmly fixed to them at right angles. The joints were secured with plates of iron, and the ends were plated with brass. The plumb lines used in setting them level, were = 3 feet and 2 inches in length, and hung in the middle of the levels, being secured in a tube from the wind, in the manner of carpenters levels; wherefore we called these by the same name. When the plumb-line bisected a point at the bottom, the ends were perpendicular. Where the ground was not horizontal, or there were logs, &c. to pass over, one end of the level was raised by a winch and pulley. The level being set, a short staff was drove into the ground (very near and opposite the plumb-line), in the top of which moved a thin plate of iron, about 12 inches long; at the ends of which were points, which were directed to the intersections of lines, drawn on the board that covered the plumb-line. By bringing the points in a line with one of the said intersections, if the level was by accident moved, it might be discovered, and brought again to its place. A level being thus marked, the end of the other was brought in contact with it, and marked in the same manner, before the first was moved; the first was then taken up, and set before the last. And so the operation was continued. Mr Dixon attended one plumb-line and staff, and I the other. The measure was carried on in a strait line, and in the proper direction, by pointing the levels to the farthest part of the visto that could be seen.

Whilst in America the two astronomers sent back a suggestion to the Royal Society that the opportunity should be taken to measure an Arc of Meridian, the first in North America. The Royal Society agreed, purchased a 'Shelton regulator clock' for the purpose, and shipped it out on the *Egdon* in 1765. The *Egdon* was wrecked in a storm but the clock survived, suffering only a broken pendulum spring, and was at length delivered to Mason and Dixon in Pennsylvania. They duly measured the 'length of degree on the meridian on the present border between Maryland and Delaware, in the peninsula between the Chesapeake and Delaware Bays'. This exercise took place whilst the Mason–Dixon line was still being defined.

Throughout their work bad weather, especially wet weather, was one of their main hazards, damaging their instruments. Even as they came to the end, still their work was dogged by damp conditions. Their diary entry for May 1768 records:

> May 20 – great dews for 4 mornings past.
> May 25 – rain last night and this morning, passed through water part of the day.
> May 26 – rain last night and part of this day. The levels continually wet.

But it was not the damp that finally brought their work to an end. Indian attacks were becoming more frequent and more dangerous. As well as a superstitious fear of the surveyors' instruments – 'star guns' they called them – there was a more fundamental source of unrest throughout the Indian nation. Angered by the push westwards and the settlement of their lands by the colonists, tribes under the leadership of the Ottawa chief Pontiac fought on against the British. Iroquois and Cherokee fought the settlers on a front that stretched from the Great Lakes to Maryland. Their resistance was sustained for some time but the push of the colonists was in the end inevitable and irresistible. For at that time, as well as the already settled lands, new territories were being discovered and colonised. Frontiersmen such as Daniel Boone, like Jeremiah Dixon a Quaker, ventured even further out into the wild lands. In 1767 while Jeremiah and his colleague were still laying down their line, Boone set out in search of the territory known by the Iroquois Indians as Ken-Ta-Ke (The Great Meadow). So it was that Kentucky was discovered, when eventually Boone crossed through the Cumberland Gap and came upon that new land.

So at last Mason and Dixon's great endeavour was at an end; despite the attentions of the Indians and the weather, their commission had been successfully completed. On 6 June 1768 the work was finally halted, 245 miles west of the Delaware River. They had spent in total 1,737 days in the field. Their meticulous survey which had taken nearly five years to finish ended with the simple, matter-of-fact diary entry for that day: '– Began at the 6th mile post, and measured northward through the Swamp of Nanticoke. – Crossed the river to the mark left the 31 May. – This finished the line A–B.' The cost to the Houses of Penn and Baltimore for their services over the five-year commission was £3,500. The line Mason and Dixon had laid down would eventually bear their names so that on one side of the Atlantic, at least, the magnitude of their achievement would be recognised by history.

Both surveyors remained in America for some time carrying out further observational work for the Royal Society. From the Brandywine River in Pennsylvania they made observations 'for the determining of the going of a clock sent thither by the Royal Society, in order to find the difference of gravity between the Royal Observatory at Greenwich, and the place where the clock was set up in Pennsylvania'. Further observations followed, of the end of an eclipse of the moon, and of 'some immersions of Jupiter's first satellite, observed at the same place in Pennsylvania'.

On the Mason–Dixon line, souvenir hunters were quick to remove the marker stones and use them as doorsteps and kerb stones. Efforts were later made by the authorities, who recovered many of them and replaced them in their original positions. Since the Mason–Dixon survey, disputes have still occasionally arisen as to the exact position of the line. Surveys made in 1849 and 1900 showed that there was no important error in the line Mason and Dixon decided upon. Another survey in the 1960s resulted in a slight shift of the line measuring four feet in 245 miles. A theodolite used by Jeremiah in the surveying work is now in the possession of the Royal Geographic Society in London.

On 4 April 1859, in New York, Bryants' Minstrels played a new tune, 'Dixieland'. Written by Irish-American Dan Emmett, the songwriter was the first known person to use the name 'Dixie'. A tradition has it that because the Mason–Dixon line represented the symbolic dividing line between North and South during the Civil War, 'Dixie' was generally assumed to refer to 'The South' encompassing the states below Mason and Dixon's line, and that the term 'Dixie' or 'Dixieland' is derived from the name of Jeremiah Dixon. Older editions of the Concise Oxford Dictionary seemed to confirm this as the entry read: 'Dixie-land – "Dixie(s) land". The USA south of Mason and Dixon's line, the former slave states. (Corrupt. of Dixon, Surveyor).'

Jeremiah Dixon's work in America was carried out at a time of increasing unrest and dissatisfaction with the British government. In 1763, the year Dixon arrived in America, few would have thought that in little over a decade the colonists would achieve their independence from the British Empire. However, the early signs of discontent with comfortable colonialism were already beginning to show.

The Seven Years War against France had just ended. The cost of the 'French/Indian War', as it was known to the colonists, had left the British Treasury with huge budget deficits. Somehow the money had to be recouped. A series of highly unpopular taxes had been imposed on the colonists by the British government, who paid little regard to the emerging elected colonial assemblies. In 1764 the British government set the 'American Revenue Tax'. This so-called 'sugar tax' placed prohibitions and restrictions on the American sugar trade and effectively granted British planters a monopoly in the market. The following year saw riots over the 'Stamp Act', the first effort by the British government to impose a direct tax on the Americans, ostensibly to raise money in the colonies to help support British troops stationed there. The colonies, however, were developing rapidly and had grown accustomed to a large degree of independence and autonomy. They were becoming rich: by 1766 Philadelphia in Pennsylvania was the richest city in America. The attempts at taxation by the British government were seen by the colonists as attempts to take away their new-found freedoms. By 1768 the first rumours of serious discontent were heard, which would eventually lead to revolution and the creation of a new nation. Jeremiah Dixon would probably not have realised it at the time, but he was working against a background of momentous social and political change, the formative years of the move towards independence of what would eventually become the richest and most powerful nation in the world.

Jeremiah arrived back at Cockfield on 21 January 1769, but his triumphant return home was to be cut short; once again a commission arrived from the Royal Society. They required Jeremiah to travel to Hammerfest in northern Norway, there to observe another impending transit of Venus. So it was that on 8 February Jeremiah once again left Cockfield and set off for London. The Mason–Dixon partnership was finally sundered. Dixon's companion on this trip would be another Royal Observatory assistant, William Bayley. Charles Mason was also to observe the transit, but he was sent by the Royal Society to Ireland, at Cavan in County Donegal, and fate would decree that the two who had given their names to the Mason–Dixon Line and to history would never again work together.

The Royal Society had purchased, for £40 each, two more astronomical clocks from Shelton. The clocks together with the observers were eventually stowed aboard the good ship *Emerald*, which sailed north under the command of Captain Charles Douglas to Norway, where at 10 a.m. on 7 May 1769 she anchored in Hammerfest Bay. Jeremiah and William Bayley proceeded to set up separate observation points about 60 miles apart as an insurance against bad weather conditions. Again Jeremiah's entries in the *Philosophical Transactions* give the best insight into the unsophisticated, almost quaint way in which the operations were begun:

> May 10th – digging holes for fixing the clock post, and stand for the transit instrument. NOTE: The ground too much frozen and rocky. Could not finish them this day. May 11th – finished the digging, and fixed up the post for the clock. Also put up that part of the observatory which moves around. NOTE: The post for the clock was three feet deep in the ground.

Everything was now in place for the observation of the transit. The weather, however, was causing severe problems. The diary entries record snowstorms and wind continually for eight days. Eventually, the day of the transit dawned, 3 June 1769. Let Jeremiah's own entries describe what he observed that day:

> 1.40 p.m. – saw the planet Venus upon the sun about half immerged. 1.43 p.m. – now totally immerged. 1.50 p.m. – seems to be completely upon the sun, but no threads of light: this was an instantaneous view, and through thin cloud. The air all the time very hazy. After this, all cloudy as before.

The observation was complete, although somewhat spoiled by the cloudy weather. Jeremiah had nevertheless recorded the necessary information for the Royal Society. On 4 June the instruments were packed up to be stowed away the next day, and the *Emerald* made ready for the return voyage. This would be Jeremiah's final voyage, home to Cockfield; the rest of his days would be spent in his home village in County Durham.

After his return Jeremiah spent his time carrying out work as a local surveyor. His nature, being of a 'retiring and unostentatious disposition', precluded him from any recounting of the importance of his previous work in America and for the Royal Society, which no doubt goes some way to account for the lack of knowledge of his work today. Jeremiah seems to have been a practical, no-nonsense man if a celebrated anecdote is to be believed. The story is told that when Jeremiah attended an interview at what has been recorded as the Royal Woolwich Academy, although this may in fact have been the Royal Greenwich Observatory, Jeremiah was examined by a panel of learned gentlemen. The initial exchange between the panel and Jeremiah was as follows: 'Sir, where did you acquire your education, was it at Oxford or at Cambridge?' 'At neither place!' 'Then where?' 'In a pit cabin on Cockfield Fell.'

Dixon did leave to his native county evidence of his work. A 'Plan of the Park and Demesnes at Auckland Castle, belonging to the Right Rev. Father in God, John Egerton, Lord Bishop of Durham, taken in 1772 by Jeremiah Dixon' at one time hung in the long dining-room at Auckland Castle. The following year Jeremiah surveyed and measured Lanchester Common. In 1774 Jeremiah's brother, George, drew up a plan for a combined canal and railway system without locks for the purpose of carrying coal. This would develop years later in the railway system proper. Despite protests from local farmers about trespass on their land, George, his sons and nephew, assisted by Jeremiah, completed a survey of the whole route, the plans for which are still in existence.

It was at this time that, according to yet another tradition, Captain Cook reappears in Dixon's life, visiting Jeremiah at home in Cockfield. One time apparently Cook had remarked that he was going to visit his 'northern friend'.

Could this indeed have been Jeremiah? A sundial which used to stand in the garden of Dixon's family home in Cockfield had carved upon it the initials J.C. Could Captain Cook have carved his own initials on the sundial or did they commemorate the visit of the great man to Cockfield? There is no hard evidence to confirm that Cook did visit Jeremiah, and the truth of this story must also remain in doubt. Captain James Cook has since gone down in history as one of the greatest of all explorers and navigators. He was to die, killed by tribesmen in Hawaii, on 14 February 1779.

Charles Mason continued for a time to work for the Royal Society. In 1772 he was sent by Astronomer Royal Neville Maskelyne to Scotland, there to find an appropriate site to conduct an experiment that Maskelyne had suggested to the Royal Society. The experiment, using the theory of the 'Attraction of Mountains', could, Maskelyne was convinced, be used as a means of determining the mass of the earth. Mason, on a commission of half a guinea a day plus expenses, arrived at Perth harbour and trekked 45 miles into the mountains to find a suitable site. The Royal Society then asked him to conduct the experiment himself, an experiment which would take four months to complete. The Society offered to double his pay, but Mason had had enough and he refused. Neville Maskelyne himself carried out the experiment; Charles Mason eventually returned to the American colonies, to Philadelphia, dying there in 1787.

Jeremiah Dixon died quietly at Cockfield a month before James Cook on 22 January 1779, aged 45 years. He left no children to keep alive his remarkable story, for he never married. The truth about Jeremiah's private life appears even more elusive than that of his professional career; however, there does appear an intriguing clause in his last will and testament dated 27 December 1778, and proved in Durham in 1779. In it Jeremiah bequeaths his copyhold premises in Bondgate, Bishop Auckland, to a certain Margaret Bland, with profits becoming due from these premises to be paid towards the maintenance of Margaret Bland's two daughters, Mary and Elizabeth, until their 21st birthday when the copyhold would go to them equally. Perhaps therein lies another as yet undiscovered chapter from Jeremiah's life.

Jeremiah Dixon had lived through a time of momentous change across the world stage. He had been only 12 years old when the '45 rising of Bonnie Prince Charles Stuart had been finally routed and England's army had been disgraced in the butchery that was the aftermath of the Battle of Culloden. France had been defeated in the Seven Years War, and in little over a decade the growing British interests in the 'New World' had been suddenly and massively expanded, then totally lost. The British America colonies had disappeared and the United States of America had emerged as a new nation. During Dixon's career General Wolfe had fallen capturing Quebec, Clive had begun to stamp British authority on India, and Captain Cook sailed the world in the name of exploration and science. Free for a time from the necessities of war, the British began to push outwards. The seeds of empire were sown.

As with much of the story of Jeremiah Dixon's life and career, the facts surrounding his death and burial are again obscured by confusion. He died in his native village of Cockfield and popular tradition maintains that he is buried in an unmarked grave, as was the Quaker tradition of his day, in the burial ground of the Quaker Meeting House in Staindrop. The old Meeting House, still standing today, backs on to the green and is now a private dwelling, but it dates from 1771 so it would no doubt have been known to Jeremiah. And so it was that no record of the spot where Dixon lies would be left to us. Indeed, over recent years controversy has risen over plans to remove Quaker headstones of a later date from the burial ground, which is now the owner's back garden. An older tradition has it that Jeremiah was actually buried in the grounds of a small Quaker chapel which stood in the village of Old Raby, near Raby Park. The chapel, along with the village, was demolished by the then Duke of Cleveland to make way for improvements to the park and road near the castle. Here again no marker remains for Jeremiah, for it is said that where the chapel graveyard once was there now stands only 'a row of stately trees' to shelter his last resting place.

A strange and sad end then for a County Durham man who was one of the greatest mathematicians of his time, whose work took him to parts of the world about which others of his day could only dream. An astronomer, surveyor, one of the most ingenious men of his age, whose intellect soared as high as the heavenly bodies he charted and whose work has remained unrecognised, his name virtually unknown even in his home county. But his name is known well on the other side of the Atlantic Ocean, and whether the tale be truth or mere romance, he will always be remembered when 'Dixieland' is heard.

> But though no sculptur'd marble marks the place where sleeps one of the noblest of his race; yet nature, in her amplitude of pride, shall for her favourite child a monument provide; there shall the spirits of true genius weep, and o'er his humble grave, their nightly vigil keep.

Chapter Fourteen

Byron, Boz and Pretty Bessie Barrett

'Pretty Bessie Barrett, Coxhoe Beauty'

In 1895 there was published volume four of the proceedings of the 'Society of Antiquaries of Newcastle upon Tyne'. In it was printed an extract from a letter to the Society, dated 3 September of that year, from the Rev. W.R. Burnet, Vicar of Kelloe. The letter described a curious find which had recently been brought to the attention of the Rev. Burnet. An odd, old window lit up a schoolroom which had previously been part of the Kelloe Vicarage. He had observed that on the glass pane of the window, which was obviously of considerable age, an inscription could be seen 'scratched, apparently by the use of a diamond'. The Rev. Burnet was also well aware of the local tradition which told that there was once a window pane in a former gallery of the church which had been inscribed with the words 'Pretty Bessie Barrett, Coxhoe Beauty'. The Vicar of Kelloe believed he had discovered the very window pane on which had been scratched, years earlier, the name of a child who would grow up to become the leading poet, champion of social justice, and ultimately tragic figure of Elizabeth Barrett Browning.

Since medieval times a mansion house had stood at Coxhoe. The passing years, the pounding of the weather and the transient fashions popular with a succession of owners meant that the original structure had been altered many times, until in the early 1720s the house was partially rebuilt. Ownership of the Hall changed hands several more times during that century, until eventually it became the temporary residence of one Edward Moulton Barrett. Barrett and his wife had just returned from the West Indies where he had made his fortune as a sugar plantation owner. It was to be only a temporary residence before moving south to a permanent home, but it was to be at Coxhoe Hall that on 6 March 1806 Edward Barrett's eldest duaghter, Elizabeth, would be born.

Edward Moulton Barrett, remembered by history, and by Hollywood, as a tyrannical and aloof father, apparently expected the same obedience from his children as he had received from his plantation slaves. Aware, however, of the early promise shown by Elizabeth, from which later would develop a great talent, he indulged and encouraged his daughter's early passion for the Classics and for writing, and a great affection would grow between the two. Elizabeth studied avidly as a child, reading Latin and Greek. She began to write seriously at an early age. Her first long poem, completed when she was only 13 years old, was dedicated to her father who had it published at his own expense. A happy childhood was, however, to end when Elizabeth reached the age of 15. The Barretts had moved their family home south to 'Hope End' near Malvern, the first of a succession of moves Barrett would make. One day whilst riding, Elizabeth fell from her pony and was severely injured. For the rest of her life she would be plagued with ill health, and little hope of improvement would be given to her by doctors.

Nonetheless she continued to write, prolifically, but her health began seriously to deteriorate. Eventually she was virtually confined to her bed. In the spring of 1840 she wrote that she had not been dressed since the previous October, and in all that time had only been lifted from her bed on to a sofa. While living for a while at Torquay, Elizabeth's brother, Edward, was drowned at sea. It was a devastating blow to Elizabeth whose already feeble health went into a dramatic decline. Edward Moulton Barrett decided therefore once again to move the family home and to settle, this time, in London in Wimpole Street, the frail Elizabeth surviving 'on a diet of obstinacy and dry toast'.

In 1833, the Earl of Shaftesbury's Abolition of Slavery Act had severe financial implications for Barrett, so much so that he predicted his own ruin, although it was said of him at the time that 'he bore the disaster of being merely rich, instead of very rich, with admirable fortitude'. Elizabeth grew up to be a gentle woman. Her views, however, on the social injustices of the day highlighted at the time by popular reformers were seen as radical. She became an outspoken critic of the government and of the existing social order, which as she saw was the main cause of all the injustice. The report on 'The Employment of Children in the Mines and Factories' was published in 1842. Elizabeth's outrage at some of the horrors contained in that report were reflected in her poems *The Cry of the Children* and *The Runaway Slave*. Her radical views and her writing were considered by some to be anti-establishment; this offended and alienated her father, and their relationship eventually began to sour.

The poetry and writings of Elizabeth Barrett had, however, by this time been widely published and circulated. Her work, apparently exhibiting anti-establishment overtones and sympathy for the disadvantaged of society, had become popular amongst writers with similarly held convictions, both in Britain and abroad. In America, Edgar Allan Poe was an admirer of her work; in England her writing came to the attention of the poet Robert Browning, who was impressed especially by her *Poems*. Elizabeth in turn had long enjoyed Browning's own work. So it was that in January 1845 the two began corresponding, a correspondence which would last for 18 months.

Robert Browning had been brought up in London and had acquired much of his education from his father's 6,000-volume library. In his youth he had read and admired the works of Shelley, Byron and Keats, and his early work had been influenced by them, his own first writings having been completed before his twelfth birthday. Browning enrolled at, then dropped out of, London University, after which he travelled extensively in Russia and in Italy. After his first critical success in 1835, he had subsequently enjoyed the company of such literary luminaries as Carlyle and Dickens.

Elizabeth began meeting Browning first openly, then in secret as her father became increasingly hostile towards the budding friendship. When friendship developed into romance, and marriage was eventually talked of, her father forbade it. To him it seemed that a poet, moreover a radical, was no fit husband for the daughter of Edward Moulton Barrett. However, in the best traditions of literary romance the couple eventually eloped and on 12 September 1846 they were married at St Pancras Church. Edward Barrett would not forgive his eldest daughter. He ordered that her clothes be thrown out into the street and that her name not be spoken in his house. Elizabeth and her father were destined never to see each other again, a force of circumstance grievous to them both. The newly married couple moved abroad, to Italy, settling in Florence at Casa Guardini. Elizabeth's frail health improved, and ever a supporter of the struggle for social justice she became heavily involved in the 'Risorgimento', the popular movement advocating Italian unity which would inspire her later works. The couple's happiness turned to joy when Elizabeth became pregnant. The pregnancy caused some concern because of Elizabeth's history of poor health, and the fact that she was over 40 years old at the time. However, in 1849 Elizabeth presented Robert Browning with a son. Their fame grew, the couple became renowned for their works, Elizabeth perhaps even more so than her husband, and on their first visit back to England they played host to, among others, Tennyson and Ruskin.

Some years later, after returning from one such visit, Elizabeth became seriously ill, and this time the Italian climate was to offer her no reprieve. On 29 June 1861 'Pretty Bessie Barrett, Coxhoe Beauty' died of congestion of the lungs while lying in her husband's arms. With her last breath she whispered the words 'Dear Pappa'. Elizabeth's early work had seemed to some radical, alarming, almost bordering on the revolutionary, but long before her death her work had come to be held in such high regard that when William Wordsworth died in 1850 her name had even been proposed for the vacant position of Poet Laureate.

Elizabeth Barrett lived a dramatic and tragic life, almost it seems the story of a fictional heroine. A century later her life story was dramatised by Hollywood when in 1934 MGM Pictures released *The Barretts of Wimpole Street*, telling the story of the invalid Elizabeth's relationship with Robert Browning and her love for, and fear of, her tyrannical father. Starring Frederick March as Browning, Charles Laughton as Barrett, and Norma Shearer as the heroine, the picture earned both best picture and best actress nominations at the Academy Awards.

Of Elizabeth's early home, Coxhoe Hall, nothing now remains. After the Barretts left the old house was transferred through a further succession of owners until it was requisitioned in World War Two and used to house prisoners of war. After 1945 the building fell into dereliction and it was finally demolished in 1956. Attempts at conservation have, however, been carried out and efforts made by the city council to restore Coxhoe Hall Wood and the former 'Long Walk', where no doubt the child Elizabeth spent many carefree days, not knowing then the twists of fate that would carry her to the ultimate triumphs of her later years.

Many years after the Barretts had left Coxhoe, the worthy Reverend Burnet obtained from Kelloe Church records a copy of Elizabeth's certificate of baptism. He forwarded the copy to the Society of Antiquaries. The record informed the Society and all future generations that 'Elizabeth Barrett, born 6th March 1806, baptized 10th February, 1808, first child, daughter of Edward Moulton Barrett esq., of Coxhoe Hall, native of St James', Jamaica, by his wife Mary, late Clarke, native of Newcastle upon Tyne' was 'received into the congregation at Kelloe Church'. A commemorative brass plaque telling of the event can be seen in St Helen's Church, Kelloe, to this day.

['Two hundred boys at twenty guineas each per annum']

The reputation of the so-called 'Yorkshire Boarding Schools' had, by the 1830s, become notorious throughout the land. Stories of these establishments, and of the terrible conditions that the young boy pupils had to endure while attending them, had escaped from the remote northern schools and spread, even as far as London. Their shameful reputations offended social reformers, outraged by the dreadful stories of cruelty, disease and woefully inadequate sanitary conditions. None of the masters of these schools listed any qualifications in their advertisements. To others in the

Establishment, however, such stories were condemned merely as malicious gossip. One young man, only 25 years old but already a writer of some standing, determined to investigate the validity of these claims; so it was that early in the year of 1838, Charles Dickens began his journey north to establish for himself the truth behind the rumours and gather material for his novel, *Nicholas Nickleby.*

Such a 'Yorkshire School' was Shaw's Academy in the village of Bowes, near Barnard Castle. In 1823 the school's proprietor, William Shaw, had defended and lost a legal action taken against him in the Court of Common Pleas relating to conditions at his establishment. It was proved that boarders at his school were losing their sight as a result of acute malnutrition, deprivation and neglect. Shaw had been found negligent and had suffered heavy damages, but was nonetheless allowed to continue to take boys into his school, 200 of them at 20 guineas each a year.

Charles Dickens, pseudonym 'Boz', arrived after a cold, gruelling coach journey through a snowstorm with travelling companion and illustrator of his stories Halbot K. Browne, pseudonym 'Phiz', at the George and New Inn at Greta Bridge. The date was Thursday, 1 February 1838. The next morning they proceeded, again in a snowstorm, to Barnard Castle where Dickens had arranged lodgings at the King's Head Hotel, which still stands in the Market Place today. He had previously made enquiries about the local 'Yorkshire Schools' under the false pretext that he was seeking a recommendation for a friend who wished to board his son at one of them. Arrangements had been made prior to his arrival and Dickens was to meet several people of standing in the town to discusss the 'attractions' of the local boarding schools.

The local people, however, were noticeably reticent about giving such recommendations. One solicitor Dickens met initially praised Shaw's Academy, then had a change of heart, returned and told Dickens that he couldn't in all conscience allow another boy to be sent to that place. William McKay, who had previously been an employee of William Shaw, told terrible stories of the hardships the pupils endured at Shaw's Academy. According to McKay the boys were subjected to hard labour and harder punishment; their food was rotten, often maggoty; they slept on straw in overcrowded rooms and were allowed only one blanket each as protection against the fierce cold of the northern winter nights; there was no heating and no toilets and the boys were frequently subjected to beatings. The bleakness of these reports and the hopelessness of the boys seemed too terrible to be true, so Dickens decided to visit Bowes to see for himself the horrors of Shaw's Academy.

On reaching the village the next day, Dickens witnessed a number of gaunt, half-starved-looking boys, some working in the nearby farmyards, others wandering in the road. Enquiries at the local inn confirmed that they were indeed boarders at the Academy. On reaching the establishment itself

Dickens was, however, to be disappointed. William Shaw had heard a rumour of their coming and received them with great suspicion, and after a short, brusque exchange he refused their request to tour his Academy. He then hastily escorted them from the premises. So it was that the investigating author was denied the opportunity to examine the much-maligned school himself. He had, however, seen enough. With the persistent and numerous rumours, the evidence of McKay and others, the images before his own eyes as he had witnessed the pathetic schoolboy figures in Bowes Village, and the refusal of Shaw to open his doors to them, it seemed to Dickens that the terrible stories, and his own worst fears, had been confirmed. He had the material he needed for his novel.

Dickens returned to Barnard Castle and made ready for his departure. Before leaving he browsed a while around the old market town. Eventually he came across a shop bearing the name 'Humphrey's – Clockmakers'. Displayed in the window was the apprentice piece of the shop owner's son, 'Master Humphrey's Clock', which was to give Dickens the idea for another of his literary works. A commemorative plaque can be seen today on the site of the clockmaker's shop near St Mary's Church. At length Charles Dickens and Halbot K. Browne left for Darlington, there to catch the Newcastle to York stagecoach. And, as he left, in his mind Dickens's characters were already gathering substance. Shaw's Academy it is said was the model for Dotheboys Hall. Headmaster Shaw himself became the detested Wackford Squeers, though Dickens always claimed the character was actually a composite of several people. In Dickens's mind the poor boys he had seen in Bowes Village began to develop new characters and to know new names: Browdie, Dorker, Smike.

Nicholas Nickleby was published in April 1838. Fifty thousand copies were sold on the first day, and one result of Dickens's tale and of his vivid portrayal of life at Dotheboys Hall was that many of the 'Yorkshire Schools' – called, incidentally, 'London Schools' in the north of England – began to close within a few short years. William Shaw, however, lived on, eventually dying in Bowes, and his gravestone can still be seen in St Giles churchyard in Bowes Village. Charles Dickens returned to London; fame and fortune were to be his, but tragedy also left its mark on his life, and his connection with County Durham and the north of England was to continue for many years.

Frederick Dickens, Charles's younger brother, was, by all accounts, an extremely likeable and popular man. A flair for acting and impersonation made him a favourite with his friends. Frederick was also, however, totally irresponsible. Constantly in debt, he regularly relied on his celebrated brother Charles to bail him out. Frederick drifted from job to job, never holding one down for any length of time. When he announced that he was to take a bride, Charles was apparently horrified, and opposed the marriage. Undeterred the good-natured Frederick married Anna Weller in 1850. It was not long before Dickens became unable to support himself and his new wife. His pleas to Charles for financial aid were initially successful but when it proved that Frederick was virtually incapable of earning his own living even the benevolent Charles Dickens eventually ceased his subsidies, saying that he 'refused to sink money into the unfathomable sea of such a marriage'. The debts began to build up, Frederick's financial problems began to look insurmountable, and further pleas to Charles for help resulted in the same response: 'I have already done more for you than most dispassionate persons would consider right or reasonable.' Not to be put off, Frederick started to borrow money from his brother's friends until, when eventually his situation became seemingly irretrievable, he deserted Anna and it was left to Charles to provide for her.

Charles Dickens himself had by that time become famous as an author and social commentator and his novels would eventually become known worldwide. Achieving celebrity status he began touring the country, giving public readings of his works. He was a regular and popular visitor to northern England where he gave public readings at all the major towns. Audiences at the old town hall in Darlington heard Charles Dickens recite his works, as he did again in Durham and at Sunderland. He formed his own theatre company to raise funds for the establishment of a Guild of Literature and Arts. When performing in Newcastle in 1852, tickets costing 12s. 6d. were sold on the street for ten times their face value. On 24 September 1858, Dickens was back in the north giving public readings from his novel *A Christmas Carol*. It was said by one commentator that 'those who have not heard it read by Mr Charles Dickens can not know how much more beautiful this beautiful story becomes, when given in the author's own manner'. Dickens returned in 1861; he was it seems fond of the northern audiences, saying: 'For while they laugh to shake the roof, they have an unusual sympathy for the pathetic and passionate.'

The success of Dickens's theatre company prompted Charles to give his wayward brother Frederick employment. Unfortunately, like all the other jobs before, it didn't last long, and by 1860 Frederick had arrived in Darlington. He had contacts in the town and eventually did get a job as a journalist for a local newspaper. But it was in Darlington that Frederick began to suffer from congestion of the lungs. His condition became chronic and eventually, on 28 October 1868, Frederick Dickens died at the age of 48. He was buried in Darlington's West Cemetery. The loss was grievous to Charles, who wrote of his brother:

> He lost opportunities I had put his way, poor dear fellow, but there were unhappy circumstances in his life which demanded great

allowances. It was a wasted life, but God forbid that one should be hard upon it or upon anything in this world that is not deliberately or coldly wrong.

['Bad, mad and dangerous to know']

It was the spring of 1812. The large house in London, the home of Viscountess Melbourne, was alive with the polite conversation of fashionable members of London society. In one room stood two very different people. An animated and adoring circle of admirers surrounded Lord George Gordon Byron, poet, leading 'Romantic' and self-styled champion of liberty. Across the room, engaged in society gossip, a young woman fidgeted uneasily; a highly intelligent and serious-minded young woman only 20 years old, she was becoming increasingly bored and irritated at the seemingly endless and meaningless tittle-tattle. The young woman, Lady Anabella Millbanke of Seaham Hall in County Durham, would soon be introduced to Lord Byron. Byron was at once taken with the serious young lady and, through their conversation, became impressed with her obvious academic ability and attainments; Annabella was equally attracted to the flamboyant and notorious Lord Byron. But Byron's affair with Lady Caroline Lamb was still ongoing; his was a restless soul, and though their very oppositeness was a mutual attraction, this was to be an ill-fated meeting which would eventually bring grief to both of their lives.

Born in 1788, the son of 'Mad' Jack Byron and the Scottish heiress Catherine Gordon, Lord Byron had been educated at Trinity College, Cambridge and had travelled widely in his youth, basing his famous work *Childe Harold's Pilgrimage* on his own early journeys. He had become a leading member of the 'Romantic' movement of poets and writers of the early nineteenth century, for a time the darling of fashionable London society, and the icon of many budding young poets and artists throughout Europe. His style of living, however, had begun to outrage the Establishment. His often scandalous behaviour, his very public affair with the already married Lady Caroline Lamb, and his politics, which some considered bordered on the revolutionary, all served to alienate him from powerful sections of society. In his time he would be a fierce critic of the established order and of the victorious powers who would, as he saw it, fail miserably to build the 'new order' following the defeat of Napoleon. To Byron it seemed that old repressions would simply be restored. Of Wellington and the so-called 'Victory Peace', Byron was to say: 'Never had mortal man such opportunity except Napoleon, nor abused it more.'

Sir Ralph Millbanke was a country squire, with estates in Durham and Yorkshire. He was active both in Parliamentary and county affairs and he had been married 15 years before his wife had presented him with their only child, Anabella. Much of her youth had been spent quietly at Seaham Hall on the Durham coast where she had grown up a sensitive and reflective young woman. Extremely well read, she had studied drama, poetry and, encouraged by her parents, had proved her excellence in mathematics. The soberness of her upbringing would later be reflected in her' dislike of London society. Uninterested in and somewhat unresponsive to 'polite' company, she was described by one duchess as being 'really an icicle'.

Anabella and Lord Byron began to meet regularly and their growing attraction led, in October 1812, to Byron's proposal of marriage, to his 'Princess of the Parallelograms'. From the beginning it seemed a strange match: the dashing, romantic figure of Byron and the sober, studious Miss Millbanke who was considered not quite the type of society beauty likely to be a bride for Byron. Indeed, Byron's mistress, Lady Caroline Lamb, had written that 'Byron would never pull together with a woman who went to Church punctually, understood statistics and had a bad figure'. Much to people's surprise, however, the single-minded young Anabella refused Byron's initial offer of marriage and it was to be two years later before she agreed at last to become Lady Byron.

On Anabella's acceptance of the proposal, Lord Byron was invited to the Millbankes' family home at Seaham Hall. During his visit it was further agreed that the wedding itself should take place at Seaham. So it was that a special licence was obtained and on 2 January 1815 Lady Anabella Millbanke married Lord George Gordon Byron in the upstairs drawing-room of Seaham Hall. To some it appeared the match was doomed from the very start. It was said that during his time at Seaham before the wedding, Byron had occupied himself largely by wandering alone in the grounds of the Hall. During the marriage ceremony itself, one guest noted that Byron, kneeling in front of the clergyman and repeating his solemn vows, seemed lost as if 'a mist was before his eyes and his thoughts were elsewhere'. As the couple left for their honeymoon, Byron said to his new wife, 'Miss Millbanke, are you ready?', a slip noticed by all apparently except the new Lady Byron, and which many considered an ill omen for the newly-weds' future together.

Lord and Lady Byron left Seaham for their honeymoon and travelled to Halnaby Hall, the Millbankes' residence in Yorkshire, halting only briefly at Rushyford just south of Ferryhill for 'a glass of port and a change of horses'. But they would soon return to Durham for another celebration. On the occasion of Lord Byron's 27th birthday the couple were back at Seaham Hall. For a time they were happy, content with each other's company, but gradually Byron began to grow restless with the quiet life at his wife's father's home. It became irksome to him. He wrote of his time on the storm-lashed Durham coast and of his life with his new bride and her father as being 'nothing but

County Meetings and shipwrecks'. He began to correspond regularly with his friends in London, his words betraying his irritation and boredom: 'I have today dined on fish, which probably dined upon the crews of several colliers lost in the recent gales.' Of course Anabella was quite happy at Seaham, disliking as she did the London society to which her new husband yearned to return. Byron, however, began to find his father-in-law increasingly uninteresting and wearisome. He wrote to a friend:

> My papa, Sir Ralpho, hath recently made a speech at a Durham tax meeting. And not only at Durham, but here several times since, after Dinner. He is now, I believe, speaking it to himself (I left him in the middle) over various decanters, which can neither interrupt him nor fall asleep.

By March 1815 they had left; in less than a year the doomed marriage would end and Byron and Anabella would begin a lengthy, acrimonious and very public separation. Byron was accused by his wife of cruelty, Anabella claiming his behaviour was the result of his insanity. Eventually Byron left England where his bitter separation, his growing personal debts and the rumours of more scandalous affairs had begun to tarnish the once shining image of the great 'Romantic'. But in spite of vitriolic words and shocking accusations made against him throughout the course of the separation, Byron it seemed bore no malice toward Anabella. When it was all over, he wrote of her to a friend:

> I must say it, in the very dregs of all this bitterness, I do not believe there ever was a better, or even a brighter, a kinder or a more amiable and agreeable being . . . I never had, nor can have any reproach to make her while with me. When there is blame, it belongs to me; and if I cannot redeem it, I must bear it.

Byron travelled to Italy where he met Teresa Guiccioli who became his mistress, and in 1819 he began actively to support the Italian revolutionary movement. Finally settling in Greece his 'Holy Grail', the struggle against the established order, saw him elected in 1823 as a member of the 'Greek Committee'. Giving money and advice Byron attempted to help that country in its fight for liberation from the Turks. A year later on 19 April 1824, Lord George Gordon Byron – 'bad, mad and dangerous to know', as Lady Caroline Lamb had described him – died of marsh fever at Missolonghi, aged 36 years. In true Byronic fashion, his heart was buried in Greece. However, when his body was returned to England for burial, his interment was refused both at Westminster Abbey and at St Paul's Cathedral. In the end the Establishment which he had so often criticised and mocked saw to it that the scandalous socialite and revolutionary poet would not rest with the great and the good of his country.

For a time Anabella lived on at the Millbanke home of Seaham Hall, and Fordyce tells us that in later life she became a patron of education. Eventually, however, six years after the separation, the Millbankes sold Seaham Hall to Frances Anne Vane-Tempest. For County Durham in general, and Seaham in particular, major changes lay ahead.

Part Five

Chapter Fifteen

Of Cavaliers and Coalfields

'Believe me, I am, your sincere friend – Vane Londonderry.'

The statue of 'The Man on the Horse in Durham' has been a centrepiece of the old Market Place for many years. Tourists and visitors to the city wander idly by and gaze up in curiosity at the dashing military figure on his fine horse. Local people rushing through the Market Place in the course of their daily business, or scurrying by during a snatched lunch hour, hardly notice the statue is there at all, so familiar has it become. Of all those who pass by, few know anything about the man whose effigy bestrides the great horse, and even fewer know of the curious history of the statue itself and of the abiding legend which surrounds it.

A plaque on its base tells the curious that the statue represents Charles William Vane Stewart, 3rd Marquess of Londonderry, Commander of Hussars and Adjutant-General to the Duke of Wellington, 'Fighting Charley' to his family. Unveiled on 2 December 1861 in the presence of his widow, Frances Anne, and family friend, Benjamin Disraeli, the statue marks the achievements of a remarkable man who had been by turns soldier, diplomat and entrepreneur in the early Durham coalfields, a man who was later described by Disraeli as combining

> the greatest energy of character with a singular softness of heart . . . He was a man of very enlightened mind, a man who thoroughly understood the characteristics and necessities and wants of his age, and a man who truly understood that in a commercial country like England the aristocracy of the country should place themselves at the head of that great commercial interest.

To many local people at the time, however, this seemed a curious and ill-formed eulogy, for this was the man who had vigorously opposed popular reform, the coal owner who had forbade official inspections of his mines and who had even opposed the raising of the school leaving age on the grounds that 'a boy of 12 should be learning his trade, not wasting his time in reading and writing'. The enlightened role of the 3rd Marquess of Londonderry as patron and friend to the Durham miners was by no means obvious to all.

Charles William Stewart was born in Dublin on 18 May 1778. He was the younger half brother of the 2nd Marquess of Londonderry, Robert Stewart, Viscount Castlereagh, and for most of his early years he had lived somewhat in the shadow of that illustrious statesman. The brilliant Castlereagh was one of the principal figures in the government during the time of the Napoleonic Wars. He had begun his political life as Chief Secretary for Ireland and was later appointed to the Cabinet as Secretary of State for War. However, he resigned his position after a bitter argument with Foreign Minister George Canning which led to them fighting a duel in which neither was actually hurt. Castlereagh returned to government in 1812 when he joined the Foreign Office. It was from this position that he began the delicate work of bringing together by careful diplomacy the previously disparate enemies of Napoleon Bonaparte, and thus he forged the alliance which would bring about Bonaparte's final defeat. In the years after the wars he was to dominate British politics. He was made Leader of the House of Commons and by 1815, as Churchill put it, 'Britain and Castlereagh stood at the head of Europe'. When, in 1818, the Duke of Wellington was elected to the government, he and Castlereagh dominated a lacklustre administration.

Times were to change though. Castlereagh began to suffer increasingly from mental instability. A persecution mania convinced him that there were those trying to destroy him with allegations of homosexual conduct. His condition rapidly deteriorated until, on 22 August 1822, he 'did with a knife of iron or steel stab himself on the carotid artery and gave himself one mortal wound of which he did then and there instantly die'.

There were few amongst the working-classes who mourned his passing. Brilliant though his statesmanship may have been when concerned with matters of foreign policy, he had been a man who had dealt harshly with civil disorder at home. In the Irish Rebellion of 1798, Castlereagh had played his full part in the subjugation of the 'rebels', earning himself the title 'Bloody Castlereagh'. He had been an autocrat who was totally insensitive to public opinion; indeed public opinion was a thing for which he had no respect. He was strongly suspected to have been complicit, along with Wellington, in the infamous Peterloo Massacre when, in Manchester on 16 August 1819, the local mounted militia were given orders to attack hundreds of people attending a peaceful open air meeting about reform legislation. Innocent people were ridden down by the mounted troops and many were killed or injured. The name of Castlereagh had become despised. It was said that as his funeral procession passes by on its way to his burial in Westminster Abbey, 'indecent cheering' broke out amongst the watching crowds. The man who had been the chief political architect of his country's victory over Napoleon had become hated by many of his fellow countrymen.

The year of Castlereagh's suicide, 1822, saw his younger half brother, Charles Stewart, at the Congress of Verona with the Duke of Wellington. It would be he who succeeded as the 3rd Marquess of Londonderry, and it would be his statue that eventually stood in the Market Place at Durham City. Only time would tell, however, if he would prove any more sympathetic towards the working-classes and towards the gathering momentum in favour of reform right across British society. So it was that the statesman was succeeded by the soldier.

Charles Stewart had been commissioned into the army when only 16 years of age. Within a year he had risen to the rank of major in the 106th Foot. In time he transferred to the cavalry and began a brilliant career as a cavalry commander. He fought in Wellington's Peninsular Campaign against the forces of Napoleon and he commanded the Hussar Brigade which covered the famous retreat of General Sir John Moore to Corunna in northern Spain, the retreat which dragged Napoleon's armies into the remote provinces of the north and saved much of the British expeditionary army from destruction. It was a desperate retreat, with the French army continually harassing, and in such appalling, freezing conditions that, as was recalled by a Highlander, 'the silence was only interrupted by the groans of the men who, unable to proceed further, laid themselves down in dispair to perish in the snow'. After Moore's death at Corunna, Lord Stewart (as he then was) became Adjutant-General of the British Forces in the peninsula, under the new commander, the Duke of Wellington. As a Major General, and Adjutant-General to the 'Iron Duke', he was a recklessly brave fighter, 'The Bold Sabreur' as he became known to his military kin. Twenty-five battles he had taken part in between 1796 and 1814, and after the final defeat of Napoleon at Waterloo he would, in June 1815, be with his half brother, Castlereagh, at the peace conference in his official role of Ambassador in Vienna.

It was while he was in Spain in 1812 that he learned of the death of his first wife. He had married Lady Catherine Bligh, daughter of the Earl of Darnley, eight years previously. They had one son, Frederick, who would eventually become the 4th Marquess. Lady Catherine was only 37 years of age when she died. It was in that year of 1812 when Castlereagh had rejoined the Cabinet that he had despatched his half brother Charles Stewart as Minister to the Court of Berlin, with special liaison duties to the Prussian and Swedish armies. However, Charles Stewart was first and foremost a military man and his wishes to see further action would soon be granted. Marshal Blücher, who would eventually command the Prussian forces at the Battle of Waterloo, gave to Stewart the command of his reserve cavalry and he again went into action against the forces of Napoleon in October 1813 at the so-called 'Battle of the Nations' at Leipzig. For his role in this engagement, Stewart was awarded the Order of the Sword from Sweden, and the Orders of the Black Eagle and the Red Eagle from Prussia.

In 1814, again with the patronage of Castlereagh, Stewart was appointed to the Embassy in Vienna, and it was around this time that he met Frances Anne, only daughter of Sir Harry Vane-Tempest and Anne Countess of Antrim and heiress to extensive landed and mining properties in County Durham. They were married on 3 April 1819. Stewart added her family name Vane to his own. As ambassador and wife they travelled widely throughout Europe, living in a style befitting their station, and made personal friends in many of the Imperial Courts. In 1822 a Great Congress was called in Verona, an incredible gathering the object of which was ostensibly to discuss the future direction of Europe following the Napoleonic Wars. At Verona, Stewart and Frances Anne did indeed mix in the very highest social circles. The delegates included three kings, two emperors, three reigning grand dukes, one cardinal (representing the Pope), one viceroy, three foreign secretaries, 20 ambassadors and 12 ministers. It was at Verona that Stewart and Frances Anne struck up a lasting friendship with Emperor Alexander I of Russia, and it was because of that friendship that, in 1830, on the advice of Wellington, Stewart was appointed Ambassador to the Imperial Court of St Petersburg.

The year of the Verona Congress, 1822, was also the year of Castlereagh's suicide, and so it was that in that year Charles William Vane Stewart became the 3rd Marquess of Londonderry and heir to that family's Irish estates. He continued to serve as ambassador in Vienna for another year but eventually returned to England and to Frances Anne's estates in Durham. Here the new Lord Londonderry would begin his new occupation as coal entrepreneur.

He vigorously pursued his interest in making money, and living in the Imperial style to which he had become accustomed. Described variously as a determined, stubborn individualist with a vain and pompous nature, his father had been a fervent Tory and indeed Londonderry himself was instrumental in the foundation of the Durham County Conservative Association in January 1833. He soon warmed to his new adventure. In 1820, only a year after his marriage to Frances Anne, he wrote enthusiastically to an adviser that after reading the colliery accounts of the first year he saw 'so much greater a net profit than we in our most sanguine moments had ever calculated upon'.

The main collieries of the Londonderry coalfield were at Rainton, Penshaw and Pittington. Stewart also opened new pits near the coast, notably at Seaham, some of which were among the deepest in the world at the time. Business prospered, the Londonderry empire began to expand. At the peak of his operations he owned 11 pits, two railways, lime quarries and a steamer, as well as some 12,000 acres of land in County Durham, in addition to his estates in Ireland. Over 2,000 pitmen and other workmen were in his employ. On 28 November 1828, he laid the foundation stone of the north-east pier of the inner harbour at Seaham, the town and port that he founded, to be an outlet for his coal traffic.

The family lived in almost regal splendour. They had two homes in the north, two in London, as well as residences in Ireland. Their main home they made at Wynyard Hall, about four miles north of Stockton. When the old hall burned down in 1841, Londonderry replaced it with a palatial new house, laying out parkland, gardens and ornamental lakes as an overt symbol of his rank, wealth and power. They entertained on a lavish scale: royalty, statesmen, and captains of industry spent time at Wynyard, and it was said that when the Londonderrys went to Stockton races 'the procession of coaches was equalled only by those of royalty'. In 1827 Londonderry had erected a 127-foot-high obelisk to commemorate a visit to Wynyard Hall by the Duke of Wellington. The inscription made the point for all to see: 'Wellington – the Friend of Londonderry'.

He had on 23 March 1823, in addition to the titles he already held, been created Earl Vane and Viscount Seaham, but throughout his life he was never averse to asking for additional favours and honours, something which he thought, because of his distinguished military and diplomatic service and his new rank as leading coal owner, he obviously deserved. Nor was he averse to allowing public displays of the long lists of his honours. The memorial inscription on the Seaham harbour foundation stone told everyone that:

Charles William Vane, Third Marquess of Londonderry, Viscount Castlereagh and Baron Stewart of Mount Stewart, and Ballilawn in Ireland, and First Earl Vane and Viscount Seaham of the United Kingdom of Great Britain and Ireland, K.C.B., G.C.H, K.B.E., K.R.E., K.S.G., K.S., K..T.S., etc, etc laid the Foundation Stone of Seaham Harbour. A.D., 1828, Nov. 28th.

He pestered a succession of prime ministers, first Lord Liverpool then both the Duke of Wellington and Robert Peel. He had been granted most of what he wanted earlier in his career, with the benefit of the patronage of Castlereagh, then to an extent of Wellington, but as the years went by his demands for honours began to strain even his relationship with Wellington.

When in January 1842 the Duke of Cleveland died he left vacant the position of Lord Lieutenant of the County of Durham. Prime Minister Peel offered the position to Londonderry. It was accepted, rather grudgingly, as it was an honorary position which he felt rather lacked the gravitas of a post more suited to a man of his standing. However, he thanked the Prime Minister and hoped that in the future, 'entirely independent of what may be fairly due to my position and possessions in the north, my military and diplomatic services might not go unappreciated'.

By the standards of his day Londonderry was an above-average employer. Indeed, he thought of himself as being positively benevolent towards his miners. He considered it to be his bounden duty as employer to care for his workforce. This paternalistic *noblesse oblige* did indeed bring certain benefits to the exploited pitmen of the time; conditions in his mines were certainly no worse than in others, in fact they were better than many. However, one must consider that conditions in the mines generally at this time were usually appalling. When accidents occurred in pits, as they frequently did, Londonderry fervently believed that it was the sole responsibility of the owner to provide for the victims and their families: 'It is for the benefit of the company the lost men toil'd and fell, and it is a sacred duty on their part alone to support those left behind.'

In 1823 there was a disaster at Londonderry's Rainton pit, 56 lives were lost. Over the next nine years he paid out over £2,000 in compensation to the victims and their dependants. The relief fund was still paying out over 20 years later. Miners in Londonderry's pits also received free medical treatment and free housing, although some of that was of questionable quality. The situation in Coxhoe was highlighted in a report on the state of workers' accommodation. It showed that the dwellings had no yard, consequently no lavatory. The cart which delivered coal to the front door also removed the 'waste products' from the back door. In 1819, spare stables at Chilton Moor had been converted into workers' houses; that way it was estimated that savings of £3.18s. 'a year' could be made by not having to pay the miners travelling expenses from Penshaw. It was not until 1844, coincidentally the year of the Great Strike, that Londonderry decided to improve the conditions in his workers' houses. It has to be said that some of the dwellings did have yards, some even their own gardens, a real innovation at the time. However, by 1844 reports were coming back of dreadful conditions, of 'scenes of immorality, prejudicial to health . . . the children appearing in a forlorn state of wildness'. These squalid scenes were a world away from the grandiose style in which the Londonderrys lived, where at Wynyard the 'great and the good' dined off gold plate, and no extravagance was too excessive.

So long as the miners remained in service to Londonderry, free education was provided for them and their children. Starting with night schools, day schools were eventually made available. Three new schools were specially built, one for each pit at Penshaw, Rainton and Pittington, and in the eight years before his death over 3,300 children had received a basic education at Londonderry's schools. Indeed, Frances Anne eventually stipulated that before young boys would be allowed to go down the pits, they must have attained a certain standard of education. Today's observer may wonder why; after all, what benefit could those boys possibly derive from having to take their newly acquired education down into a dark hole in the ground, where they would spend half of their young lives? There are those who would argue that providing any education purely for the good of the workforce was a visionary, reforming step to take; cynics might suggest that if the exercise was purely for the good of the miners then indeed it was a step to be praised. However, some have pointed out that Londonderry, by taking the high moral ground, by demonstrating what a caring, benevolent and forward-thinking employer he was, would reap the acclaim of a reform-minded society, with all that such acclaim might bring his way. Who benefited most from Londonderry's education scheme is open to question.

Londonderry could never understand how, given such benevolent paternal care of his workers, the miners could possibly turn against him and give their allegiance to the union. It has been said that both the Marquess and Frances Anne had a 'genuine affection for their pitmen, whom from time to time they felt they were regretfully obliged to punish, like wayward children'. Once in 1842, when addressing his miners at Penshaw, Londonderry said to them: 'When you have thus placed your proprietor, by the sweat of your brow, the first man in the coal trade, is it possible I should look upon you without feelings of gratitude?' Two years later he began evicting his striking miners from their houses. In return for his care, Londonderry expected his men to show a 'proper sense of gratitude'. In return for what he provided them, the miners were expected to obey their master at all times, and maintain the flow of wealth-creating coal. They were certainly not expected to transfer their loyalty to 'an upstart union'.

An above-average employer, judged by the standards of his day, Londonderry may have been, but he was no champion of reform. Few accused him of being a visionary. He vigorously opposed reform legislation through his seat in the House of Lords, especially his *bête noire*, the introduction of Independent Government Inspectors of Coal Mines. He argued that the introduction of inspectors constituted overt and unwarranted interference by government in the running of private enterprise. He based his argument on the claim that his pits were efficient and safer than most, he therefore did not need government inspectors to tell him how to run them. He had a point. The mines of the Great Northern coalfield were some of the safest in the country, Londonderry's was amongst them. The claim was made against him, however, that by opposing official safety inspections he was attacking a proposal which would save 2,000 miners' lives a year.

In the 1830s and '40s there was growing public embarrassment, and some concern, at the use of child and female labour in the coal mines. Lord Ashley (later the Earl of Shaftesbury) persuaded Parliament to set up a Royal Commission to investigate the condition of children in mines and factories. The first report was delivered in 1842. What the findings showed shocked popular reforming attitudes. The Commission reported that in some coalfields children as young as four years old were employed; there were stories of six-year-old girls being required to carry loads of up to half a hundredweight, children forced to crawl through passages only eighteen inches high and being used as 'hurriers', pulling with chains heavy tubs of coal. The northern pits were to a greater degree exonerated of such practices, but the findings of the Commission led to the introduction of the Mines and Collieries Act of 1842. This Act set limits on the age of children employed underground. Boys had to be over 12 years of age. The use of women and girls was forbidden altogether. The Act again provided for the independent inspection of mines.

Again Londonderry opposed the legislation. His main objection was not the age limit on children; the provisions regarding women didn't concern him personally as he didn't employ any underground, but to the issue of inspectors he remained vigorously opposed. During a debate in the House of Lords he is reported to have said that, for his part, 'if an inspector came to me and asked permission to inspect my works, I should say, get down how you can, but when you get down, you may get back how you can'. The debates were heated. One time, as contemporary diarist Charles Greville reported, Londonderry exploded into 'such a fury that he rose, roared, gesticulated, held up his whip, and four or five Lords held him down by the tail of his coat to prevent him flying on somebody'.

The Marquess published his view on the Bill in a lengthy open letter to the *Morning Chronicle*. A young writer and author named Charles Dickens wrote a damning review of Londonderry's letter:

> It is scarcely necessary to mention that, in reference to the Mines and Collieries Bill (as we learn from his letter), everybody was wrong except the Marquess of Londonderry; because whenever there is one intellect so vastly in advance of the rest of the world as the Marquess of Londonderry's it is universally felt and admitted by all men to be . . . A moment's reflection upon the stupendous character of Lord Londonderry's mind set us right and showed us not only that this is quite intelligible, but that it must be and is inseparable from the existence of such a triton among minnows of creation as the most

noble Marquess, 'whose humble services', as he observes, 'are before the public and Europe', and whose consolation, under all the Lilliputian arrows aimed at his mighty head by pigmies, is to be found 'in the recorded testimonials of great and enlightened warriors and statesmen' – which are neatly framed and glazed at Wynyard Park, and may be seen on application to the housekeeper any Wednesday afternoon between the hours of two and four o'clock.

The document which contained the report on conditions in the mines also contained some specially commissioned illustrations, several of which showed squalid scenes of women at work in the pits. Dickens wrote of these in the *Morning Chronicle*:

> The 'disgusting' pictorial woodcuts' which accompanied the report still haunt the nobleman of taste, who complains 'that they were seen in the salons of the capital', and it was 'in the very worst taste' for any lady or gentleman to look into the rooms at Wynyard Park and see those brutal forms reflected in the glittering plate and polished furniture, and even bordering, in fantastic patterns, the pages of the bankers book of the most noble, the Marquess of Londonderry, in account with Coutts & Co.

Londonderry did not employ women in his pits, in fact there were none employed in the northern coalfield. There were, however, a large number of children underground in north-east England. A study of four pits, including Londonderry's at Rainton, Penshaw and Pittington, revealed that 235 'trapper boys' were employed to open and close air doors and allow the passage of coal tubs; of these, 135 were less than ten years of age, four were under seven years old.

Growing unrest in the coalfield led to a strike in 1831. There was anger on the part of the miners when they demanded increased pay and better conditions. They also saw their physical labour financing the vast fortunes and lavish lifestyles of their patrons which showed up in so stark a contrast with their own. The miner's life was concerned with hard work, danger and a meagre existence. So it was that after ten years of uninterrupted coal production the miners came out. It was a bitter strike, there were instances of violence on both sides. John Buddle, Londonderry's coalfield agent, wrote to Londonderry saying: 'The pitmen boast they will hold out to the last extremity, and live on grass before they give in.' Buddle was also aware of the military presence in the region which could, if given the order by the magistrates, be used to quell the miners' anger. He wrote: 'We have plenty of military in the county, a squadron of cavalry at Newcastle, 300 infantry at

Sunderland, to keep the peace of the county, if the Magistrates will but do their duty.' But the trade at that time was in decline, demand was low, and in consequence Londonderry became the first owner to negotiate with the striking miners. Within three weeks he had conceded to the demands of the men. The settlement was to cost him about £3,000 a year and he was roundly criticised by the other northern coal owners.

The Great Strike of 1844 was to be a markedly different affair. The main trouble was ostensibly the 'yearly bond'. By this system miners were obliged to sign an annual contract to their coal owner by which they were legally bound, under payment of a substantial financial penalty, to work continuously at one colliery for that year and be held liable to various fines and conditions. The coal owners on the other hand were not held liable even to guarantee a full year's employment or wages to the miners. There had been general unrest in the preceding years. Coal owners of the South Wales coalfield had attempted to reduce the wages of their miners. The pitmen had made several attempts at strike action, achieving little, but the unrest was growing and spreading. The miners were now being organised by the National Miners Association of Great Britain, and in 1844 the miners struck; all the pits in Durham and Northumberland lay idle. Londonderry was again quick to negotiate with the miners' leaders, but by this time he had been appointed Lord Lieutenant of the County. He felt he now had broader responsibilities to the northern coal owners generally, rather than responsibility just for his own pits. This time he made no concessions, feeling he must take strong measures to dampen 'this rebellious spirit in the pits'.

On 28 November 1828, he had laid the foundation stone of Seaham Harbour. This was to be his model town and port, from which the export of coal would be made more efficient and more profitable. Consequently, at the outset of the strike Londonderry had vast quantities of coal stockpiled, waiting to be shipped from Seaham. Unlike the other coal owners, who had little, Londonderry had virtually the only coal available for sale. When the probability of a strike had first threatened, coal prices in London had rocketed and would remain high throughout the strike. Londonderry was able, therefore, to make for himself a large killing on the market. Consequently there was no hurry for him to get his miners back to work. They were on strike, he was paying them no wages; at the same time he was making enormous sums of money, selling his coal at inflated prices. Londonderry took some kudos from the publicised fact that he was the first of the coal owners to negotiate with the miners and he was the last to begin evicting them. Indeed, it was some time after the other owners had started that Londonderry began his own evictions. Once the strike ceased to be profitable for Londonderry, it had to be broken.

On 3 June, 12 weeks into the strike, Londonderry posted a notice to the pitmen of Penshaw, Rainton and Pittington collieries. He addressed his remarks to 'the most deluded and obstinate victims of designing men and crafty attorneys'. He went on to appeal to the striking miners:

> I have been amongst you, I have reasoned, I have pointed out to you, the folly, misery, the destruction awaiting you by your stupid and most insane union. I gave you two weeks to consider whether you would return to your work, before I proceeded to eject you from your houses. I returned to Pensher, and I found you dogged, obstinate and determined: indifferent to my really paternal advice and kind feelings to the old families of the Vane and Tempest pitmen who had worked for successive ages in the mines . . . You heeded me not. I have now brought forty Irishmen to the pits and I will give you all one more weeks notice. And if by the thirteenth of this month a large body of pitmen do not return to their labour, I will obtain one hundred more men, and proceed to eject that number, who are now illegally and unjustly in possession of my houses: and in the following week another 100 shall follow.

Perhaps rather incongruously he then signed his notice: 'Believe me, I am, Your sincere friend. Vane Londonderry.'

The evictions had begun. At first it was the so-called ringleaders, troublemakers and their families that were ejected from their houses; leaders of the union would soon follow. On 25 June, 13 families were evicted from their homes in Pittington, more would soon be ejected at Penshaw and Rainton. Londonderry brought workers over from his estates in Ireland. On 30 June, about 200 'black leg' workers began work in Londonderry's pits. The miners, however, refused to be intimidated and remained on strike.

Further evictions were to take place before the strike was ended and Londonderry took the extra measure of instructing the shopkeepers of 'his' town of Seaham to stop trading with and especially giving credit to the striking miners. From this action many have later claimed that Londonderry effectively starved his miners back to work. The strike was eventually ended. The miners did not achieve the abolition of the 'yearly bond', indeed they wouldn't do so for another 25 years. The emergent National Miners Association of Great Britain was crushed by Londonderry and the coal owners. Londonderry's actions during the strike have been defended by some. It is argued that he did initially try to negotiate before taking any action against his workers, unlike other coal owners; he was slow to begin evictions, he saw the miners as being misguided, swayed away from his paternal care by the sinister influence of their union. He did his best to convince them of their folly and it was only when his efforts to that end failed that he resorted to the harsh measures used so readily by the other coal owners. However, his actions during the 1844 strike, more than anything, blackened the name of the 3rd Marquess of Londonderry, and caused it to be despised through generations of County Durham pitmen.

The radical writer Harriet Martineau spoke of Londonderry's 'genuine goodwill towards his serfs on the one hand, his Imperial friends on the other, and all between who would take him as he was'. Serfs his miners were, and serfs it was their duty to remain. The word serf is a medieval term which refers to bonded workers of a feudal overlord. In the context of the culture of his time, that of a nineteenth-century paternal feudalism, it has been said of Londonderry that 'he embodied the paternalistic attitude of so many contemporary businessmen towards their employees, whereby they were treated well as long as they kept their station in society'. Londonderry was an individualist who, like many of his contemporaries, was concerned about accumulating vast sums of money, essentially through the labour of others, whom he regarded as his charge. In the end he was prepared to be ruthless with any who stood in his way.

The estimated income from the Londonderry estates was about £75,000 a year, three-quarters of which came from coal mining. During his 35 years as head of the family, the 3rd Marquess spent in excess of £2.5 million, almost half of which was accounted for by lavish personal spending, a sharp contrast to the life of his eight-year-old 'trapper boys' sitting in the darkness of his pits, working a 12-hour shift for 10d.

When, on 1 March 1854, Charles William Vane Stewart, 3rd Marquess of Londonderry, Earl Vane and Viscount Seaham, died at the age of 76, few workers in the Durham coalfield mourned his passing. A rather terse contemporary report tells us that on the day of his funeral, 'at Durham, Sunderland, Stockton and Seaham Harbour, the funeral of the Lord Lieutenant of the County was observed by the closing of shops, tolling of bells and other public manifestations'.

Chapter Sixteen

Fighting Charley and the Blind Beggar

'Good Sirs, look to the horse!'

In 1858, four years after the death of the 3rd Marquess of Londonderry, his widow, Frances Anne, commissioned a grand statue of her beloved husband. It was to be a lasting memorial to the benefactor of the people of Durham. The sculptor she commissioned was an Italian, a Milanese named Raffaelo Monti. A celebrated sculptor of the time, he specialised in working with marble and had exhibited at the Royal Academy in 1853. However, unknown to Frances Anne, Monti was at the time on the verge of financial ruin. To Monti the commission coming when it did must have seemed a godsend. He determined that this would be his finest piece. He would use an innovative new technique, the statue he would make of plaster then the surface would be electroplated with copper. This would be the first time this method was used in such a work. Monti knew that a brilliant piece of work completed for this particular commission might lead to further commissions and greater rewards, and finally put an end to his financial troubles.

And so Raffaelo Monti began his great work. It was eventually completed in 1861, and it was indeed a masterly piece of sculpture. Unfortunately for Monti, its completion had come too late, for even as the great statue stood finished in his studio Monti was finally declared bankrupt. All his assets including his studio and his completed work were seized. Frances Anne had paid an advance to Monti of £2,000 for the statue; she was obliged to pay another £1,000 to acquire it from Monti's creditors, 'a force of circumstance of which she disapproved in very strong language'. She later presented it to the City Corporation, of which Londonderry had been mayor. The statue itself was an heroic equestrian work, representing a fine proud charger being ridden by a dashing Hussar. It was indeed the 3rd Marquess portrayed as the 'Fighting Charley' of his younger years. The statue was finally positioned in the Market Place and unveiled in the grand ceremony on 2 December 1861, with Frances Anne and Benjamin Disraeli looking on.

The statue eventually acquired a fame of its own; after all, the name of the Marquess of Londonderry was notorious throughout the county. The quality of the workmanship was universally admired, and the boast of the sculptor that his work was perfect gave rise to a legend which has its roots in the arrival in Durham one day of a blind beggar. The story of the subsequent events became a popular folk tale and visitors to the city were rarely allowed to leave without first hearing the story.

The crowd of onlookers grew as the day wore on. Rumour had spread around the city as to the curious spectacle taking place in the Market Place. There were gasps as the blind man again lost his footing and almost fell to certain injury. Most of the onlookers were bemused and at the same time expectant as to what the blind man would find as he slowly groped around the statue, inching his way, seeing horse and rider in his mind's eye, slowly studying through his fingertips every detail of the 'perfect work'.

The statue of 'The Man on the Horse' had become quite celebrated. Many visitors had come to admire it and the townsfolk were justifiably proud of the latest addition to their Market Place. The sculptor had declared it his greatest work. Indeed he was so sure of its perfection he had stated publicly that if a fault was found on the statue, he would end his own life. This, of course, acted merely as an encouragement to all and sundry to examine the statue in the hope of finding the slightest fault, the smallest mistake that would ultimately test the sculptor's word. Many people tried, from the rich and powerful to the humble and penniless. No fault could be found, and the sculptor basked in the warmth of praise and congratulation. As more and more people tried but could find no fault with his work, the sculptor became increasingly confident that he was right; his work was indeed perfect.

Examinations of the statue grew to such fever pitch that 'experts' were invited to the city to assess its accuracy. Horse experts looked at the anatomy of the animal. The size and proportions of the body, the limbs, bones and muscles were all true; they could find no fault. Military experts were brought to examine the regalia worn by the rider. The coat of arms, the Hussars uniform, the weaponry were all exactly as they should be; they could find no fault. It was even said that an old manservant of Lord Londonderry was brought to the Market Place, and he admitted that the likeness was perfect, 'as if his master had been turned to stone'. None could find any fault in the statue: the sculptor had indeed created a perfect work; or so it seemed.

Time passed and the novelty of the new statue and of the solemn oath of the sculptor faded from the minds of the local people, that is until one day when there came to Durham a blind beggar. No one knew where he had come from, he was just a penniless drifter, wandering from town to town, relying on charity to keep body and soul together. He remained in Durham for some time and he eventually heard the story of the statue. Before he'd arrived he had never heard of the work, or of its creator, but the rumour of the perfection of the statue and the oath of the sculptor interested him.

He eventually asked to be taken to the Market Place so that he too could examine the work, and with blind eyes and searching fingers discover the fault that would disprove the sculptor's claim. People said he was mad, that it was a waste of time. If others had looked with their eyes and found no fault, how could he, who could not see the road in front of him, possibly hope to do so? Nevertheless, the beggar insisted and early one morning he was taken to the Market Place and helped up on to the base of the statue. He asked all those present to leave him. He needed no more help. Then, as the onlookers shook their heads in silent disbelief and amusement, he began slowly and gingerly to run his fingers over every minute detail of the sculpture. Later in the morning the curious townsfolk returned. The beggar told them to return again, later. Midday came and went and still the blind man inched his way painstakingly around horse and rider. Late afternoon now, and shadows began to creep over the scene; still the blind beggar continued without rest or food. The sun disappeared and darkness drew around, but darkness had no meaning to him. He eventually approached the end of his examination and claimed that he had finished his work. He asked to be helped down. A crowd had now gathered and jostled around him, eager to know what, if anything, he had discovered. The blind man said nothing, he asked only to be taken to the sculptor.

For his part the sculptor was as curious as anyone about this mysterious beggar who had, with blind eyes, the audacity to attempt to find fault with the masterpiece. As the beggar had wished, he was brought before its creator. Confident of his work, the sculptor asked disdainfully what then was a blind man's opinion of his work. The beggar simply congratulated him on such a marvellous piece of sculpture. To create something as magnificent as that with such skill was indeed something of which to be proud. The horse, the rider, every detail was perfect. Perfect that was, except for one small fault!

There were gasps around the room. The sculptor's heart jumped, he knew he had made his solemn oath; for a moment there was absolute silence. Slowly and with great humility the blind man said, 'Good Sirs, look to the horse; its mouth is open as if in the heat of a gallop, but the horse has no tongue!'

A cry rang out among the assembled company. They turned and as one dashed out to the Market Place to confirm for themselves what the blind man had discovered. They came upon the statue and looked closely, shining their lights into the horse's mouth. Now they knew what to look for. Then they saw that the blind beggar was indeed speaking the truth, the horse had no tongue. The sculptor's 'perfect' work was flawed. The revelation of the blind man was the talk of the town, at least for a time. Gradually, however, things settled down and the novelty of the event that had taken place began to fade. People returned to their everyday lives quietly satisfied that the swaggering boast of the sculptor had at last been disproved, and by a blind man. The blind beggar himself left Durham as anonymously as he had arrived, never to be seen again; and it is said, though I will not say it is so, that the sculptor, true to his oath, took his own life.

In 1952 the City Corporation commissioned the repair of the deteriorating statue. The council bore most of the cost, the rest being met by public donation. It is not recorded whether workmen and conservators confirmed the absence, or otherwise, of the horse's tongue. The story of the blind beggar's discovery and of the sculptor's resulting suicide became a popular local tale, which would fade, only eventually, through the uncertainty of memory into the obscurity of time.

Go into the Market Place today and look up at the statue. Look especially at the horse's mouth. It is difficult to see from the Market Place flagstones whether or not the horse does indeed have a tongue. To be certain you would have to climb up and follow in the faltering footsteps of the mysterious blind stranger whose discovery, as legend records, sent the statue's creator to his doom.

Chapter Seventeen

The Tsar of Russia, the Nova Scotia Miners and Mr Timothy Hackworth

'As honest a man as ever walked.'

The young man shivered in the biting November wind, and winced as the cold, dirty water splashed over him, soaking his clothes. He was only 16 years old and never before had he witnessed a spectacle such as this, nor would he ever again.

He stared incredulously at the distinguished company assembled. Members of the royal family, the aristocracy, leaders of the Church and over a hundred people stood there motionless on this freezing day at the end of 1836, holding lighted tapers as chanting choristers of the Russian Orthodox Church filled the air with sacred sounds and High Priests solemnly performed the ceremony of baptism. There, in a place of honour, stood the Tsar himself, looking on with quiet satisfaction. The priests, firstly invoking special blessings on the Imperial family, turned to the subject of this strange christening. For the 'baptism' was not of a Russian royal prince, nor even of a distinguished new member of the Orthodox Church; but here, at the Tsar's Imperial Summer Palace at Tsarskoye-Selo near St Petersburg, the object of the priests' prayers was a 'double trunk' engine steam locomotive, built in Shildon, County Durham by Timothy Hackworth, the father of the cold, wet young man and, as some would have it, the real 'Father of the Railways'.

Timothy Hackworth was born in the village of Wylam on 22 December 1786 and was a contemporary of George Stephenson, the other great railway pioneer of the time. Hackworth's father had been a foreman blacksmith at Wylam Colliery and the young Timothy had started his working life there as an apprentice. After his father's death, when Timothy was just 17 years old, the young man gradually rose himself to become foreman smith. In 1815

Hackworth eventually left Wylam after a dispute with the colliery managers. He had been asked to carry out work on a Sunday. Hackworth, a devout Methodist, refused to work on the Sabbath, the result being that he lost his employment. He eventually secured a position at George Stephenson's Forth Street engine building works, and there he saw the construction of 'Locomotion No. 1', the first engine built for the Stockton and Darlington Railway. It was whilst he was manager of the Forth Street works that people began to take note of Hackworth's engineering ingenuity.

When he was 38 years old, the Committee of the Stockton and Darlington Railway Company offered Hackworth the position of 'Superintendent of Permanent and Locomotive Engines', and this was the post he held at the time of the official opening of the Stockton and Darlington line. In 1826 Hackworth moved his small team to Shildon, there to set up a permanent repair and maintenance workshop for the company. Seven years later the Railway Committee gave Hackworth permission to set up his own locomotive building works while retaining his position as manager and engineer of the railway. Thus came into being the Soho Works at Shildon, and the inventiveness of Hackworth as a pioneer engineer would be given full expression. The genius of Hackworth, the things that perhaps set him apart from the other great names of the early railways, were his innovation, his continual development of new ideas and, above all, his brilliant engineering. It was at Shildon that Hackworth built the *Royal George*, the machine that finally established the supremacy of the locomotive over other forms of transport, and the *Sanspareil* which Hackworth entered in the locomotive trials at Rainhill, near Liverpool, in October 1829.

This would be an ill-fated adventure for Hackworth. His *Sanspareil* would be matched against three other specially designed locomotives – the *Novelty* entered by Messrs Braithwaite and Ericsson; the *Perseverance* entered by Timothy Burstall; and George Stephenson's *Rocket* – competitors for the distinction of being the first locomotive to be used on the newly constructed Liverpool and Manchester Railway, and a prize of £500 was being offered. Hackworth's locomotive, however, was not to complete the trials, suffering a burst cylinder provided ironically by Stephenson and Company. A contemporary chronicler recorded, as indeed history records, that Stephenson's *Rocket* was eventually awarded the prize, 'although but for the mal-adventure of bursting one of her cylinders, (very imperfectly manufactured by Stephenson & Co), the "Sanspareil", would most assuredly have asserted her superiority then, as she afterwards did assert it'. After the 'Rainhill Trials', George Stephenson and his *Rocket* went on to achieve railway immortality; a disappointed and somewhat dejected Timothy Hackworth returned to his Shildon works, there to make new and better locomotives.

Hackworth engines were destined to work all over the world, but

Timothy Hackworth himself was no traveller. In 1824 he had been offered the post of Superintendent of Engineering Operations on an expedition organised by speculating groups of bankers and merchants, to work gold and silver mines in Central America and the West Indies. His commission would include the sinking of mines and the construction of engines and machinery. Hackworth declined the offer and the position was eventually taken by George Stephenson's 21-year-old son Robert, who was sent off to Colombia. The venture was a failure and almost all the speculators lost money. However, the event had proved fortuitous for Timothy Hackworth because it was in the absence of Robert that George Stephenson had offered Hackworth the post of manager of his Forth Street engine works.

The demands of his work did not allow Hackworth much time for holiday; indeed much of what free time he had he spent as a lay preacher on the local Methodist circuit holding prayer meetings in his cottage at the Soho Works, and travelling as far as Barnard Castle to preach. However, in September 1836 he did allow himself a short holiday. He travelled to London with his 16-year-old son, John Wesley Hackworth, and while there he took the opportunity to visit various engineering works he had wished to see. For the young John the trip to London was but the beginning of an epic journey, as custodian of his father's engine, which would take him to Russia and the Court of the Tsar.

John Wesley's journey was an eventful one. The engine, crated up and packed away together with Hackworth and a small team of engineers, eventually arrived on the Baltic coast in freezing weather conditions. Travelling by sleigh to St Petersburg, in weather so severely cold that the spirit bottles broke, the party later recounted that they had frequently, and somewhat alarmingly, been the object of the attentions of packs of wolves. On arrival at St Petersburg, the Shildon men assembled the engine and began a few days of trials. Then disaster struck. One of the engine's cylinders cracked. A foreman by the name of George Thompson was given the unenviable responsibility of travelling the 600 miles to Moscow, there to make a pattern for a new cylinder and have it cast, bored and finished at an armaments factory. Thompson then returned to St Petersburg and fitted the new cylinder to the engine.

The now fully restored machine was taken by young John Wesley Hackworth and his men to Tsarskoye-Selo and the Imperial Summer Palace for the official 'baptism'. For the ceremony, the 'holy water' was obtained by the priests from a nearby bog with a golden censer and sanctified by repeated immersions of a golden cross. The priests first prayed that on all occasions of travel by the new mode the royal party would be well and safely conveyed. Then came the blessing of the engine. As one priest carried the censer of holy water another wielded a huge brush, dipping it into the censer and with large brushstrokes making on the engine and the wheels the sign of the cross. The solemn rites completed, the remains of the holy water were thrown over the whole locomotive, and the unfortunate John Wesley Hackworth.

The Church of Russia was content, the Tsar having already assured the Church leaders that the locomotive would run only on holy days and holidays. What attitude the Church of John Wesley Hackworth and his father would have taken to that is not recorded. So it came about that the Hackworth locomotive, designed and built by Timothy at his Soho workshops in Shildon, was ceremoniously started up, and the onlooking crowd of Russian nobility witnessed the first steam locomotive ever to run in their country. The Tsar himself was well pleased. He remarked to the young Hackworth that back in 1816 he had witnessed the running of Blenkinsopp's engines on the colliery line from Middleton to Leeds, and said that he 'could not have conceived it possible so radical a change could have been effected within 20 years'. John Wesley Hackworth and his team returned home to Shildon with the proceeds of the sale: £1,884 2s. 9¾d.

The young Hackworth came home with more than just the money. After his return from Russia he began to sport a beard, much to the disquiet of his father, the sober, sensible but nevertheless, for a nineteenth-century Wesleyan lay preacher, very liberal-minded Timothy Hackworth. The wearing of a full beard was quite unfashionable at the time. However, Timothy regarded the matter as one of greater importance than mere fashion. The wearing of a beard was a mark of at best vanity, at worst eccentricity. Once writing to his wife from Durham, Hackworth criticised a fellow lay preacher he had heard, describing him as a 'dandy young man with hair under his chin'. Hackworth confessed to his wife: 'I was not edified.'

Russia was not the only country to obtain a Hackworth machine as its first working locomotive. In 1838 he built the *Samson*, the *Hercules* and the *John Buddle* for the Albion Coal Mining Company of Nova Scotia. The *Samson*, the first to be shipped, was taken to Nova Scotia on the brig *Ythan* from Newcastle by a Captain Tutton. The locomotive arrived at Pictou on 27 May 1839, and was ferried to the Albion mines on barges. It was put together by George Davidson who had helped construct the machine at Shildon. So it was that in September 1839 the *Samson* became the first locomotive to run in 'British North America'. Davidson remained as driver and eventually settled permanently in Nova Scotia. For this engine Hackworth received £2,140.

The *Samson* would go on working for more than 40 years, and it is a measure of the quality of Hackworth's engineering that the locomotive would still be going strong after all that time, after working on average 113 days each year, clocking up over 4,700 miles each year, and hauling annually nearly 22,000 chaldrons of coal. In 1893, 43 years after Timothy Hackworth's death, the Baltimore and Ohio Railroad Company exhibited the *Samson* at the

Raby Castle ~ once home of the House of Neville and one of the most important castles of medieval England.

Memorial to the murdered Brass childen in Merrington churchyard. The inscription shows that the word 'executed' has been removed.

Cockfield - birthplace of Jeremiah Dixon.

LEFT: *Confederate flag - 'Look away Dixieland'.*

RIGHT: *The 3rd Marquess of Londonderry - 'Fighting Charley'.*

Soho Cottage, Shildon - home of Timothy Hackworth and now the Hackworth Museum.

A replica of the Sanspareil *steaming on part of the original Stockton-Darlington line.*

Banners at the Miners' Gala.

JOHN BURN
AGED 21 YEARS.
WILLIAM LAMBTON,
AGED 21 YEARS.
JOHN JARVIS LAMBTON,
AGED 17 YEARS.
HUGH ARMSTRONG,
AGED 19 YEARS.
THOMAS ARMSTRONG,
AGED 16 YEARS.
WILLIAM PATTISON,
AGED 19 YEARS.
WILLIAM SMITH,
AGED 18 YEARS.
JOHN SLOGGETT,
AGED 17 YEARS.
JOHN LAWSON,
AGED 16 YEARS.
GEORGE STEPHENSON,
AGED 16 YEARS.
EDWARD ROBERTS,
AGED 15 YEARS.

FAR LEFT: Both men and boys died in the Tudhoe Colliery explosion of 1882 - the names of the youngest victims are carved on the memorial.

LEFT: Tomb of St Cuthbert in Durham Cathedral.

BELOW: Tomb of The Venerable Bede in Durham Cathedral.

LEFT: The statue of Neptune stands today in Durham's Market Place.

BELOW: The Way - contemporary sculpture representing the journey of St Cuthbert's monks to Durham.

World Fair in Chicago, the engine leading the procession of locomotives. A plate on an accompanying carriage still bore the maker's name: 'Timothy Hackworth, New Shildon, Durham, August 1838'. Also at the exhibition driving the *Samson* was the aged George Davidson who had continued to work his beloved engine until 1882.

Timothy Hackworth died on 7 July 1850 after a short illness. By the time of his death he had built up his Soho Works into one of the most well-equipped engine works of the time. Up until his father's death, John Wesley Hackworth had worked as works manager. Afterwards John sold the Soho Works and moved to Darlington, building a successful business manufacturing stationary engines. In his later life he set up as a consulting engineer and eventually moved to London. He died two years before his father's *Samson* was exhibited at the Chicago Exhibition. A contrast to his father, John Wesley Hackworth lacked Timothy's patience and even temper, for John 'was quick to wrath, and easily stirred to indignation', but he shared at least some of his father's engineering genius.

Timothy Hackworth, it is said, was a quiet, unassuming, publicity-shy man, 'as honest a man as ever walked'; an engineer, lay preacher and philanthropist whose great achievements have been largely, and some would argue unjustly, overshadowed by those of the Stephensons. His contribution to the world's railway heritage remains vast. His individual achievements and inventions are far too numerous to be done full justice in this short passage, but they are today remembered in the Timothy Hackworth Victorian Railway Museum at Shildon, on the site of his original Soho Works. Timothy Hackworth's home now serves as the museum building and on certain days it is possible to look out of the bedroom window, back seemingly across 160 years, and once again wonder at Hackworth's *Sanspareil* steaming along the Stockton and Darlington railway line.

No grand monuments have ever been erected to Timothy Hackworth; his effigy has never been placed in the centre of a great city, his face never seen on a banknote, but it is said that on the day of his funeral in Shildon churchyard almost all the population of the town came to pay their last respects. Perhaps that in itself would have been tribute enough for him.

Part Six

Chapter Eighteen

St Cuthbert and the Lost Bombers

'Modern-day myth, or modern-day miracle?'

In the spring of 1942, RAF Bomber Command introduced a new tactic in their escalating campaign against Nazi Germany. Large formations of heavily armed bombers began to attack German towns and cities. These attacks – 'concentrated incendiarism', as Chief of Bomber Command, Arthur Harris, called them – were inflicted over a comparatively short space of time and the resulting amount of damage was usually extremely high. No one, however, resident at the time in Durham could have imagined that two of these RAF raids, on the medieval German cities of Lübeck and Rostock, would eventually lead to the making of a modern-day legend in their own city.

On the night of Palm Sunday, 28/29 March 1942, Bomber Command attacked Lübeck. In medieval times the old port had been the chief exchange and distribution centre for the Hanseatic League, the loose amalgam of north European cities which had dominated trade for nearly 200 years. Much of the city's medieval core was still intact, and there were large numbers of seventeenth- and eighteenth-century warehouses still standing. Starting at 10.30 p.m. and for the next three hours, 234 bombers dropped 304 tons of bombs. Only 20 minutes after the first wave of bombers had gone in, other crews reported that fires had spread right across the 'Altstadt', the island upon which the old medieval part of the town was situated. The raid succeeded in destroying vast quantities of stores bound for the Russian campaign. It also succeeded in burning to the ground an area of 200 acres, the greater part of the old town. Lübeck's medieval cathedral was destroyed.

Bomber Command then turned its attention to the next target. For four nights in early April, Rostock was pounded. Precision bombers, Manchesters of 106 Squadron commanded by Squadron Leader Guy Gibson, later to command 'The Dambusters', attacked Rostock together with the new four-engined Lancasters carrying high-explosive bombs. The official target was a group of Heinkel munitions factories. In the first attack all the bombs were dropped within an hour. Observers reported fires raging in the harbour, the smoke from which was rising 8,000 feet into the sky. By the final night of the raid it was estimated that 70 per cent of the city had been destroyed, 100,000 people had been made homeless, and again the medieval part of the city had been obliterated.

The reaction of Adolf Hitler to the raids was swift and predictable. He ordered immediate revenge bombings, terror raids aimed at British centres of historic and cultural interest. A new type of Nazi offensive was about to be launched. Hitler gave the order for these retaliation raids on 14 April 1942, saying to Goebbels: 'There is no other way of bringing the English to their senses. They belong to a class of human beings with whom you can talk, only after you have first knocked out their teeth.' The German tourist guidebooks. the *Baedeker Guides*, contained information on all such British historic cities and towns.

After the destruction of Lübeck and Rostock, the Deputy Head of the German Foreign Office press department, Baron Gustav Braun von Stumm, had said: 'Now the Luftwaffe will go out for every building marked with three stars and more in Baedeker.' The idea stuck, and the new Luftwaffe raids became known as the 'Baedeker raids'. Goebbels was reputedly furious at the statement, fearing it to be a propaganda mistake showing the Nazis to be little more than vindictive, malicious vandals. Hitler, however, was insistent, telling Goebbels that the raids would go ahead 'night after night until the English are sick and tired of terror attacks'. People living in the historic cities of Britain braced themselves for the coming onslaught.

Targets for the attacks were chosen using certain criteria. The cities were chosen because they were prominent or easy to find. They were always within 50 miles of the coast. Historic cities were 'soft targets' anyway, being virtually undefended. Most of the raids would take place only on bright, moonlit nights, even though the Junkers and the Dornier bombers were preceded by Luftwaffe 'Pathfinder' units using new electronic targeting equipment, and the attacks would last for only half an hour to an hour.

The bombs of the Baedeker raids began falling, on Exeter and Bath. Over 400 people died. In Exeter the old centre of the town was destroyed. Though apparently using only a small number of aircraft, the bombing of the Luftwaffe was very accurate and it was confirmed by Intelligence sources that the German bombers were indeed using a recently developed electronic beam to guide them to their targets. On the night of 27/28 April, Bath and Exeter were joined in the destruction by Norwich which was bombed and machine-gunned for more than an hour. A clear sky and a brilliant moon illuminated York the following night, giving the bomb aimers an easy target. Seventy-nine people died. After York it seemed that Durham could well be their destination. The local defence organisations needed no warning, and on 30 April people in Durham held their breath and wondered what the coming night would bring. What did happen that night would later be considered by some as a modern-day miracle, and by others as a modern-day myth. The arguments for and against continue, no doubt, unto this day.

As a legitimate target for the Baedeker raids, Durham City certainly conformed to their primary considerations, namely that a target must possess some or all of the following features: a major cathedral, monastic remains, a castle, city walls, medieval housing, and a congested town centre. Above all, it must have an historic core, concentrated within an area small enough to be devastated by a limited attack force. The events of the night of 30 April/1 May 1942 were eventually to be recorded in a brief descriptive passage, by an unknown writer, in a 1945 edition of *The Leader* magazine. In that article it was revealed that on the night in question, early in the morning of 1 May, Durham City and the cathedral were bathed in bright moonlight and would have been a perfect target for the enemy. However, as aircraft were heard approaching the city, a thick white mist suddenly rose up engulfing both the cathedral and castle, hiding them from the bomb aimers' view. The enemy planes circled around for some time looking for their target, but eventually gave up and turned eastwards, leaving the city and the cathedral undamaged. The unknown writer of this account said that some had considered what had happened to be a miracle, ascribing it to St Cuthbert who lay behind the High Altar in the cathedral, and comparing it to the appearance of the 'Angels of Mons' in the Great War. A somewhat embroidered account of the original article was then published in the *Durham County Advertiser* in May 1945. The response to that article highlighted the diverse interpretations of what actually happened, interpretations given by different people all of whom, early that May morning, had either been at the same place or had witnessed the same phenomenon.

One lady wrote that looking out over Durham City from her home, high up near the village of Cassop, she had witnessed the whole event. She maintained that the ominous droning of the bombers' engines, familiar and fearful, could already be heard even before the mist began to rise. She at least was convinced of the origins of this rapid and miraculous transformation, from bright moonlight to dense mist, saying: 'Truly, I saw the hand of God.' The chief ARP warden, who was on duty that night, was more sceptical. He insisted that the 'mysterious' mist was in fact a common sight to the wardens of Durham. Given certain conditions of climate, it had risen quite naturally from the river below the cathedral scores of times before. He contended that if St Cuthbert had indeed miraculously brought about this whole event to foil enemy bombers, then he had rather carelessly left the top of the central tower sticking out above the layers of mist. The chief warden was convinced that if the Germans had been determined to bomb Durham Cathedral, they would have simply returned on another, clearer night. A simple mist, he suggested, would not have stopped the Luftwaffe. He maintained that the bombers droning menacingly overhead were merely lost.

South Street stands directly to the west of the peninsula. Situated high above the river, it overlooks the western towers of the great cathedral. It was from this perfect viewpoint that a young lady member of the Royal Observer Corps stood on fire guard duty that night. Her description of the events seemed to confirm the original story. Shortly before 3.00 a.m. the air-raid siren began to wail its piercing tone. Suddenly a white mist began to swirl up from the river below her and clouds covered the moon. The whole scene, which up until minutes ago had been bathed in bright moonlight, was dimmed and shrouded as the mist rose. It covered first the western towers and the castle, then the central tower. No part of the central tower, she maintained, was visible. The mist had risen so quickly that others she had spoken to after the event had suggested that it must in fact have been a deliberate smokescreen. The mist continued to hang over the peninsula as the bombers circled overhead. When at two minutes past four in the morning the all-clear was sounded, the mist dispersed. At that, the young lady returned indoors; she later described the feelings she had had: 'As I closed the front door I paused for a moment removing my tin hat, and stood in silence; and with bowed head thanked God for our deliverance . . . I shall believe to the end of my days that I witnessed a miracle.' Both a Home Guard officer on duty that night and a city councillor, who was at the time Officer in Charge at ARP County Control Headquarters, confirmed what had happened. The initial warning had been received at 2.33 a.m. A number of bombers were heard circling above the mist, eventually turning east and dropping high explosives at Grange Colliery, Belmont and on the loop of the River Wear at Finchale believing it, some said, to be the loop of the Wear around the cathedral.

What then is today's reader left with? A fanciful account of a natural, if curious, phenomenon or a timely demonstration of divine intervention? After the Baedeker raids on other historic cities, especially the raid on York only the previous night, it was surely reasonable to assume, given the criteria of a Baedeker 'target', that Durham would also now be attacked. Therefore when the civil defence authorities were warned that large numbers of enemy bombers had crossed the County Durham coast at several points, it was surely also reasonable to assume that some, if not all, of the aircraft were headed for the cathedral city. All reports later confirmed that aircraft were indeed heard in the skies over Durham. Everyone who responded to the newspaper article agreed: that on a night which had previously been clear and moonlit, a mist had risen suddenly, even as the enemy bombers approached, and obscured to a great degree the cathedral and peninsula. The same night other parts of the region were bombed in a concentrated raid on the north-east. In Sunderland people died as high explosives rained down. The shipyard areas of Jarrow, South Shields and Newcastle were extensively bombed. But on Durham not one bomb was dropped; the historic core of the city was left totally unscathed.

Each individual who was present early in the morning of 1 May 1942 formulated their own personal interpretation of what happened. Some attributed the event to coincidence, confusion and the vagaries of localised climatic conditions: the mist had risen from the river naturally, the bombers heard overhead were simply lost, it was mere coincidence that the mist materialised at the time it did. To others, however, who witnessed the mist suddenly form and rise into a clear night sky, there to shroud the cathedral even as the engines of the enemy aircraft could be heard approaching, and later to disperse only at the sound of the all-clear, other forces were at work. Some have ascribed what they saw that night to the miraculous workings of St Cuthbert. After all, did not the monk, Symeon of Durham, tell us that 900 years ago St Cuthbert had brought forth a similar mist to sow confusion and fear in the forces of the aggressor of that day, and it had halted for a while the march of William the Conqueror.

Today's perhaps more pragmatic reader may consider this. The chief warden himself said that during the course of the war many hundreds of enemy bombers must have flown over Durham City, both on misty nights and in bright, clear conditions; indeed, it was thought that the Luftwaffe aircrews used the cathedral and the distinctive loop of the river around the peninsula as a navigation point. The cathedral and the city must therefore have been to them a familiar and easy target. Given the fact that there was so much hostile air activity over the city – hundreds of Nazi bombers aided, according to British Intelligence, with electronic targeting devices – does not the real wonder lie in what the chief warden later told the *Durham County Advertiser*, namely that 'in our five years of war, the only bomb to fall within our boundaries . . . exploded harmlessly beside a sewage bed'. Surely the fact that throughout the whole duration of the war neither city nor cathedral was damaged by one single bomb is in itself a miracle.

'True believers' will remain 'true believers', no matter what convincing, if apparently mundane, evidence is produced which throws doubt or pours scorn upon that which they believe. 'True sceptics' will remain 'true sceptics', regardless of any curious but genuinely recognised factors that make logical, matter-of-fact explanations seem uncomfortably unconvincing in the eye of the neutral. They will insist that there is always a rational explanation, even for that which on occasion defies the norm.

Chapter Nineteen

Lest We Forget

'Remember before God the Durham miners who have given their
lives in the pits of this county.'

So begins the inscription on the memorial to the Durham miners, presented
to the cathedral in 1947. Alongside it hangs a solitary miner's lamp, below
which is kept a Book of Remembrance which contains a thousand names, one
miner's life for every year of Durham's millennium.

It would surely be impossible to complete a book about a thousand years
of Durham's history without mention of the Durham pits and the Durham
pitmen. It is not, however, my intention in this short piece to explore in detail
the history and development of the Durham coalfield. There have been a
number of excellent books published on this subject written by those
infinitely better qualified to write about it than this particular author. I wish
only to write a short chapter in recognition of the Durham miners and their
families who have, over the centuries, lived and died in an industry and a way
of life that is no more. If this piece is written more from the heart than from
the head, I make no excuses for it.

On the feast of St Cuthbert, in March 1183, by order of Hugh Pudsey,
Bishop of Durham, the *Boldon Buke* was commissioned. Following the
'Harrying of the North' by William the Conqueror, there had been virtually
nothing left for William's *Domesday Book* commissioners to record in the
lands between Tweed and Tees. The *Boldon Buke*, so called because the first
entry referred to the village of Boldon, was commissioned a century later as
an appendix to *Domesday* relating to the northern counties.

As early as the twelfth century more than one reference can be seen in the
book relating to the early extraction and working of coal in what is now
County Durham. One entry records that at Wearmouth, the smith held 12

acres to work iron for ploughs, and to work for coal. A further entry tells us that in Escomb, near Bishop Auckland, a certain coal miner provided coal for the iron work of the ploughs of Coundon. This evidence of primitive coal workings, seen alongside such other entries as one describing the possessions and entitlements of one 'Ralph the Crafty', keeper of the Bishop's hawk eyries in Weardale, gives an idea of exactly how long coal has been mined from the ground in County Durham.

With the onset of the Middle Ages, the extraction of coal began to increase. From one 'miner' simply digging down and taking coal from layers just below the surface, more complex structures eventually began to develop with several men working one 'mine'. In 1460, during the Wars of the Roses, there is a record of ten miners working together in a pit at Raby, and in medieval times the monastery of Durham granted rights for the digging and taking of coal on their land. As coal extraction grew, trade increased with foreign ships sailing in to the River Tyne. Indeed, at that time most of the coal produced was exported to Flemish and Dutch ports, to France and to Germany. In exchange the traders brought grain for the people of Durham and Northumberland.

Over the coming centuries more mines were sunk, more coal extracted, the importance of the coal trade grew. Eventually, mine owners and coal traders became rich. The coal of County Durham gradually became one of the country's main sources of fuel; indeed it was instrumental in the fuelling of the Industrial Revolution, the engines of empire, and the forging of raw materials into the ships, aircraft and guns of two world wars. The size and productivity of the Durham coalfield reached its peak just before the Great War, with over 300 pits and almost a quarter of a million people employed in mining and associated industries. At one time there were eight pits within sight of Durham Cathedral. By then the early struggles were over, but the miners' 'Holy Grail' of a nationalised mining industry would not become a reality for over 30 years.

In the early days the miners of Durham saw vast fortunes accrued by colliery owners, as a direct result of their own hard labour. The lifestyles of their employers would often be lavish, luxurious and excessive; in contrast, the life of the miners would often involve hunger and squalor. In the nineteenth century early attempts at strikes and the organisation of a miners' union were smashed by the colliery owners, some of whom became despised by the miners – 'With tyranny and capital, they never seem content' – and it was not until 1869 that at last the Durham Miners Association was formed, in the Market Tavern, then the Market Hotel, in Durham city centre. The first Miners' Hall opened in North Road, Durham, in 1875 and then, on 23 October 1915, the Durham Miners Association moved its headquarters to Redhills, to The Miners Parliament.

Their struggles, however, were to go on. Disputes continued to be resolved in the manner in which they had been resolved in the past: a confrontation with the militia or the magistrate. In the General Strike of 1926, the striking miners were subject to 'Emergency Regulations'. As many colliery owners sat as magistrates, punishment for the union leaders was harsh, and victimisation against them was commonplace after the strike. Eventually the bold 'new vision' of the immediate post-war period gave the miners what they wanted, and in 1947 the remaining 127 pits of the Durham coalfield were nationalised. One effect of nationalisation was increased safety consciousness in the mines. By their very nature the pits were extremely hazardous places in which to work. From the earliest of days, death had been no stranger to the miner. Any death in the pits was tragic, but when a major disaster struck, usually by way of underground explosion, the tragedy was made all the more bitter, for in the pit disaster it was not uncommon for two or three generations of the same family to be lost as grandfather, father and son were claimed by blast, fire or gas. The 'pitmen's poet' Tommy Armstrong recorded the tragedy of such an event in his poem *The Trimdon Grange Explosion*, written to commemorate those who died in the disaster at that pit on 16 February 1882:

> Men and boys left home that morning,
> For to earn their daily bread;
> Little thought before the evening,
> They'd be numbered with the dead.
>
> Let us think of Mrs Burnett,
> Once had sons but now has none;
> By the Trimdon Grange Explosion,
> Joseph, George and James are gone.

Joseph Burnett was 23 years old. His brothers, George and James, were 19 years old and 17 years old respectively. In all, 74 died in the disaster at Trimdon Grange.

It was not uncommon for rescuers to descend into a pit soon after an explosion and see scenes both harrowing and poignant, young boys lying dead alongside their fathers and grandfathers. At the Tudhoe Colliery explosion, only weeks after Trimdon Grange, the first body to be brought out was that of a young miner named Michael Cairns; his brother Robert and his father James had also died. Rescuers at Tudhoe later came across the bodies of two miners lying clasped in each other's arms, having simply laid down to die together as they realised that the 'after damp', the deadly build-up of carbon monoxide gas caused by the explosion, had surrounded them and there would be no escape. Most tragic of all, the body was found of a young boy, William Patterson, who had only weeks before moved to Tudhoe after surviving the explosion at Trimdon Grange. The Bishop of Durham, Bishop Lightfoot, conducted the funeral service of some of the Tudhoe victims and asked that the bereaved take time to pray also for their fellow mourners at Seaham and at Trimdon Grange.

Stories such as these are commonplace and can be recounted many times over, as the list of Durham pit disasters is a long one. The following are just ten, selected merely to represent the ten centuries of Durham's millennium, and to help illustrate the sacrifices made by Durham miners over a period of 250 years.

1708 Fatfield	69 dead
1794 Picktree	30 dead
1812 Brandlings Main	92 dead
1823 Rainton	59 dead
1850 Houghton	26 dead
1871 Seaham	26 dead
1880 Seaham	164 dead
1882 Trimdon Grange	68 dead
1882 Tudhoe	37 dead
1909 West Stanley	168 dead
1951 Easington	83 dead

The full list of Durham's pit disasters runs to over 30 with more than 1,600 men and boys killed, but there are many more miners not commemorated in the lists of disaster victims: those who died alone, killed by shot blast, roof fall or some other unlooked-for accident; those who simply succumbed to hearts strained or bodies broken by years of hard physical labour; or those who died with lungs congested by the black dust of the pit.

The outward symbol of the unity and strength of the Durham miners has traditionally been the annual Durham Miners Gala, the 'Big Meeting', held on the racecourse in Durham every July. The first-ever mass gathering of Miners Lodges was held in 1871 when 5,000 miners attended an open-air meeting in Wharton Park. In its heyday a constant stream of Lodge banners lined Durham's narrow streets as they marched behind the bands in colourful procession, passing their political leaders, their heroes, who saluted back from the balcony of the Royal County Hotel. Tens of thousands of miners and their families would, for one day in July, swell the population of the city so much that Durham effectively belonged to them. Inevitably the decline in the industry meant a decline in the numbers attending the gala. Today it still takes place, but not now as a celebration of a Durham coalfield which is no more, but as a visible, tangible reminder of the triumphs and tragedies of a bygone age.

I remember, as a child, being taken by my parents to the 'Big Meeting'. It was in the early '60s and the memory remains vivid, marching behind the band and the Lodge banner with my father, as my grandfather had done before. Now, in the '90s, at least for the time being, the gala continues. The people still turn up, but where once there seemed to be hundreds of colliery banners, only a handful are now paraded. Thousands of people still come to Durham on gala day, but there used to be hundreds of thousands. The procession of 'Bands and Banners', which in former times took most of the day to pass by, now goes by in a couple of hours. Today, when the last banner passes on its way along Old Elvet and off down to the racecourse to keep its yearly appointment with the politicians, the old men, dressed as they have always been in best suit, tie and new cap bought specially for the occasion, stare out into the empty road as if watching banners of yore go by. Perhaps they are remembering the words of an anonymous Bearpark miner:

> Bands playing different tunes,
> As Banners floated by;
> Some folk cheerfully waved,
> While others stopped and cried;
> To see a Banner draped in black,
> Another man had died.

The good humour of gala day still remains, but now it is tinged with a poignancy, even a solemnity that was absent in the heyday of the 'Big Meeting'. On the racecourse, the politicians and union leaders still make speeches from the platform. The faithful and the merely curious still congregate to hear them, but the once-stirring rhetoric now sounds hollow and soulless, their words more a eulogy than a celebration. By early afternoon, as the traditional parade leaves for the cathedral and the annual service dedicated to the Durham miners, all that is left are the chip vans and the amusements. What has passed has been a proud but sad shadow of what has been lost.

The coal industry in County Durham was not just an industry, it was a way of life. The traditional Durham village communities were built around their pits. Right across the county most villages had a pit, or to be more accurate most pits had their own village, for the pit and the village were one. They relied upon each other for their continued mutual existence. When the pit died, the village would inevitably face a period of decline. And the pit, the shared workplace of the community, would give to its people a sense of common identity now gone. To talk today of community spirit, of the unity of the old close-knit pit villages, smacks of cliché; there are those who would suggest that perhaps it is just a romantic notion of something that everyone remembers, but never really was, a cosy collective vision induced by nostalgia for what is no more. Nevertheless, for many thousands of people over many years in Durham County it was a reality.

To others, however, the extent to which the power and influence of the miners eventually grew and the increasing politicisation of their union was disliked and mistrusted. To them the miners became a force to be feared, despised and crushed. In October 1992, the government announced what in effect was to be the closure of the British coal industry. Already by then the greater part of the Durham coalfield had disappeared. The announcement finally doomed not just the few remaining pits, but delivered the *coup de grâce* to an already vanishing way of life. Many disputed the government's reasons for the closure, some will always do so. Was the real motive behind the closures based on economic or political realities; there are many who in their own minds are convinced of the answer. No doubt at some future time history will confirm for us the truth. So it came about that 23 November 1993 was to be a fateful day for the oldest pit in the county, for on that day Wearmouth, where coal had been extracted since the days of Ralph the Crafty, was scheduled for closure.

For many people, when the pit wheels stopped turning so did their world. There are others, however, who, while mourning the passing of that spirit of unity forged in the early struggles for decent basic pay and conditions, do not mourn the passing of the pits. Indeed few will mourn the passing of the grim landscapes, the spoil heaps and the pollution. As a way of earning a living it was dark, it was dirty, and it was the most dangerous of all. Perhaps in the heyday of the coalfield it was a proud and accepted tradition that a son would eventually follow his father down the pit. However, there were also those miners who wished the opposite, that sons of theirs would break away, seek other employment, and find opportunities that they never had. For many years the sad fact was that to do so wasn't possible. If they wanted to work at all, the pit was all there was.

So now the Durham miners are gone, their history, from exploitation to justice to demise, is now but a memory. It is up to new generations born in a 'county built on coal' to remember those who met their unlooked-for deaths deep in the darkness of the Durham mines. If the last vestiges of the annual Miners' Gala are brought finally to an end, the Durham miners would indeed still be remembered, thanks to the various new monuments now being erected. However, the most poignant and telling of all epitaphs to those men and boys who lived and died in the Durham coalfield are the memorials scattered around the county's graveyards, for it is these that show us the real cost of a county's and country's wealth.

The Durham countryside is green again. Farm animals now graze on a landscape once blighted by pit wheels and spoil heaps. Years of sympathetic reclamation work have helped heal the scars left by the mining industry. The River Wear, once so polluted by colliery effluent that as it meandered through Durham City it was described as a 'black sewer', now runs clean. In its waters salmon and sea trout have long since returned to their native runs. And where clean water flows, the breeze blows clearer air. For the mines are no more, as are the miners. But let us hope, in County Durham at least, the memory of their early struggles, the hardships of their lives and all too often their premature and cruel deaths will linger long in the memory of their children, grandchildren and successive generations, on into the next millennium; lest we forget!

Chapter Twenty

Nine Hundred Years

'With records stored, of deeds long since forgot . . .'

It seems incongruous to start the final chapter of the book where chapter one ended, just as incongruous as it would seem to start the last chapter of a book about a thousand years of history with the title 'Nine Hundred Years'. However, this chapter begins after the erection of the first simple shelter for the relics of St Cuthbert, and the clearing of the rock. For this was but the prelude to the momentous event which would happen almost a hundred years later when England was ruled by a foreign race, a race that would bring fire, sword and destruction but also new ideas about architecture and design, and a new dual significance to the great religious buildings: as monuments glorifying both the power of God and their own power on earth.

On 11 August 1093, 98 years after the monks of St Cuthbert had arrived on the Dun-holme, the foundation stones were laid of the great Norman cathedral which, more than anything, has come to symbolise Durham. To the sophisticated generations of today, the sight of the cathedral towering over the city is still an inspiring one. To the uneducated and illiterate peasants of eleventh- and twelfth-century Durham living squalid, mean lives in ramshackle dwellings, ever close to disease and death, the sight of the cathedral, its size, power and majesty, must have been almost incomprehensible. As incomprehensible as it would be to end a book about one thousand years of Durham's history without a chapter devoted to telling stories of Durham's greatest treasure.

Much has been written about Durham Cathedral. Hundreds of books, thousands of words have down the ages told in scholarly works of its history and significance. Many authors have written about the 'half Church of God, half Castle 'gainst the Scot', and the rich history, truth, half-truth and legend that has been handed down. I trust that none would begrudge this author a few hundred words of his own. To start, we must once more travel back across the millennium, back to the first settlement on the 'high wooded rock'.

The first shelter for the relics of St Cuthbert, made of tree boughs, was quickly replaced. In AD 998 only three years after the arrival of the monks a new stone church was dedicated. The White Church, as it became known, was a grand Saxon structure not completed until 1017; it would stand for almost 100 years until its eventual destruction by the Normans to make way for the great cathedral that we know today. The completion of the White Church and the placing in it, on 4 September 999, of the remains of St Cuthbert saw the beginning in earnest of the stream of pilgrims that continues to this day. It was to the White Church that Cnut the Great made his pilgrimage and from which William the Conqueror fled in terror, and it was to the White Church that in the year 1022, during the reign of Cnut, the remains of the Venerable Bede were brought to rest with those of St Cuthbert.

> With God's help, I Bede the Servant of Christ and Priest of the Monastery of The Blessed Apostles Peter and Paul at Wearmouth and Jarrow, have assembled these facts about the history of the Church in Britain, and of the Church of the English in particular, as I have been able to ascertain them from ancient documents, from the traditions of our forebears, and from my own personal knowledge.

So Bede told of how he had been able to complete what was arguably his greatest work, *The Ecclesiastical History of the English People*, chronicling the life and turbulent times of the early Saxon royal houses and the Anglo-Saxon people. Bede was born in the year 673, in the grounds of the monastery at Wearmouth. An early contemporary of Cuthbert, he was 13 years old when Cuthbert died. As a member of the Benedictine monasteries at Wearmouth and Jarrow from 680 to 735, Bede was to become the greatest writer of his time, and he was England's first true historian; indeed Bede it was who first used the name of England to describe the emerging nation state of his day. The twin monasteries of Jarrow and Wearmouth, under the influence of Benedict Biscop, the first abbot, and his successor and Bede's teacher and mentor, Ceolfrith, had become one of the major centres of Christian learning, with a vast library, accumulated mainly by Biscop, which at the time was one of the most extensive in Europe.

As a monk Bede never travelled further than Lindisfarne in the north or Whitby in the south, but as a scholar and writer he became revered throughout western Christendom and his work was in great demand. He said that his 'constant pleasure lay in learning, teaching or writing'. His output was prodigious. As well as writing pages on history, philosophy and the Church, he gave us the first complete account of the life of St Cuthbert. His works are prized. King Alfred the Great had Bede's *History* translated from its original Latin into common English, as he considered it one of the books 'most necessary for all men to know'. And it is said that when King Athelstan placed gifts in the coffin of St Cuthbert in 934, one of those gifts was a copy of a gospel translated by Bede, for he had also translated the Gospels into English and indeed his final work was a translation of the Gospel of St John.

The story is told that two weeks before Easter in the year 735, Bede was 'seized with an extreme weakness'; however, he continued dictating his work to his scholars. Gradually the sickness grew worse and he said to his students: 'Learn with what speed you may, I know not how long I may last.' With his life drawing to a close and his translation of St John's Gospel nearing completion, he urged his scholars to 'take thy pens and write quickly'. On Ascension Eve Bede's pupil, Cuthbert, said to him that there was one more sentence to be written. This Bede, with failing breath, slowly dictated. Cuthbert then told him: 'It is finished now.' Bede replied: 'You speak the truth, all is finished now.' With that the 'Father of English history' passed quietly from earthly life. Through Bede's work at Jarrow and at Monkwearmouth, the northern monasteries had become at that time a centre of European learning.

Aelfred was sacrist of the White Church of Durham. One of his main preoccupations was collecting the relics of saints and renowned northern holy men. He had previously made several annual journeys to Jarrow, to the tomb of Bede. On one visit, after some days there in prayer and meditation, he left early without his brethren and returned in secret to Durham. The bones of the Venerable Bede were later discovered to have been taken. Aelfred never again returned to Jarrow. Once, when asked if he knew of the whereabouts of the earthly remains of Bede Aelfred replied: 'No one can answer that question so well as I. You may be assured, my brethren, beyond all doubt that the same chest which holds the hallowed body of our Father Cuthbert also contains the bones of Bede our reverend teacher and brother.' Aelfred had indeed stolen the remains of the Venerable Bede from Jarrow, and had brought them back to Durham, there to lie in the same coffin as those of St Cuthbert. He had added to his collection. During his time he had also 'collected' the bones of Oswin from Tynemouth, and those of Boisil, St Cuthbert's prior from Melrose.

An earlier chapter told of the coming of the Normans and the terrible fate that awaited the rebellious northerners as William the Conqueror ruthlessly imposed his authority. The north had been subjugated by the year 1070; two years later saw construction work begin on the Conqueror's castle at Durham. In 1076 both the castle and the Earldom of Bamburgh were transferred to

Walcher, the first Norman bishop. Durham thus became the centre of Norman administration in the north. However, Walcher was later murdered, and in 1091 William II (Rufus) transferred royal rights and powers to the then Bishop of Durham, William of St Carileph. These new Palatine powers, combining the authority of the Earldom of Bamburgh and the Bishopric of Durham, authority both temporal and spiritual, military and religious, were vested in one man; thus appeared the Prince Bishops of Durham, a dynasty which would last for over 700 years. The Prince Bishops' seat would be the new castle, and Durham would become the capital of what amounted to virtually an independent kingdom.

The Prince Bishop would rule over the Palatinate as the king would, raising his own army and leading them into battle, levying his own taxes and printing his own coinage; examples of coins printed at the Durham mint can still be seen in the Cathedral Treasury. The Prince Bishop would develop his own law courts and his own 'Parliament'. He would reign supreme over an unstable part of the country, far away from the direct control of the king. The centre of Norman power and authority had been established, the fortification of the castle and the sovereignty of the Prince Bishop. What, however, was still needed was a visible statement, a tangible symbol, a demonstration to all of that power and authority.

In the year 1081, William of St Carileph had been appointed Bishop of Durham. He was from the first alarmed at the way of life of the incumbent community of St Cuthbert's monks at Durham, for they were indeed a community in the fullest sense of the word. The monks led very unmonastic lives. Many were married with families of their own. Their lifestyle bore little resemblance to that of the ascetics of St Cuthbert's own Celtic tradition, or to the strict orders of the Benedictines of Bede's monasteries at Jarrow and Monkwearmouth. Carileph moved to change this. He sought the counsel of the King and Queen, and of Lanfranc, Archbishop of Canterbury, finally journeying even to Rome to petition the Pope. His plan was approved and on 26 May 1083 William of St Carileph replaced the existing and potentially troublesome community of St Cuthbert with a new Benedictine monastery. Thus did the 'Black Monks' of Durham appear. St Carileph hoped to maintain the tradition of the Benedictines and of Bede of learning and scholarship, but with the existing independent and worldly community of St Cuthbert it was unlikely he would be able to achieve this.

The great cathedral of today was the product of St Carileph's inspiration and his patronage. It is not known whether he was responsible for the design, but the Normans were architects of great vision with their own ideas about architectural design. They brought craftsmen of great skill and patrons of great wealth. At Durham it was decided that, as had been the practice at other great religious sites, their own monument would be built on the site of the existing Saxon church, by doing so emphasising the continuity of worship under the new Norman hierarchy and at the same time destroying the Saxon heritage, eroding further any sense of a collective Saxon identity and the concomitant danger of lingering Saxon nationalism. So it was that the Saxon White Church, built by St Cuthbert's own people, was destroyed and the foundation stones of the great Norman cathedral were laid on 11 August, in the year 1093. The scene that day must have been a slightly peculiar one to the people of Durham. Carileph was of course present. No stranger to intrigue and controversy, he had from the beginning thought to replace the White Church with a grander structure. However, he had been forced to wait until 1091 and his return from exile before putting his plans into action. His original appointment had been made by the Conqueror, but after William's death Carileph had been involved in a rebellion against the King's son, William Rufus, and had subsequently been forced into a three-year exile, before making his peace with the new King. As well as Bishop Carileph and the Saxon Prior Turgot, there was present at the ceremony King Malcolm III of Scotland – Malcolm Canmore, the MacDuncan, slayer of Macbeth. Events already in the past which would be dramatised in Elizabethan times by William Shakespeare.

Four times before during his 40-year reign had Malcolm led his forces south to war with the English, as the people of Durham knew only too well. He had come in the wake of King William's brutalities, and in 1070 had laid waste to a land already reeling from the wrath of the Conqueror. Twice more in the space of 20 years would his armies bring death and destruction. He had sworn fealty and allegiance to the Conqueror, as his father had done many years before to Cnut, but he had returned again nevertheless to plunder the English realm. He had attacked as far south as Chester-le-Street in 1091, only two years before, and yet here he was, standing in an honoured place at the laying of the foundation stones of Bishop St Carileph's new cathedral. Malcolm it seems had rested at Durham on a journey south to meet and discuss peace terms with William Rufus. The Saxon Prior of Durham, Turgot, was also confessor and spiritual adviser to Malcolm's wife, and Turgot would also be present at the ceremony. The subsequent peace conference failed. Malcolm returned to Scotland, and barely three months after the foundation ceremony at Durham he invaded for a fifth time, this time finally meeting his death at Alnwick in Northumberland.

And so it was that Bishop Carileph, King Malcolm and Prior Turgot laid the three foundation stones of Durham Cathedral. The work had started on the monument which would finally give visible substance to Norman authority: 'Eternal certainty carved into every arch, each massive pillar, the certainty that Normandy is King, and God its Suzerain Lord.' William of St Carileph witnessed only the first three years of building work on his cathedral.

Late in 1095 while at Windsor he became ill, and died on 2 January 1096. Throughout the early building work the Prince Bishop had funded the project from his own personal wealth. Already by the end of those first three years, a major part of the construction had been completed. Eventually, preparations were made for the placing of St Cuthbert's coffin in its honoured position in the new cathedral. Ranulph Flambard was by that time Prince Bishop, the Saxon, Turgot, still the Prior. It was decided that before the coffin was entombed for ever, it would be opened. Turgot and nine specially chosen monks were delegated to the task.

When, on 24 August 1104, they dutifully lifted the lid, they were met with the same sight as had been beheld by the monks of Lindisfarne when they had opened the coffin over 400 years before, in 698. Cuthbert, it was said, lay on his side as if he slept. Various treasures were about him. The bones of Bede and the head of St Oswald were also there. Of the treasures, the monks removed from the coffin only the Corporax cloth which Cuthbert had used in the performance of the Eucharist, the same cloth which would, over 240 years later, be flown as a banner for the English forces at the Battle of Neville's Cross, and later still in the year 1513 on Flodden Field. The bones of Bede would eventually be removed and would, in 1370, be buried separately with great reverence in the tomb where he still lies today. It is interesting to imagine the scene on 29 August 1104 when Cuthbert was finally laid to rest in his place of honour within the new cathedral. Present again was Prior Turgot, and also present was King Alexander of Scotland whose father, Malcolm, had laid one of the foundation stones 11 years before. After the death of William of St Carileph, funding for the project had become less generous and more uncertain. However, construction continued, and in the year 1133, after only 40 years, the cathedral, apart from the Galilee Chapel and the Chapel of the Nine Altars which were later additions, was completed.

Around the tomb of St Cuthbert a great and elaborate shrine was erected. It continued to attract vast numbers of pilgrims, and thus great wealth. The mystique of Cuthbert had not been diminished by the coming of the Normans, and now the combination of the power of the saint and the grandeur of the cathedral was to make Durham a major centre for pilgrimage throughout the Middle Ages. The cathedral and the monastery prospered, and the shrine of the Great Saint was to become, according to the *Rites of Durham*, 'one of the most sumptuous monuments in all England'. Throughout the unfolding years the magnificence of the cathedral and the sanctity of St Cuthbert drew pilgrims in their thousands and the community at Durham became very rich. Noble visitors arrived as well as the common folk. Kings and queens were numbered amongst those who came to pay homage. However, there were some regal pilgrims whose light shone less brightly than did others, and the reasons for their coming to Durham were varied; some were definitely more welcome than others. In the year 1213, King John arrived at Durham with an army, on his way north to Scotland. He resided at the castle for several days. Such an unpopular monarch was he, and has he remained, that one chronicler recorded the visit with just a few terse words: 'On this day, King John, he of ignoble memory, visited Durham.' In 1255 King John's successor, Henry III, came to Durham ostensibly to pay homage to St Cuthbert. The story is told that while he was there he helped himself to treasure, gold and jewels from the shrine. Explaining to the monastery that he needed to repay some sizeable debts, he assured them that he was merely borrowing it. None of the treasure was ever seen again.

Mighty kings visited the shrine of the saint as well as monarchs of ignoble memory'. In 1298 Edward I, 'Hammer of the Scots', was in the north after defeating the Scottish army of William Wallace at the Battle of Falkirk. On his return he came to Durham and while there, obviously mellowed by the contentment of victory, 'forgave the Prior and Convent of their subsidies owing to him of £1,012 9s. 11½d'. He returned two years later and mediated in 'bitter dissensions' between the Bishop and the convent.

The mighty Edward III, grandson of the Hammer of the Scots, had a long association with Durham. In 1327, on his first expedition against the Scots, he made a visit to the cathedral and stayed for two days. He returned with another army six years later, and on 1 April 1333 lodged in the Priory. His wife, Philippa of Hainault, rode up from Knaresbrough to meet him, a meeting about which a well-known story is recounted.

> The Queen, being unacquainted with the custom of this Church, went through the Abbey gates to the Priory. And after supping with the King, retired to rest. Whereby the monks informed the King of St Cuthbert, and the King ordered Philippa to rise and in her undergarments she returned through the gates and went to the Castle, after most devoutly praying that St Cuthbert would not revenge a fault, which she had, through ignorance, committed.

The story alludes to the tradition held by the Durham monastery of St Cuthbert's alleged dislike and mistrust of women, even, it seems, of a queen. On this occasion Philippa, not daring to return to the castle by passing through the cathedral where Cuthbert lay, passed around the eastern end and made her way back to the castle through what is now Dun Cow Lane, so as not to give further offence to the great saint. To this day can be seen a line of marble set in the cathedral floor, near the font, signifying the easternmost point to which female pilgrims were allowed to approach St Cuthbert's shrine.

In 1436 St Cuthbert was visited by one Aeneas Sylvius Piccolomini, who would later become Pope Pius II. A still later visitor was the pious, sick and ill-fated King Henry VI. As the Middle Ages drew on, the royal patronage continued. Richard III, justly or not one of the most reviled of English kings, alleged murderer of his brother and his nephews, also paid homage. Before his accession the King, son of Cecily Neville the 'Rose of Raby', was an annual visitor to the shrine of St Cuthbert as Duke of Gloucester; indeed he was a member of the 'Fraternity of Cuthbert' to which the membership was limited only to the most prominent of lay people. He and his duchess, Anne, were frequent visitors to the shrine and as members of the Fraternity were entitled to participate in all religious ceremonies performed by the monks of Durham, and be addressed as Brother or Sister. Obviously this enhanced greatly the Fraternity members' image of piety.

Early in the year 1541 a sledgehammer crashed down on the coffin of St Cuthbert, and with that crude blow the age of the splendour of his shrine was ended. The Reformation had arrived. In 1539 Henry VIII had ordered the dissolution of the monasteries. On New Year's Eve 1540, Durham Cathedral was surrendered to Dr Lee, Dr Hewley and Master Blithman, the King's commissioners. They would have no truck with the myths of antiquity, and set about destroying both St Cuthbert's shrine and the legend of his incorrupt body. They were, however, in for a shock. When they finally smashed open the coffin and uncovered the saint's remains, the sight they saw made them waver, unsure whether to proceed. They sent word of their discovery to the King and awaited instructions. They reported that they saw there the body of the saint over 850 years after his death, 'whole uncorrupt, with his face bare and his beard, as it had been a fortnights growth, and all his vestments upon him as he was accustomed to say Mass, and his metwand of gold lying beside him'. Eventually instructions came to the commissioners to re-inter the coffin, and the monks of Durham once again laid to rest the body of their saint. They buried the body of St Cuthbert where the broken-down and destroyed shrine had previously stood, covering his grave this time with the simple grey slab that we see today.

Or did they? There is an abiding story which has been recounted down the years that the monks, fearing the despoliation of their saint's mortal remains, removed his body from the coffin, replaced it with the bones of a person unknown, and reburied those. St Cuthbert's body was then taken by the monks and buried at some other secret location in the cathedral, a location the knowledge of which may have been handed down through the centuries to selected successors of those few conspiratorial monks.

The coffin of St Cuthbert would be opened again, for 'serious research', in the nineteenth century. In 1827 the contents were again exposed. In the coffin there remained only a skeleton, perhaps adding fuel to the rumour that the preserved body of the saint had indeed been previously removed. In the coffin were found an ivory comb, a portable altar, and a golden pectoral cross, each of which can now be seen in the Cathedral Treasury. Also there were the embroidered silken stole and maniple which had been placed in the coffin at Chester-le-Street by the Saxon King of all the English, Athelstan, almost 900 years earlier. Under examination, traces of a substance resembling skin were seen adhering to the skeleton.

Was there then any substance to the story of the relocation of St Cuthbert's body at the time of the Reformation? If what Henry VIII's commissioners reported was indeed the truth, then obviously the saint's body was still extremely well preserved. Whatever the agent that had maintained that preservation for over 850 years – be it some chemical 'fluke', or the body having been embalmed, or indeed divine intervention – that same agent had apparently deserted the saint some time before 1827. Why would the commissioners even report their findings if they were not true; after all, they were representatives of the 'new thinking' of Henry VIII's new Church, and it was their business to 'debunk' such superstitious legends of the old order, not to confirm them. Why would they lie to the King about such a story? Henry VIII was many things, but he was certainly not a man to be trifled with. Was it really a surprise that the next time the coffin was opened the former perfectly preserved body of the saint had been reduced merely to bone? Was it not the case that those particular bones had been secretly placed in the empty coffin by the monks of Durham in the early 1540s? The argument could no doubt be finally settled by modern scientific analysis, but to drag into the present the misty world of legend and long-forgotten deeds which is woven into the very fabric of Durham Cathedral's history and place it under the sharp focus of today's science, would surely be to despoil the food of imagination. It may be the case that St Cuthbert's body is interred not where tradition has it, but lies in a high place and looks towards the west. However, to all that visit the cathedral today, the bones that lie under that plain grey slab are indeed the bones of St Cuthbert. So it should be, and so no doubt it will remain.

Following the Reformation, the fortunes of the cathedral went into decline. The religious excesses of the late sixteenth century and the narrow Puritanism of Cromwell's Protectorate half a century later were both reflected in the despoliation and neglect of the cathedral. In later centuries, however, the process began to be reversed and the cathedral began once again to be cared for and treasured. Nevertheless, the glories of the old age had gone for ever.

As we have previously seen it was Oliver Cromwell who first planned the foundation of a University of Durham. However, he died before his scheme came to fruition and it was to be in 1832 that the last of the Prince Bishops of Durham, William Van Mildert, together with the Dean and

Chapter, co-founded Durham University, the third oldest in England. He gave to the new university his castle that 760 years earlier William the Conqueror had ordered to be built, and which would become the seat of the first Prince Bishop. A centre of military might and authority had eventually become a centre of education, and in some way the tradition of the original Benedictine monks, and indeed of Bede, of learning and scholarship was to be continued at Durham. The link with the university is just one example of how the life of the cathedral is today intertwined with the lives of the local community. For many years coal mining was the major industry in the region and the miners always maintained close links with the cathedral. In 1947 a special memorial dedicated to the many Durham miners who lost their lives in the pits was placed in the cathedral. Every year on the day of the Durham Miners Gala a special service is held, and a Miners Lodge banner hangs permanently in the cathedral. The county's own regiment, the Durham Light Infantry, has a chapel dedicated to it where those who did not return from 210 years of battle are remembered: the fallen of the Peninsular Wars, of Inkerman and Sevastopol; those who were lost in the slaughter of the Great War at Ypres, the Somme and Passchendaele; and those who died in the great battles of World War Two at Dunkirk, at Tobruk, at El Alamein and Kohima.

Indeed, the cathedral of today is more than just an international centre for pilgrimage and tourism, it is very much a cathedral for local people. Moreover, it is in itself a working community, as it was 900 years ago. It is a community of clerics and lay people, from stonemasons to artists, groundsmen to stewards and guides. Above all it continues to be a living church maintaining the emphasis on religious service. Thankfully, despite the hundreds of thousands of tourists the cathedral receives each year, it has never been allowed to become merely a museum, a storehouse and showplace for ancient relics. Today Durham Cathedral seems to have time for everyone, from the great university to the smallest primary school, from the great pomp and ceremony of religious and civic occasions to private meditation in a quiet corner.

St Cuthbert's Day, 20 March 1993, marked the beginning of celebrations commemorating 900 years of the great cathedral. Throughout that year the celebrations continued, involving many people and groups, a great cross-section of the community. They included everything from village fêtes to grand civic services, events organised by local groups to visits by academics from overseas. When the celebrations ended, many more people had contributed to, and joined in with, the continuing story of Cuthbert's church.

In 1984, to mark the 150th anniversary of the Royal Institute of British Architects, 50 experts were commissioned to assess some of the world's leading man-made structures. From that assessment Durham Cathedral was placed first on the list, ahead even of the Taj Mahal and the Parthenon. The site of the cathedral and castle was, in 1987, dedicated by UNESCO (the United Nations Educational Scientific and Cultural Organisation) as a World Heritage Site, one of only a handful in Britain – Stonehenge is another – and one of only 400 worldwide, along with the Pyramids of Egypt. The cathedral itself has been described as a 'glory of Christendom'; Ruskin called it 'one of the wonders of the world'; Nikolaus Pevsner said the sight was 'one of the great experiences of Europe . . . the group of Cathedral, Castle and Monastery on the rock can only be compared to Avignon and Prague'. The superlatives have always flowed, and there is no doubt that today the cathedral is regarded as probably the finest example of Norman architecture in Europe. As the plaudits increase in number and the tourism awards roll in, it is interesting to consider what Cuthbert of Lindisfarne would have made of it all. Would he indeed have been happy at being venerated in the way he has since been; with the wealth and power that the community at Durham gained through his name; and with the glory of his jewelled shrine? Possibly not. He now lies under a simple slab inscribed only with his name; perhaps he would have settled for that.

Speaking as someone who lives and works in Durham City it is easy to become rather blasé about the cathedral, its status and its history. After all, if you see it every day, at times you begin not to notice it. But what is always noticeable when visiting the cathedral is the special atmosphere of the place. There seems to be an overpowering sense of 'ancientness', unlike some of the other great cathedrals. Durham is not the largest cathedral, certainly not the most ornate, but it has an atmosphere unique to the building itself, to its history and setting. Above all, the cathedral is a paradox: it seems to stand upon its lofty site where 'Cuthbert's folk' arrived 1,000 years ago, aloof from the humdrum world and the small concerns of the passing generations, yet at the same time it is very much at the centre of the history, culture and life of the local people, as well as being a symbol of the region with which the 'Cuthbert's folk' of today can readily identify.

Many events have taken place over those 1,000 years: the slaughter and destruction of wars; the rise and fall of empires, of kings, queens, statesmen and tyrants; religious and political upheavals. Durham Cathedral has seen them come and seen them go, and through them all has stood silent and majestic on its seat high above the River Wear.

And so the millennium has passed and another year goes by in the realm of the Prince Bishops. A thousand years on and they lie there still, Cuthbert and Bede, forever enshrined in this glorious monument. Indeed, the cathedral is a monument to many things: to the vision of William of St Carileph and his architects who designed it; to the skill of the masons who built it; to the power and wealth of the Norman nobility who patronised it; but most of all to the memory of a humble Northumbrian Celtic monk called Cuthbert whose life and holiness inspired it. In the words of Sir Walter Scott: 'Grey Towers of Durham, yet well I love thy mixed and massive piles, half Church of God; half Castle 'gainst the Scot; and long to roam these venerable aisles with records stored, of deeds long since forgot.'

Here's to the next 1,000 years!

Bibliography

Major Sources

The Boldon Buke – A Survey of the Possessions of the See of Durham made by order of Bishop Hugh Du Puiset. 1183

The Monthly Chronicle of North Country Lore and Legend. 1887–1891

Archeologia Aeliana – The Journals of the Proceedings of the Society of Antiquaries of Newcastle upon Tyne. From 1822

Allan, G. *Historical and Descriptive View of the City of Durham and its Environs.* 1824

Boyle, J.R. *The County of Durham.* 1892

Brockie, W. *Legends and Superstitions of the County of Durham.* 1886

Cox, T. *A Compleat History of Durham.* 1730

Denham, M.A. *The Denham Tracts.* 1892–1895

Fordyce, W. *The History and Antiquities of the County Palatine of Durham.* 1855–1857

Grice, F. *Folk Tales of the North Country.* 1953

Hutchinson, W. *The History and Antiquities of the County Palatine of Durham.* 1785–1794

Page, W. *The Victoria History of the County of Durham.* 1905–1928

Richardson, M.A. *The Local Historians' Table Book of Remarkable Occurrences.* 1841–1846

Richardson, M.A. *Reprints of Rare Tracts.* 1847–1849

Surtees, R. *The History and Antiquities of the County Palatine of Durham.* 1816–1840

Sykes, J. *Local Records.* 1866

Other Sources

Collectanea Dunelmensis

The Neville Family of Brancepeth and Neville's Cross, from 1028

Arthur, T. *The Wonderful Tradition of the Lambton Worm*: 1875
Bates, C.J. *Bamburgh Castle, its History and Architecture*: 1894
Brooks, F.W. *The Council of the North*: 1966
Broumley, J.W. *The Lords of Raby and Staindrop*: 1957
Brown, Curtis M. *Evidence and Procedures for Boundary Location*: 1981
Chronicle Publications *Chronicle of America*: 1990
Churchill, Sir Winston S. *The History of the English Speaking Peoples*: 1956
Cooper, L. *Great Men of Durham*: 1956
Dodd, J.J. *The History of the Urban District of Spennymoor*: 1897
Emery, N. *The Coalminers of Durham*: 1992
Fuller, T. *The Worthies of England*
Geeson, C. *A Short History of Kelloe Church and District*
Hamblen, T. *A Chapter in the History of Railway Locomotion and Memoir of Timothy Hackworth (The Father of Locomotives), and a List of Some of His Principle Inventions*: 1875
Hilton, J.A. *Catholicism in Elizabethan Durham*: 1977
Hind, A.L. *The Story of the Lambton Worm*
Hughes, Sarah S. *Surveyors and Statesmen: Land Measuring in Colonial Virginia*: 1979
J.L. International Publishing *Chronicle of Britain*: 1992
Kapelle, W.E. *The Norman Conquest of the North: The Region and its Transformation 1000–1135*: 1979
Kingsley, C. Saint Godric, Hermit of Finchale, in *Durham Pictures and Papers*
Layson, J.F. *The Great Engineers*: 1881
Lipscombe, H.C. *History of Staindrop Church and Monuments*: 1888

Londonderry, Edith Helen Vane-Tempest-Stewart, Marchioness of *Frances Anne: The Life and Times of Frances Anne, Marchioness of Londonderry and her Husband, Charles, the Third Marquess of Londonderry.* 1958

Low, J.L. *Historical Scenes in Durham Cathedral:* 1887

Maitland, A. *St Cuthbert's Mist.* 1983

Mander, R. *The Story of Elizabeth Barrett.* 1980

Meadows, P. and Waterson, E. *The Lost Houses of County Durham.* 1993

Musgrove, F. *The North of England.* 1990

Myerscough, Rev. J.A. *Memoirs of Missionary Priests*

Myerscough, Rev. J.A. *The Martyrs of Durham and the North East.* 1956

Nef, J.U. *The Rise of the British Coal Industry.* 1966

Pollard, A.J. *North Eastern England During the Wars of the Roses.* 1900

Raistrick, A. *Quakers in Science and Industry.* 1950

Rice, Fthr. F. *One of the Greatest Stags in the Forest.* 1978

Rothnie, N. *The Baedeker Blitz*

Sharp, Sir Cuthbert *The Worme of Lambton.* 1830

Sharp, Sir Cuthbert *Sunderland Tracts of Other Times.* 1842–1848

Sharp, Sir Cuthbert *Memorials of Rebellion.* 1840

Sharp, Sir Cuthbert *The Rising of the North.* The 1569 Rebellion: 1840

Sharp, Sir Cuthbert *A Leaf from the Pilgrimage of Grace.* 1842

Stephenson, W. *The Lambton Worm, a Legendary Tale.* 1830

Stranks, C.J. *The Life and Death of St Cuthbert.* 1964

Sturgess, R.W. *Aristocrat in Business, The Third Marquess of Londonderry as Coalowner and Port Builder* – Durham County Local History Society: 1975

Swallow, H.J. *De Nova Villa: or the House of Neville.* 1885

The Surtees Society *Jacob Bee's Diary.* 1683

'W.D.' *The Intimate Story of the Origin of the Railways.* 1925

Weld, C.R. *History of the Royal Society.* 1848

Wood, M. *In Search of the Dark Ages.* 1981

Wood, M. *Domesday: A Search for the Roots of England.* 1986

Yale University Press. *The Pageant of America – A Pictorial History of the United States.* 1925

Young, R. *Timothy Hackworth and the Locomotive.* 1923

Journals, Articles and Other Publications

Charles Dickens in Teesdale. The Story of Nicholas Nickleby and the Yorkshire Schools, in Middleton in Teesdale Discovery Guide: 1983

The Philosophical Transactions of the Royal Society: 1760–1768

Handbook of Raby Castle

St John Boste and the Continuity of Catholicism in the Deerness Valley. St John Boste Celebrations Committee, Newhouse: 1993

Bomber Command Continues: Air Ministry Account of the Offensive Against Germany: 1942

Charles Dickens and the Yorkshire Schools, in North Magazine: 1971

Durham Cathedral, in Durham County Joint Curriculum Study Group: 1976

Brown, P. Durham Cathedral: Some Strange Stories, in the *Sunday Sun*, 15 August 1937

Heesom, A.J. Entrepreneurial Paternalism: The Third Marquess of Londonderry and the Coal Trade, in *University of Durham Journal*: 1974

Heesom, A.J. The Third Marquess of Londonderry as an Employer, in the *North East Group for the Study of Labour History, Bulletin No. 6*: 1972

Hollis, H.P. Jeremiah Dixon and his Brother, in the *Journal of the British Astronomical Society*, Vol. 44: 1934

Lomas, R.A. Durham Cathedral, in *Friends of Durham Cathedral 59th Annual Report*

Smith, D. The Lord, The Cobbler and The Lady, in *North Magazine*: 1974

Stokes, P. The Day the Coalfield Died: 24 November 1993, in the *Northern Echo*

University of Durham Publications *North Country Life in the Eighteenth Century*: The North East 1700–1750

University of Leeds School of History *Northern History*, Volume XXI

Welch, N. Charles Dickens and his Fruitful Travels in the North East, in *North Magazine*: 1973

Welch, N. The Third Marquess of Londonderry, in *North Magazine*: 1972